Eating Like a Mennonite

Eating Like a Mennonite

Food and Community across Borders

MARLENE EPP

McGill-Queen's University Press
Montreal & Kingston • London • Chicago

© McGill-Queen's University Press 2023

ISBN 978-0-2280-1893-3 (cloth)
ISBN 978-0-2280-1894-0 (paper)
ISBN 978-0-2280-1950-3 (ePDF)
ISBN 978-0-2280-1951-0 (ePUB)

Legal deposit third quarter 2023
Bibliothèque nationale du Québec

Printed in Canada on acid-free paper that is 100% ancient forest free (100% post-consumer recycled), processed chlorine free

This book has been published with the help of a grant from the Canadian Federation for the Humanities and Social Sciences, through the Awards to Scholarly Publications Program, using funds provided by the Social Sciences and Humanities Research Council of Canada.

We acknowledge the support of the Canada Council for the Arts.

Nous remercions le Conseil des arts du Canada de son soutien.

Library and Archives Canada Cataloguing in Publication

Title: Eating like a mennonite : food and community across borders / Marlene Epp.

Names: Epp, Marlene, author.

Description: Includes bibliographical references and index.

Identifiers: Canadiana (print) 20230218717 | Canadiana (ebook) 20230218725 | ISBN 9780228018933 (cloth) | ISBN 9780228018940 (paper) | ISBN 9780228019510 (ePUB) | ISBN 9780228019503 (ePDF)

Subjects: LCSH: Food – Religious aspects – Mennonites. | LCSH: Food habits – Religious aspects – Mennonites. | LCSH: Food – Social aspects. | LCSH: Mennonite cooking.

Classification: LCC BX8128.F66 E67 2023 | DDC 394.1/2 – dc23

This book was designed and typeset by Peggy & Co. Design in 11.5/15 Adobe Minion Pro.

Contents

Figures vii

Acknowledgments ix

Introduction:
Eating Like a Mennonite 3

1 Eating Encounters:
Mennonites Move across Time and Place 30

2 Mennonite Women Can Cook:
Gendered Notions of Foodways 73

3 Recipes and Beyond:
The Cookbook Phenomenon 112

4 Food Trauma:
Memories of Hunger and Scarcity 150

5 Breaking and Baking Bread Together:
Food and Religious Practice 186

Conclusion 223

Notes 227

Bibliography 253

Index 281

Figures

0.1 Norm Ediger Signature Series Mennonite Sausage, sold by Drake Meats, Saskatchewan, 2022. Source: Drake Meats, Drake, SK.   5

0.2 Mennonite children in Mexico, 1955. Mennonite Archives of Ontario, Waterloo, ON. Photo: John Friesen. Item 1994-14-263.   8

0.3 Sign at Steinbach, Manitoba, Pride Parade, 2016. *Canadian Mennonite* magazine. Photo: Beth Downey Sawatzky.   19

1.1 Advertisement at Mennomex store, Aylmer, Ontario, 2022. Source: Mennomex, Aylmer, ON.   31

1.2 Selina Frey at Mennonite Relief Sale, Ontario, 1970. *Hamilton Spectator*. Mennonite Archives of Ontario, Waterloo, ON. Photo: Derek G. Hopwood, Item 1989-1 46.   39

1.3 Helena Harms Hiebert, Paraguay, c1948–50. Mennonite Library & Archives, Fresno, CA. Photo: C.N. Hiebert. Item M66-008.   54

1.4 Members of Grace Lao Mennonite Church, Kitchener, Ontario, 2012. Photo: Marlene Epp.   60

1.5 Mennonite women preparing *foufou*, Mbuji-Mayi, Democratic Republic of Congo, 2012. Photo: Marlene Epp.   69

2.1 *Vereniki*, farmer sausage, and *plumi moos* at Mennonite Heritage Village, Steinbach, Manitoba, 2018. Photo: Marlene Epp.   75

viii   Figures

2.2   Carved "butter lamb" made by Rosella Leis, Ontario, 2022. Photo: Marlene Epp.   84
2.3   Mennonite Church General Conference, Waterloo County, Ontario, 1953. Mennonite Archives of Ontario, Waterloo, ON. Photo: David L. Hunsberger. Item DH-1475.   87
2.4   Sunnycrest Home Baking, operated by Old Order Mennonite women, Hawkesville, Ontario, 2022. Photo: Marlene Epp.   107
2.5   Mennonite men at a women's church gathering, Balodgahan, India, 2016. Photo: Marlene Epp.   109
3.1   Recipe for Russian Mennonite Borscht, 1984. Sketch by Marta Goertzen-Armin. Mennonite Heritage Archives, Winnipeg, MB. Item 6491-21-7.   119
3.2   *The Mennonite Treasury of Recipes*, 1962 edition. Source: Biblio.com.   126
4.1   *Zwieback* at a Mennonite church near Omsk, Siberia, Russia, 2010. Photo: Marlene Epp.   168
4.2   Refugee trek from Ukraine in Second World War, c1943–44. Mennonite Archives of Ontario, Waterloo, ON. Item 1992-14-3058.   170
5.1   Lucy Santiago and Glorimar Mojica near the Mennonite church, San Juan, Puerto Rico, 2019. Mennonite Central Committee. Photo: Diana Voth.   197
5.2   *Anarsa* prepared by Mennonites in India at Christmas, 2015. Photo: Marlene Epp.   205
5.3   Mennonite church meal, Reedley, California, 1960s. Mennonite Library & Archives, Fresno, CA. Item CB525-27.   214
5.4   Potluck meal at Rajnandgaon Mennonite Church, India, 2015. Photo: Marlene Epp.   217
5.5   Pig Butchering, Ukraine, c1910. Mennonite Heritage Archives, Winnipeg, MB. Item 44-01.   220

Acknowledgments

This book is the result of years of researching, reading, and thinking about the question of Mennonite foods and foodways. Some of the material has appeared in book chapters and articles, and in public talks I have given over two decades. As such, this particular project has been a long time "in the oven." I have appreciated opportunities to test my ideas in special lectures at Bethel College (Kansas), Canadian Mennonite University (Manitoba), University of Winnipeg, Essex-Kent Mennonite Historical Association, Mennonite Historical Society of British Columbia, Ontario Women's History Network; in presentations at various academic conferences; and in my own classrooms at University of Waterloo.

I am grateful to assistants who completed numerous research tasks for this project and helped out in my university classes, especially when I took on administrative assignments. They include Stephanie Fong, Aileen Friesen, Sophia Heidebrecht, Noe Ishaka, Mitchell Lee, Laura Morlock, Ellery Penner, Duncan Smith, and Jeremy Wiebe. Thank you to Conrad Grebel University College for occasional grants that allowed me to hire assistants and to undertake research travel for the book.

Colleagues and friends who offered advice, information, assistance, and encouragement include Connie T. Braun, Franca Iacovetta, Mado Fumunguya, Julia Spicher Kasdorf, Rosella Leis, Ruth Loeppky, Yoel Masyawong, Ben Nobbs-Thiessen, Cynthia Peacock, Ian Radforth, Susan Shantz, Sidonie Swana, Hildi Froese Tiessen, James Urry,

Robert Zacharias, and Carol Zook. I am grateful to the numerous people in India and the Democratic Republic of Congo, mainly women, who welcomed me into their churches and homes and always prepared amazing meals for me. These visits reinforced the importance of hospitality and commensality and ensured that theory stayed rooted in lived reality.

My faculty and staff colleagues at Conrad Grebel University College always showed generous interest and support for my food book, especially when I brought in food samples to illustrate my research findings! In particular, I acknowledge librarians at the Milton Good Library – Mandy Macfie and Ruth Steinman, and archivist Laureen Harder-Gissing. Jane Forgay, librarian at the University of Waterloo, supported my course on "Food, Culture, and History" in numerous ways. Thanks go to the various archives, named in the list of illustrations, that granted permission for my use of photos. Working with MQUP was a joy. I offer thanks especially to Kyla Madden, Lesley Trites, Kate Merriman, Kathleen Fraser, Lisa Aitken, and all the personnel in editorial, production, and marketing departments that worked on my book. Thanks to Stephen Ullstrom who prepared the index. I acknowledge anonymous readers of the manuscript whose useful suggestions made this a better book. I am deeply grateful for the publication grant from the Mennonite Historical Society of Ontario.

The correct spelling for food items presents a bit of a conundrum, and some readers will undoubtedly take issue with my choices. Many of the specific foods I discuss have varied spellings, according to personal and language choices and aberrations. For instance, the Russian Mennonite *zwieback*, which is referenced frequently in the book, can be seen as *tweeback*, *zweibach*, and so on. I have chosen the spelling most common to me, but if used in quotations, I have maintained the writer's spelling. Similarly, I apply italics to non-English-language food items, except if they are not italicized in a quotation.

I need to offer credit and love to the people who keep me well-fed! For the first part of my life, that was my mother Helen (Dick) Epp. My husband, Paul Born, and our sons, Lucas Born and Michael Born, engage in endless "food-talk" but fortunately also lots of creative and delicious food production. This book is for them.

Eating Like a Mennonite

Introduction

Eating Like a Mennonite

I often began my undergraduate Mennonite history class with a word association game: "When I say Mennonite, what comes to mind?" Some years ago, I heard "pious" from one student and was about to write this on the whiteboard, but he quickly corrected me, saying he meant "pies." His answer was not uncommon: food is often what comes to mind when the topic of Mennonites comes up.

When I gave a presentation on Mennonites, food, and community to a group of Ontario seniors and asked for their ideas about Mennonite food practices, something similar happened. At first surprised by the question, the group soon agreed on some common themes: lots of meat; potlucks; pig butchering; abundance and bounty; eating too much (mentioned numerous times); big gardens; frugality; eating "from scratch"; home cooking; nutritious and healthy; meat, potatoes, vegetables; seven sweets and seven sours; pride in cooking; cultural foods; sweets and meats (more meat than other cultures); preserving food (canning, freezing, drying, etc.). Some listed traditional ethnic foods: *borscht* and *vereniki* ("Russian" Mennonite foods); cabbage salad with cream dressing; shoofly pie; apple butter; bean soup; sausage baked in pastry; desserts of cakes, cookies, and pies. Food richness, abundance, and eating as part of community were all central to their reflections.

Mennonites help to generate these food associations themselves. Celebrated cookbook author and essayist Edna Staebler, who had

Mennonite ancestry, popularized the idea that certain foodstuffs and foodways were identifiable as Mennonite. Her cookbooks describe "those mouthwatering Mennonite meals" that are "plain but divinely flavoured and different from any other" and characterized by "simplicity, economy and experience."[1] Similarly, a Mennonite-themed heritage museum describes Mennonite food in three words – "thrifty, appetizing and plentiful."[2] In her memoir, Maria Klassen Braun recalls that a visiting relative, having forgotten Braun's house number, guessed the right house: "The smell of the simmering chicken soup told her that she was in a Mennonite home and that she had found the right place!"[3] The foreword, by a non-Mennonite, to a Mennonite woman's memoir states the generalization almost as a truism: "Special foods make up an important part of the Mennonite culture ... When Mennonite people gather to enjoy special events, there is always enough for everyone and the food is delicious."[4]

The associations are often made with humour. An old joke goes, "How many Mennonites does it take to screw in a light bulb? Ten: one to do the work and nine to plan the meal after." A popular media site called *The Daily Bonnet*, a comical news feed with a Mennonite twist, regularly has a food-focused topic. Here are a few headlines: "Taunte [Aunt] Helen's Coleslaw Declared 'National Historic Site'"; "Curry Dish Confuses Attendees at Mennonite Potluck"; "Mennonite Man Accidentally Consumes a Vegetable"; "Rhubarb-Flavoured Vaping All the Rage in Mennonite Country."[5] Many of the allusions are insider jokes that play on traditional Mennonite eating practices and foods or exaggerate stereotypes about calorie-rich yet plain-tasting cooking. At the beginning of his 2020 film *I Am a Mennonite*, filmmaker Paul Plett humorously lays out three, seemingly key, aspects that will help him understand the unifying feature of all Mennonites: faith, shared heritage, and "our love of pie" (so my student was on to something).[6]

In communities across the Americas with a large number of Mennonites, especially those distinct for their uniform dress and non-use of some modern technologies, visitors will find plentiful signage for "Mennonite sausage," "Mennonite eggs," "Mennonite produce," or "Mennonite-raised chicken," for example. Even alcoholic drinks are labelled with Mennonite or Amish (similar to Mennonites)

0.1 Example of Mennonite food labelling – Norm Ediger Signature Series Mennonite Sausage, sold by Drake Meats, Saskatchewan, 2022.

references, such as Buggywhip India Pale Ale in Ontario or Amish Four Grain Pale Ale in Pennsylvania.[7] The signs and advertisements suggest locality, community, and old-fashioned industry – producing food and drink that is connected to the land and the people working on it. This is how Old Order Mennonites and Amish tend to exist in the popular imagination – as leading simple lives, in farm-based communities, close to the land.

The image reinforces certain assumptions about Mennonite food practices as being more wholesome and healthier than mainstream, industrially produced food (notwithstanding stereotypes about rich and starchy cooking). In her study of Amish women's lives, Karen M. Johnson-Weiner argues that outsiders who think the Amish live "old-fashioned, plain, simple, separate lives unsullied by technology, closer to God and nature" *expect* this "supposed ... simplicity and authenticity" to exist in Amish food production.[8] Some of these perceptions may be partly true, but there is also much simplification. William Woys Weaver suggests that the popular "Amish-equals-organic equation" is actually an "anomaly for the community."[9] Indeed, many conservative Mennonite and Amish food producers and gardeners have turned their own growing practices toward more sustainable models *in order to respond* to the market for such food products among organic-eating locavores in the city.[10]

The supposed connection between Mennonites and a healthy diet was exemplified in an article in the *New York Times* in January 2013, which ran with the headline "Eat Like a Mennonite." The writer was participating in an experiment relating food to levels of Bisphenol A (BPA), the chemical found in many plastics, and had discovered a study that found levels of BPA in pregnant Old Order Mennonite women that were one-quarter of the United States' national norm. She attributed this to the fact that they ate more fresh food, made their own dairy products, and purchased fewer consumer goods. These points were not substantiated, and seemed to me to be an overgeneralization, but I read on. As the writer herself went through a prescribed regimen of detoxification from BPAs, her levels went down somewhat but she was never able to "out-Mennonite the Mennonites."[11] Despite its headline, the article said little specifically about Mennonite food practices and relied mostly on assumptions about the Mennonite diet to draw conclusions about its medical benefits. Even so, the headline inspired the question implied by my book title and explored throughout this book – what does it mean to eat like a Mennonite?[12]

In public forums, there is rarely anything said about Mennonites and food that is negative – quite the opposite. Food produced by Mennonites is often assumed to be of exemplary quality. Advertising a foodstuff as "Mennonite" suggests a high standard and implies qualities of Mennonites more broadly. It is a case of "representation," suggests Magdalene Redekop in a comment about a Middle Eastern restaurant in Toronto that has "Mennonite-farmed chicken" on the menu.[13] When I stumble upon critiques of Mennonite food – as in an 1890 report by an RCMP sergeant, who described butter produced by Mennonite settlers in Manitoba as "generally inferior" and not in demand by English-speaking people – I am surprised.[14]

The idea of "eating like a Mennonite" appears in other unexpected ways. In the impressive collection of recipes and stories by Norma Jost Voth, *Mennonite Foods and Folkways from South Russia*, there is a recipe-story for "Eating Watermelon, Mennonite Style."[15] That Mennonites might have a unique and particular way of eating watermelon is an intriguing thought. Having married into a Mennonite family from British Columbia that has an obsessive passion for watermelon, I now jest that my family was not really Mennonite, since we cut our watermelon into polite round slices that were then quartered (so not too much watermelon juice dripped from our faces), rather than halving the melon and cutting large wedges. The latter method was clearly more egalitarian since, according to *Mennonite Foods and Folkways*, it gave everyone a taste of what was called the "little Abraham" – the sweetest core of the fruit. For some Mennonites, watermelon is at the centre of family and community stories and reinforces collective memories. It is part of their identity, exemplifying the manner in which food, in a Mennonite context, has meaning considerably deeper and broader than sustenance alone.

A close association between identity and food exists for many ethnic, national, religious, or culturally distinct groups, though the reasons for this link vary: the association may relate to religious dietary requirements; it may result from the global embrace and spread of an ethnic or national cuisine; it may emerge from a group's historic marginalization and consequent public attitudes toward its foodways. For Mennonites, all these factors are present to a degree. Among plain Mennonites and Amish, for whom many church rules and expectations exist with regard to technology, dress, and interaction with society, food is one aspect of life without particular mandates or

0.2   Mennonite children eating watermelon in Mexico, 1955.

restrictions. As such, taking pride in food preparation or consumption, or indulging in food even to excess, is not subject to disapproval. Likewise, for modernized Mennonites, food is an element of daily life that is not circumscribed by explicit religious dictates, even if some choose dietary regimes that reflect their personal ethics and values.

The purpose of this book is to explore the relationships between Mennonites and food. It is less about *what* Mennonites ate – though certainly culinary history appears throughout – than about what food has meant and means for Mennonites in diverse places and times, and why.

Who Are Mennonites?

A conversation about what it means to "eat like a Mennonite" is complicated by the questions "who are Mennonites?" and "which Mennonites are we talking about?" The Mennonites are a small Christian denomination that emerged as a radical movement during the Protestant Reformation in sixteenth-century Europe. They believed that only mature persons who voluntarily confessed Christian faith should be baptized, which was contrary to the prevailing practice of infant baptism into the church. As a result, they were originally called by their critics "Anabaptist," which means "re-baptizer." Their rejection of infant baptism put them into direct conflict with both the church and state of the day and thus Anabaptism became a clandestine religious movement that emerged and grew from centres in Switzerland, Germany, the Netherlands, and Moravia. Eventually, most Anabaptists were called Mennonites, after Dutch church leader Menno Simons. Hutterites and Amish, discussed periodically in this book, are also of Anabaptist descent and share many characteristics and beliefs with Mennonites.

Along with believers' baptism, the core tenets of Anabaptism included discipleship – following Jesus's life as example – and nonresistance (pacifism), which meant they would not take up arms during wars. They developed their set of beliefs from their communal reading and interpretation of the New Testament, and believed that both faith and good works were necessary for salvation. Anabaptists maintained a separation from affairs of the state and between the church and the world, and would not hold civil office. In order to maintain purity within the church, Anabaptists practised varying degrees of discipline toward members who deviated from the rules established to maintain that separation from society. For their beliefs, considered heretical in the sixteenth century, Anabaptists were severely persecuted. Many were arrested, imprisoned, and executed by both Roman Catholic and Protestant authorities.

Over time, Mennonites adopted many different positions on where to draw the line of nonconformity and separation vis-à-vis state and society; this resulted in numerous Mennonite subgroups – fifty or more in North America alone. Some groups are culturally assimilated and their members not markedly different from their neighbours in lifestyle, while others adopt a visible nonconformity through their dress codes, modes of transportation, and other customs of living.

Migration to lands where their beliefs and practices were protected became a hallmark of the Anabaptists, later Mennonites. Some went eastward from northern Europe and created communities in present-day Poland, Russia, and Ukraine. These are often referred to as "Russian" Mennonites, many of whom migrated to Canada and the United States in several waves beginning in the 1870s. Some of these later migrated to Mexico and Central and South America.

Other Mennonites left Europe and crossed the Atlantic Ocean westward to find new homes in America. Beginning in the late-seventeenth through the mid-eighteenth century, about 5,000 Mennonites from Switzerland migrated to Pennsylvania with promises of land and religious freedoms, including exemption from military service. Their descendant communities spread into the states of Virginia, Indiana, Ohio, and further west. Similar assurances were given to Mennonites by Upper Canadian officials, prompting a migration northward beginning in the late eighteenth century. Because of their ancestry, these Mennonites are often labelled "Swiss" or "Pennsylvania German."

The labels "Russian" and "Swiss" are problematic for many reasons: the nation-state designation runs counter to the actual ethnic and cultural characteristics of Mennonites in those places; the Swiss identity is related to centuries-old history, so has limited meaning, while the Russian identity fails to capture the twentieth-century Soviet era, not to mention an independent Ukraine, where the majority of Mennonites in this category situate their ancestry. Nevertheless, I will continue to use these labels, as they are simple and widely recognizable, at least by Mennonites themselves. Another naming complication is that many Mennonites around the world prefer to call themselves Anabaptist, finding more affinity with their sixteenth-century religious ancestors than with the cultural attributes associated with the Mennonite label.

Mennonites were founded as a religious group and this remains a primary identity marker. Yet because of the way in which Mennonites chose to live – separated, sometimes isolated physically and psychologically, and in self-sufficient communities – along with a long history of migration, their ethnic and religious practices merged in some contexts. As a result, scholars often describe Russian and Swiss Mennonites as an ethno-religious group, as do Mennonites themselves. Such cultural markers as language, dress, architecture, family stories, or foodways, which evolved from the intersection of religious belief and ethnic experience, became significant features of community identity at various times and places. At the same time, Mennonites who do not descend from Russian or Swiss historic streams have brought other ethnic and cultural identities and practices to contemporary Mennonite foodways. We meet them in the chapters ahead.

While Mennonite narratives historically emphasized religious freedom and nonconformity as motives for migration, all of the above relocations were part of global movements of white settler colonialism. As they migrated across the globe, Mennonites sought economic opportunity – mainly land on which to settle and farm – and they participated, even if unknowingly, in state-led processes that displaced Indigenous peoples.[16] Settler colonialism and imperialism was the larger context for Mennonite migrations to North America from the seventeenth through the nineteenth centuries. As Reina C. Neufeldt demonstrates, Mennonites, as racially privileged settlers, were "implicated subjects" in the colonial plan.[17]

For the church, empire-building included the spread of Christianity to colonized nations. Beginning in the mid-nineteenth century, Mennonites from Europe and North America participated actively in missions to Asia, Africa, and Latin America. They also launched their own efforts to "plant" churches on these continents, leading to the contemporary presence of Mennonites across the globe. Today there are more Mennonites in the global south than north, with significant populations in India, Indonesia, Ethiopia, and the Democratic Republic of Congo, for example.[18] In North America, colonial histories included enslavement of Black people forcibly transported to America, so that by the mid-twentieth century there was a substantial population of African-American Mennonites in the United States. American territorial expansion and the domination of Hispanic peoples also resulted in a significant number of Latino Mennonites today. With the rise of global migration to the west in the twentieth and twenty-first centuries, Mennonite churches and communities with "new" ethnic and national identities originating in southeast Asia, India, and Latin America, have multiplied. And so the historic dominance of Russian or Swiss attributes in Mennonite ethnic tradition and culture no longer exists.

Putting Food in Context

This book emerged from my growing interest in food studies in North America and around the world. Food as a topic for research emerged in earnest in the 1980s, building on work by anthropologists in the mid-twentieth century. Scholars from many disciplines are increasingly asking questions beyond what people ate – questions about the role of food in encounters between peoples, about how food shapes national and regional identities, about the use of food in public policy, and about the relationships between food and social class, food and sexuality, food and conflict, and food and religion.

Food offers an obvious (perhaps too obvious) glimpse into the social history of daily life. It is ubiquitous and omnipresent – physically, psychologically, and economically. At a very simple level, food consumes an enormous amount of historical time. Only quite recently – in the second half of the twentieth century – have the preparation, consumption, and preservation of food taken relatively little time. Our degree of removal from our food sources, and our quest for convenience, suggest a certain taken-for-grantedness about food and its centrality to human existence. In contrast, a pre-modern era demanded an intimacy and familiarity with the growing, harvesting, preserving, and preparing of food that is largely foreign to twenty-first century urbanites such as myself. My husband and I have tried to nurture a chaotic vegetable patch in our front yard, enjoying at least a few weeks of our own raspberries, cucumbers, tomatoes, and peppers, and each year we preserve a small amount of food purchased from local farms or farmers' markets. However, our quest to consume less processed food and return to an ephemeral "simpler" way of eating is by choice, not necessity. Our survival does not depend upon it.

In addition to the questions that concern culinary historians – the what and the how and the when – an array of food studies scholars are exploring the meaning that can be gleaned from *foodstuffs* – the things we eat – and *foodways* – the attendant practices and customs.[19] Kitchener, Ontario-based chef Teneile Warren, who explores the diasporic patterns of African and Caribbean foodways, emphasizes that food must always be understood "in context."[20] While foodstuffs are in and of themselves interesting, it is an analysis of foodways that offers understanding into human behaviour, both individually and collectively. We eat certain foods at specific times and in specific contexts because food is imbued with cultural, religious, social, and political meaning. As one food philosopher has stated, "Eating is an act that unites our physical, cultural, and reflective natures."[21] Yet food is so ubiquitous and so everyday that we overlook its potential to offer meaning. In this book I seek to understand the many meanings behind the idea that one can "eat like a Mennonite."

Food, Identity, and Inclusivity

In 1826, the French philosopher Jean Anthelme Brillat-Savarin wrote, "Tell me what you eat and I will tell you what you are," a simple reminder that the food we consume is formative for mind and body. Over time, the aphorism has been modified to "you are what you eat" and underlines the relationship between food and identity. Anthropologist Claude Fischler says simply, "Food is central to our sense of identity." He proposes that through the incorporation of foodstuffs "we become what we eat"; this process of incorporation is "the basis of collective identity and, by the same token, of otherness."[22]

Studying food historically means not only understanding *what* or *when* or *how* people ate, but exploring food as both "material items and symbols of identity"; according to Hasia R. Diner, it means a "journey to the heart of [a group's] collective world."[23] Laurie Bertram, who has written extensively about the material culture of Icelandic immigrants, says that one noteworthy foodstuff, the cake *vínarterta*, is an "enduring symbol" of that group's North American identity.[24] Even while the art of preparing *vínarterta* declined in Iceland, its resurgence among immigrant communities symbolized their defiance of discrimination and their assertion of the integrity of their ethnicity. For some immigrant groups, such as Germans in North America at the turn of the twentieth century, food practices persisted even while other signposts of ethnicity, such as language, declined. Barbara Lorenzkowski describes how one generation of German immigrants criticized another because the "only concession to their proud German heritage [was] the sauerkraut they served at their dining tables."[25]

The role of food in personal and group identity is evident in my own life and family history. My research and personal reflections grow out of my investigations, over several decades, into the history of Mennonite women and Mennonite identities and social practices more broadly. This book is at once a work of history, ethnography, and auto-ethnography. I grew up in a Mennonite family and married into one as well. My four grandparents and my in-laws survived food scarcity and famine in the former Soviet Union and migrated to Canada in the mid-1920s and late 1940s respectively. My grandparents grew into adulthood in a region that passed through revolution, world war, and civil war in just a decade, suffering the violence, disease, and food insecurity that characterized that era. My husband's parents and his extended family arrived in Canada as part of a large, displaced persons movement, having lived through years of repression in Stalin's Soviet Union, forced famine in Ukraine in the early 1930s, and a refugee flight from their homes in the midst of the Second World War. They knew what it was like to experience near starvation and many years of inadequate food. My in-laws engaged in "food-talk" almost constantly as a way of dealing with their recollections of the past and hopes for the future. Such food-talk – about buying, preparing, and consuming food – serves to "construct identity and imaginary belongings," writes historian Andrea Pető.[26] The intensity of food-talk may increase, perhaps ironically, during times of severe food scarcity. While my in-laws ate well in Canada – some might say richly – there always seemed to lurk a fear that there would not be enough food, or that they would be unable to prepare their traditional "Russian Mennonite" foods.

The personal linkages between food and identity were further prompted by my experience of ethno-tourism. On each of four trips I have made, first to the former Soviet Union in 1981 and after 1990 to Russia and Ukraine, I watched North American Mennonites (most of whom had Russian Mennonite ancestry) delight in the foods that elicited idealized memories of a homeland, and renewed or reinforced their sense of cultural identity. Among these are traditional Ukrainian dishes such as perogies and *borscht*, foods absorbed with modifications into Mennonite culture during their time in those lands. On one of those trips, I read Donna R. Gabaccia's 1998 book *We Are What We Eat: Ethnic Food and the Making of Americans*, in which she situates food and hybridity at the centre of the immigrant experience.[27] I realized that my own Mennonite identity was shaped as much, if not more, by culture and ancestry as by theological concept or doctrinal precept. I came to understand that Mennonite foodways reflected both a hybrid cuisine and a collective social memory that changed over time.

My research has occurred in contexts where I watched Mennonites prepare and consume food and witnessed the curious association of Mennonites and food practices. I attempted to broaden my knowledge beyond the expected ethnic categories of Russian and Swiss to include the foodways of Mennonites with varied histories, cultural backgrounds, and identities. And so I sought to understand new Mennonite communities in Canada, and travelled in India and the Democratic Republic of Congo, both countries with significant populations of Mennonites as a result of century-old mission activity. While people often thought it was odd that I was researching food, no one had difficulty responding to my conversation prompts. It is generally not difficult to get people to talk about food. In settings where I was meeting women and men for the first time, the fact that we could organize the time around food, both talking about it and eating together, allowed an easy familiarity, and even bonds of community, to emerge. Food was part of identity in these encounters, even while assumptions about what that meant needed to be adjusted.

Discussion about the links between food and identity inevitably leads one into present-day debates among Mennonites over their ethno-religiosity and what it means to be Mennonite. Church leaders and laypeople alike increasingly call for stripping Mennonite identity of ethnic and cultural features such as language, ancestral stories, insider humour, music, artistic and literary traditions, and certainly food. Some view ethnicity and culture as barriers to the inclusion in the contemporary church of people who do not have a historic (Russian or Swiss) Mennonite ethnicity. In 2017, an Ontario church leader issued a call for "no more Mennonite cookbooks!" because they carry too much cultural baggage.[28] The study of Mennonite "food and folkways," it has been suggested, leads to white ethnic chauvinism, even white supremacy, and thus the concept of Mennonites as an ethnic "peoplehood" is critiqued as "irredeemable."[29] It is important to consider how food and its meaning is a racialized question, one that I explore from my position of white ethnic privilege.

For some scholars and Mennonite church members, the label is a religious one *only*. And given the multiplicity of Mennonite racial and ethnic identities around the world, the attention given to the cultural heritage of the dominant historic ethnicities is viewed by some as not only misplaced, but wrong. Thus, to talk about "Mennonite food" is to connect categories that do not belong together. I understand this perspective and embrace the need for inclusivity, but I also believe that religious belief and practice are always embedded in culture. Rather than rejecting ethnic characteristics in Mennonite communities, I propose that more effort be made to acknowledge the diverse range of cultural practices among all individuals and communities who call themselves Mennonite or Anabaptist. Describing her "newfound belonging" in her Mennonite heritage, Elise Epp (no relation to the author) states it well: "The fear is that if we talk about 'Mennonite' names and food, we will exclude people who are from other ethnic backgrounds … But it is one thing to welcome people of different backgrounds into our communities; it is another to shy away from our own heritage … It is not lamentable that what began as a faith movement grew into a culture."[30] Elise and I may be raising the "inconvenient questions" that, as scholar Warren Belasco suggests, are inherent in the cross-disciplinary field of food studies.[31]

In light of increasingly polarized stances on social, theological, and doctrinal issues along the Mennonite spectrum, I hope that the food-related themes explored in the chapters that follow are a site of connection, rather than division. Such an approach allows for a "grateful celebration of ... cultural hybridity" as called for by poet and essayist Di Brandt,[32] instead of regret and embarrassment over a disappearing Mennonite "essence." This book's agenda is, in part, to explore the relationship between Mennonite religious faith and practice and varied Mennonite cultures, as revealed in foodways. I hope to contribute to Felipe Hinojosa's call to "deterritorialize Mennonite studies" and to be "relational"[33] in thinking about the formation of Mennonite identity as something that happens through encounters across racial, ethnic, and gender boundaries and binaries. Indeed, Hinojosa's own perspectives were shaped by his growing up in a Latino Mennonite church where people "blended their faith and culture by incorporating the cultural elements of music, rhythm, dress, and language into their faith experiences."[34] Hinojosa's experiences confirm what food theorist Massimo Montanari maintains, that "every identity is a dynamic, unstable product of history."[35] Emphasizing that instability has the potential to challenge the systemic racism pervading Mennonite historical narratives. Here, foodways are not incidental but central to the conversation. Gabby Martin, of Black and Syrian parentage and adopted by Mennonites in Saskatchewan, struggles with the need to "prove" her Mennonite-ness because of her "appearance." One tactic she uses is to "explain ... that I know how to make *schmaunfat* [cream gravy]."[36] A traditional Mennonite food, in this case, is a bridge to understanding, even if Gabby felt she needed to learn this foodway in order to fit in.

Religion and food scholars Michel Desjardins and Ellen Desjardins observe that "Canadians tend to be more interested ... in tasting 'local Mennonite food' or supporting the Mennonite sale of fair trade coffee, than they are in attending Mennonite church services."[37] This may also be true for individuals with a Mennonite family background. While some take issue with the idea that there is a thing called Mennonite food, we should not ignore the phenomenon of what is called "food roots" – individuals exploring the food traditions of their ancestors as a way of finding identity in a post-religious era. This may be why many young adults, whether of recent or long ago Mennonite background, are keenly interested in their cultural food traditions. Some of these are embracing Mennonite foodways because so little else about being Mennonite is engaging them, particularly in a North American context.

For non-gender binary individuals, traditional Mennonite foodways provide a connector to ancestry and community in cases when church institutions reject their sexual identity(ies). For example, Alicia J. Dueck offers the idea that queer Mennonites who feel themselves outside the normative categories of Mennonite identity with regard to sexuality maintain their sense of belonging as Mennonite because of cultural touchstones such as Mennonite foodways.[38] Similarly, queer Mennonite writer Daniel Cruz suggests that Mennonite ethnicity, while "tenuous," may be valuable because it "keeps the possibility of staying within the Mennonite community alive" for individuals who were rejected by that community for theological reasons.[39]

Many individuals who may not be actively involved in church life and who might call themselves cultural Mennonites speak about food traditions as what ties them to their history and also, however tangentially, to their religious identity. The 2020 travel narrative of Cameron Dueck, who motorcycled from Canada to Bolivia visiting conservative Mennonite communities along the way, is not explicitly about food, but descriptions of his food expectations and experiences recur throughout the book.[40] Memoirist Rhoda Janzen is nostalgic about family foodways, musing that it would be "pleasurable to revisit the very Mennonite foods" that she recalls as causing "shame" when she brought them to school in her youth.[41] Writer Darcie Friesen Hossack observes that "being Mennonite is why I will never be skinny" and describes her Russian Mennonite grandmother, who taught her to cook and love the rich foods from her background.[42] This identity dilemma is referenced in Ernie Harder's collection of family stories,

0.3 Sign with traditional Russian Mennonite foods at Steinbach, Manitoba, Pride Parade, 2016.

when he acknowledges that his expanding family has a diversity of identities and varying degrees of affinity for their Mennonite roots. However, he writes, "If rituals and traditions anchor one's identity, then for us and our children's generation one of the most significant factors in preserving 'Mennonite ethnic identity' involves food!" He tells of grandchildren making traditional Russian Mennonite foods (*zwieback* and *rollkuchen*) for their grandmother's birthday even though this might be the "extent of their outward Mennonite identity."[43]

Conversely, the loss of traditional Mennonite foodways may be accompanied by a loss of identity. The third-generation descendants of Nicolai and Katharina Rempel, immigrants from the Soviet Union to Canada in the 1920s, were described by a second-generation family member as shedding their identity because, along with the decline of four-part hymn-singing, "croissants had replaced the zwieback."[44] Others more roundly reject their connection to the Mennonite religion but maintain Mennonite-ness as a cultural label. For example, in 1989 writer John Weier, in an essay in a Mennonite periodical, listed eleven observations about why he did not consider himself Mennonite, yet paused to say, "Well, maybe I really am," in noting that "I still really like *holobuschi* [cabbage rolls]! And chicken will always taste better done with *bubbat* [cake-like poultry dressing] the way Mom made it when I lived at home."[45] Canadian radio personality Helen (Sawatsky) Frayne said, "I don't consider myself a Mennonite though I spring from that tradition. I'm a seeker, an observer, a sceptic. Even so, once or twice a year I make Plume Mooss (a Mennonite fruit soup) and Papanat (peppernut cookies, tiny and spicy) which my children enjoy." Frayne described Mennonites as "pacifists, good cooks or fine singers," thereby combining cultural and religious traits.[46] For Weier and Frayne, traditional foodways were a caveat to their rejection of Mennonitism.

Yet another perspective comes from Mennonites who have found their way "from Mennonite cooking to Mennonite churches."[47] Mexican American Lupe De León became a Mennonite "via the Kool-Aid and cookies route," whereby invitations to church by missionaries in his south Texas community in the 1950s were accompanied by bags of groceries.[48] Historian Felipe Hinojosa said his family first met "ethnic Mennonites" while picking tomatoes on Mennonite-owned farms, an encounter that is about socio-economic class as much as food.[49] One factor in the twentieth-century growth of Anabaptist and Mennonite adherents – individuals with varied ethnic backgrounds – in the United Kingdom was "food and the generous sharing of it," according to Andrew Francis. He observes, "we ate our way into Anabaptism."[50] Here, the food practices of commensality and hospitality, which Francis identifies at the site of Mennonite origins, rather than particular recipes, are what creates the connections. There are humorous takes on this association as well. Artist Victor Klassen introduced his friends to "Mennonite sausage" and because of their enthusiasm, suggested, "the Mission Board should use it as an enticement for converting people to Mennonites."[51]

It has long been an adage for immigrants of many backgrounds that, while assimilation into a new society proceeds, language may be the first cultural feature to vanish, and food is the last. For most Mennonites whose ancestors migrated to North America, the German language has long been forgotten, but traditional recipes can easily be maintained as a signpost of identity. The fact that, in most societies, eating has historically been a commensal activity – performed in families, households, neighbourhoods, and other gatherings – further underscores the relationship between Mennonites and food. As cultural theorist Magdalene Redekop notes, "community ... when all is said and done [is] perhaps the most enduring of Mennonite values."[52] In a modern, secular, individualist society, people who reclaim their Mennonite roots through foodways are also searching for community and a sense of belonging. Describing foodways as "Mennonite" serves to reinforce Mennonite identity – whether religious and/or ethnic. At the same time, a collective idea of Mennonite-ness fortifies an imagined cuisine that is part of that identity.[53] Even so, these linkages are not static but are constructed, dismantled, and reinvented across time and place and memory.

Food, Memory, and Collective History

Religion scholar Pamela E. Klassen has referred to the "Mennonite romance with food" as a way of retaining connections to places that are distant and elusive.[54] Indeed, food helps us to remember the past, whether it is pleasure-ful or traumatic, and thus plays an important role in shaping memory and constructing identity. Sensory memories of food are often retained more vividly than other recollections of daily life.[55] Applying this idea, I suggest that remembering food eaten in past eras often prompts the remember-er to then *prepare* particular foods, which promotes the reproduction of those memories. Food memories thus construct identity in the present as well as past, as eating and memory interact in a dialogical manner. As I found in my research on Mennonite women refugees of the Second World War, narratives about food served as a device to organize memories, shroud traumatic experiences, and create familiarity when individuals remembered the unfamiliar and insecure terrain of uprooting and resettlement.[56] Poignant and vivid food memories exist for those Mennonites with a personal history of forced or voluntary migration, who maintain a sense of a lost homeland with its traditional remembered foodways. As Nadia Jones-Gailani observes about Iraqi women in diaspora, with whom interviews always involved the presence or memory of food and drink, foodways "occupy the very centre of longing, as migrants seek comfort in the act of consuming, savouring the nostalgic memories evoked by foods they associate with home."[57]

Discourse about food, both concrete and metaphorical, is abundant in the memory sources of Mennonites, such as written memoirs, autobiography, and oral interviews. Since food is central to collective and individual identity, it may be especially important to document in oral and written memoirs because it functions as a means of recall that is part of daily routine, rather than an extraordinary event. For individuals going through traumatic events such as starvation, political repression, violence, war, and displacement, activities as basic as cooking and eating can bring relief, sometimes even humour, to personal narratives that otherwise appear tragic and hopeless. Fear, pain, sadness, and despair do not disappear, but can be veiled by detailed descriptions of "what we ate that day." In my interviews, narrators who had experienced traumatic displacement as refugees were more inclined to talk about the food preparation over a fire at the end of a difficult day than they were to describe the fear of the bomb blasts they heard in the distance, terror surrounding sexual violence, or the knowledge of friends and family who had died or been left behind. Even for Mennonites who have no direct experience of oppression or hardship, intergenerational trauma might manifest itself in ideas and attitudes about food. In the midst of the war on Ukraine in 2022, a woman of Mennonite background reflected on baking Ukrainian Easter bread, called *paska*, in the tradition of her ancestors who fled Ukraine in the 1920s. Comparing these times of tumult separated by one hundred years, she described the smell of baking bread, in her childhood and after visiting a Mennonite museum, as "a wholly appropriate smell" that connected past and present.[58] Memory thus serves to associate particular foods with feelings, events, and emotions of one's past life.[59]

While this book does not deal extensively with Mennonites' emotional relationship to food, this is an underlying theme. For example, Mennonites who struggle with eating disorders can feel themselves separate from notions of collective identity that place food consumption at the centre of abundance, generosity, and community. One woman with anorexia nervosa said in a 2013 blog that she "almost didn't become a Mennonite because of the food." After moving to a new community, she was interested in joining the local Mennonite church, but hesitated because of the congregation's practice of eating Sunday breakfast together and her own struggle with eating food prepared by others.[60] I'm certain there are many other stories about Mennonite identity and food that are painful, rather than pleasurable, but are silenced because of overriding stereotypes, held by and about Mennonites.

Searching for Food and Meaning

Although food is ubiquitous in our everyday lives, it is often absent in historical sources, particularly in institutional histories and archival sources. The invisibility of food is indicative of its everydayness; yet once you begin looking, you can find references to the preparation and consumption of food almost anywhere. Thus, the evidence and examples I offer are an exercise in selection. Personal memoirs, diaries, family history, autobiography – often referred to collectively as "life-writing" – provide a rich repository for memories, reflections, anecdotes, and analyses of food practices in Mennonite households. Some contain recipes, a phenomenon more common in recent memoirs, or "foodoirs."[61] Oral histories also provide rich glimpses into eating practices.

Creative writing – poetry, novels, creative nonfiction – often illuminates foodways better than traditional historical sources.

Eleanor Hildebrand Chornoboy's novel about the Mennonite migration to Canada in the 1870s is replete with food references as the book's characters relish traditional Russian Mennonite dishes consumed in times of abundance and longed for during the hardship years of early settlement.[62] According to Robert Zacharias, Alayna Munce's novel *When I Was Young and in My Prime* offers a "poignant commentary on the shifting structure of Mennonite cultural identity, mediated at key moments through a deep concern with Mennonite food and foodways."[63] Julia Kasdorf's poem "When Our Women Go Crazy" and David Waltner-Toews' "Tante Tina" poems are full of images regarding Mennonites' love/hate relationship with food.[64] And so this study draws occasionally on creative writing for memories and other imaginative perspectives.

Cookbooks are among the best sources about foodstuffs and foodways if one learns to read them as texts. Memories and recipes often come together in food and culture blogs with Mennonite themes, of which there are a growing number. Some of these illuminate unexpected intersections. *MennoNeechie Kitchen*, for example, is produced by an Indigenous individual fostered in a Mennonite home; the blog offers traditional Russian Mennonite recipes with stories and memories from the author's upbringing.[65] *Mennopolitan*, a blog by a Canadian Mennonite woman whose background is in the Low German-speaking community in Mexico, writes extensively about her cultural identity with numerous blogposts about foodways; among her descriptors is the statement, "I love to cook Mexican-inspired Low German food."[66] There are other Mennonite food blogs that consist of recipes almost exclusively, such as the popular *Mennonite Girls Can Cook*.

If I were to write a food blog, my family might suggest the title "A Mennonite Girl Who Doesn't Cook!" Not that I can't, and indeed, I regularly do. However, we joke that while I am the one who researches, teaches, and writes about food, it is the three men of my household who love cooking and do it very well. As a family, we participated for four years in a supper program for unhoused and marginally housed individuals in Waterloo Region, preparing a three-course meal for 200 people once a month for six months of the year. My husband was head cook, but our eldest son quickly took over and, with a community of friends, continued to cook nourishing and delicious meals for people who appeared to love the spicy enchiladas, our signature family dish. At the age of twenty-two, the younger son became head cook at a Mennonite summer camp, thinking outside the traditional fare to offer baked *halloumi* cheese as a vegetarian option and rainbow-coloured "Pride" bagels. Food-talk is almost constant in our household, whether it is a discussion of a restaurant meal or a debate over the stove regarding preparation methods for the meal underway. This is just to say that my own familial food landscape shapes how I think about the topic more broadly. In this, Mennonites are not unique; witness the number of books and articles about food, culture, and identity, in which authors are clearly situated as subject.

This book is thus, in part, "personalized scholarship,"[67] as I have allowed myself the privilege and indulgence of letting family stories inform my research. Some might argue that I can insert myself into the story only because of the senior stage of my academic career. This may be partly true, yet I have always believed that "the personal and emotional can be legitimate forms of scholarly writing,"[68] as Franca Iacovetta proposes. Because the body of sources used for this book is simply "the lives of others," and because I am an insider in the Mennonite community, my life, and the lives of those around me, may offer insight into understanding the meaning of food for Mennonites. I trust that readers will draw on their own experiences to compare and contrast, and think of their own lives as valuable anthropological and historical sources.

A few other caveats before we begin. While I reflect somewhat on gardening, crops, and livestock, this book is not about food production in the context of agricultural history. Numerous Mennonite community histories chronicle settlement, land-clearing, and farming activity, but many such narratives omit the preparation and consumption of food *inside* the household, which is my emphasis.[69] I have broadened my analysis beyond Canada and North America in order to consider fascinating examples of Mennonite foodways from across the globe, but my research is not comprehensive in this regard. A particular challenge for any scholar of Mennonite studies is addressing the diversity of Mennonites in their analysis. The diversity exists on wide spectrums of ethnicity, race, and national origin; of sexuality and gender identity; of evangelical emphasis and theological tilt; and of degree of separation from and nonconformity to the modern world, to name a few. And while I have tried to incorporate stories of an evangelically minded woman from Democratic Republic of Congo, alongside a horse-and-buggy family in rural Ontario, alongside a transgender person in urban Winnipeg, it is difficult to find commonalities other than a label they claim as theirs: Mennonite.[70]

The chapters ahead take up some of the themes, questions, and limitations I have identified around the meaning of "eating like a Mennonite." Chapter 1 is about eating encounters, in which I describe the modifications and adoptions in the Mennonite diet as different migrant groups crossed territorial borders – from Europe to Russia/Ukraine to the Americas, and between North and South America – in the distant and more recent past. It is here where ideas about ethnicity and religion both align and collide, and where ideas about "Mennonite food" are formed. Crossing cultural food borders also happened when Mennonite settlers encountered Indigenous peoples on the latter's lands, and when Mennonite missionaries both imposed and appropriated foodways in environments drastically different from their own. As we shall see, transformations to foodways occurred on both sides of these borders.

While much of chapter 1 refers to national or regional borders, the subtitle of the book – *Food and Community across Borders* – suggests that borders also exist across cultures, theological spectrums, ancestral histories, and gender identities. Sometimes these borders are external to Mennonites and prompt encounters with others. At other times, these borders are internal to Mennonite communities and point to the diversity and difference that exists within a relatively small denomination. Food can either create or overcome borders and boundaries.

Chapter 2 explores food and gender. I examine the longstanding associations between food and female and woman-identified natures, which is illuminated in numerous literary and memoir sources about Mennonites. To a lesser extent, I also probe the relationship between food and masculinity. Mennonite cookbooks are the subject of chapter 3. The cookbook proves to be an invaluable source for tracing the evolving ethnic identity of foodways. Reading between the recipe-instructional lines of this source shows the particularity of Mennonite foodways, but also their alignment with wider societal trends. Chapter 4 diverges from the food abundance signified by most cookbooks and food writing by looking at hunger and scarcity in the Mennonite past. Many Mennonites, especially those with histories in the former Russian empire or Soviet Union, and today in countries that struggle with food security, have experiences of near-starvation, hunger, and/or lack of adequate nutrition. These experiences, and the memories of them, have profound implications for later generations. The final chapter examines foodways in the context of religious practice, including the role of food in Mennonite religious ritual, the importance of community and commensality in eating practices, and the centrality of food in Mennonite programs of relief.

After a pause in working on this book, I returned to my unfinished manuscript during the "stay at home" months of the Covid-19 global pandemic that began in March 2020. Suddenly, conversation and activity around food took on new importance and proportion: the custom of eating out disappeared; food sector workers were celebrated as essential; concerns about food scarcity caused panic purchasing and hoarding of some foodstuffs; baking and cooking from scratch experienced a revival in many homes; gardening and food preservation similarly attracted new practitioners; food insecurity became a deeper or new reality for many people; food caring was boosted as individuals supported food banks and purchased groceries for seniors and others. New writings about food emerged, such as the blog *Historians Cooking the Past*, featuring favourite recipes and "stories of loss, community, family, and food heritages" that spoke to the current crisis.[71] It felt as if all the themes of this book on Mennonites and food emerged in traditional and novel ways in response to a completely new global environment. While I do not attempt to analyze the pandemic through the lens of foodways, or Mennonite responses specifically, I am reminded that food as physical sustenance and social signifier has meaning in all times and places.

Fresh Spring Rolls (*Goi Cuon*) with Peanut Sauce

Recipe by Dung Manh Do

Dung Manh Do and his family were refugees from Vietnam who were sponsored for immigration to Canada by the Niagara United Mennonite Church in Virgil, Ontario, in 1979.

This recipe is taken from Ellery Penner and Rachael Peters' *The Cookbook Project: Celebrating 75 Years of Meals and Memories*, an innovative collection that includes recipes from the diverse ethnic backgrounds in the church community, extending notions about "Mennonite food" beyond Russian and Swiss heritage.

Ingredients for Spring Rolls

- ½ pkg. rice vermicelli (yields 2¼ cups)
- 12 8"–9" rice paper sheets
- ½ lb. lean pork (optional), cooked for half an hour over medium heat, thinly sliced*
- 2 green onions
- ½ English cucumber, thinly sliced
- 1 carrot, peeled and grated
- 6 large Boston or leaf lettuce leaves, cut in half
- 2 sprigs fresh coriander (cilantro), coarsely chopped
- ½ cup fresh mint leaves
- ½ lb. large shrimp*

* for vegetarian spring rolls, substitute bean sprouts, thinly sliced beets, and/or fried, thinly sliced tofu

Directions for Spring Rolls

1. Cook the rice vermicelli according to directions on the package and set aside.
2. Pour 3 cups of hot water into a large shallow bowl.
3. One at a time, immerse the rice paper in hot water for 10 seconds (no longer) and then place it on a damp towel to keep it from drying out. There is no need to have more than one rice paper on the damp towel.

4. To form the roll, lay a rice paper on a flat surface. Take a small amount of cooked rice noodle, pork, and vegetable mixture, and lay it across the bottom third. Please don't overstuff as it will tear. Rice paper is very delicate after it is soaked in water.
5. Carefully fold the bottom of the rice paper up to cover the filling, then fold the left and right side. Tuck and roll it over once.
6. Lay 2 pieces of shrimp on top, then tuck and roll it over to close. The shrimp should show through the transparent rice paper.
7. Arrange the finished rolls on a platter and cover with a damp cloth.
8. Serve the rolls with dipping sauce.

Ingredients for Peanut Dipping Sauce

¼ cup creamy peanut butter
¼ cup water
3 Tbsp. Hoisin sauce

1 Tbsp. freshly squeezed lime juice
1 Tbsp. sugar

Directions for Peanut Sauce

Whisk all of the ingredients together in a medium bowl, and set aside.

1

Eating Encounters

Mennonites Move across Time and Place

Just outside the small southwest Ontario town of Aylmer, about two hours west of Toronto, is a brightly painted general store called Mennomex. The owner and founder of Mennomex, Maria Martens, was born and raised in Mexico, but her ancestors migrated to north-central Mexico from Canada in the 1920s and their ancestors from Ukraine in the 1870s.[1] The name of the store, which opened in 1997, combines her ethno-religious heritage – Mennonite – with her geographical place of birth and youth – Mexico. Mennomex offers a mix of foods from several cultural traditions. Its main fare is Mexican, with shelves full of almost every imaginable type of ground, canned, and bottled chilis, salsas, hot sauces, and pickles, and its takeout menu consisting of foods like *tamales*, *burritos*, and *tacos*. However, it also sells farmers' sausage, *vereniki* (dumplings like perogies), and soup noodles, all foodstuffs deriving from the Mennonite sojourn in the Netherlands, Prussia, Russia, and Ukraine. Also in the coolers is locally made and imported *queso menonita* (Mennonite cheese), a food item for which Mennonites are famous in Mexico. A second Mennomex opened in 2019 in the small town of Milverton, just west of Kitchener-Waterloo, attesting to the business's success, especially among the growing population of Mennonite migrants from Mexico and Central and South America who live in southwest Ontario.

Across the street from the Aylmer store was a less eye-catching restaurant called the Hacienda Roadhouse Café, now closed. Though

1.1 Advertisement for salsa at Mennomex store, Aylmer, Ontario, 2022.

its menu offered predominantly Mexican food – *tacos*, *burritos*, *tostados*, *tamales*, and so on – it also specialized in soups, especially chicken noodle soup, which was popular as take-out fare for Sunday lunch. The owner's soup recipe used homemade egg noodles, derived from his cultural identity as Russian Mennonite – even though he never visited Russia, was born in Mexico, and immigrated to Canada as a young man. Several hours down the highway, in the town of Leamington, sits another hybrid restaurant called Family Kitchen. On the menu, which features (when I visited) separate lists of "Mennonite," "Mexican," and "Canadian" foods, the text beneath the restaurant's name announces, "where we make you feel at home." Possibly more authentic than most restaurant chains that purport to serve Mexican, the Family Kitchen serves up complex dishes like *Chile Rellenos* – "two poblano peppers, peeled and roasted on an open flame, stuffed with seasoned ground beef and cheese then dipped in a homemade batter and lightly fried to perfection."[2] A quite different authenticity is served up in the "traditional" Mennonite chicken noodle soup, said in the menu to be "just like Grandma makes!"[3]

There are numerous other restaurants and food stores like this in southwestern Ontario, southern Manitoba, and other parts of western Canada. Del Rios in Winkler, Manitoba, an hour south of Winnipeg, offers "MENNONITE DISHES as good as mom's," "Dad's favourite MEXICAN PLATTER," and "CHICKEN NOODLE SOUP 30 years of delicious tradition."[4] And several years ago, I delighted to find the "Funky Menno" pizza at Pizza Haven in Altona, Manitoba, my childhood home. This "fusion" pizza includes *schmaunt fat* (cream sauce), ham, texmex cheese, farmers' sausage, bacon, and jalapeno peppers, and is drizzled with salsa.[5]

Most of these dual-themed – Russian Mennonite and Mexican – food businesses were established by a Mennonite cultural group referred to as Low German-speaking because of their distinct language dialect. These Mennonites have crossed national and foodways borders many times. Indeed, they are among the most migratory groups in the world today, since their movement is not just historical, but contemporary and ongoing, both northward and southward. They are descended from 1870s Mennonite migrants from Ukraine to the Canadian prairies and American Midwest. These Mennonites sought not only abundant, good farmland in North America but also exemption from military service and autonomy in language and education. In 1922, resisting requirements to send their children to public schools or adhere to government regulations on curriculum in private schools, about 7,000 left Canada to establish colonies and villages in north-central Mexico. Over time, some went further south to Belize, Honduras, Paraguay, and Bolivia.[6]

Beginning in the 1950s, many Mennonites "returned" to Canada from Mexico and other parts of Central and South America, perhaps 100,000 or more by the early 2000s. As they physically moved back and forth across numerous borders, they were also eating across borders – from Russia and Ukraine to Canada to Mexico and back to

Canada or on to Belize or Bolivia. Indeed, the multiple food identities of this group further stirs the debate about "what is Mennonite food?" Is it Dutch, German, Russian, Mexican, Canadian – all of these, or none of these? While Mennonites may claim some signature recipes as uniquely Mennonite, these are really the result of migrations that embed Mennonites in cultural environments that they absorb and appropriate. As food philosopher Alexandra Plakias writes, "Dishes travel from one place to another and are shaped by their journeys; contact between cultures yields contact between cuisines."[7]

Mennomex and the other businesses described above are manifestations of what food scholars refer to as "hybridity" – mixed cuisines that emerge as the product of encounters between people moving around the globe, whether within regions or across oceans, whether forced or voluntary, with different culinary practices and traditions.[8] When food cultures interact, it is almost inevitable that food adoptions and alterations will occur as people are drawn to – or repelled by – the foodstuffs and foodways that they meet. In each new cultural context, Mennonites participated in food exchanges and underwent food adaptations. Identifying hybridity in Mennonite foodways requires us to rethink the traditional emphases on Mennonite separation from the world, as well as their often-perceived isolation and self-sufficiency. Recognizing hybridity also counters disdain for all that is not-Mennonite by acknowledging the many peoples and cultures among whom Mennonites live. Mennonite-raised poet and essayist Di Brandt, in her essay "In Praise of Hybridity," makes this point, though somewhat sarcastically: "The various countries that hosted us as refugees over the centuries can't have been all that hostile if we learned nearly all our recipes from them!"[9]

Eating encounters also happened in mission settings – at home and abroad – when Mennonites were compelled to adopt new cultural forms, even while the colonialist agenda suggested they should impose Western norms considered superior. This chapter explores the formation and transformation of Mennonite culinary practices as Mennonites encounter other peoples and cultures in the process of migration, colonialism, and missions.

Zwieback, Sauerkraut, and *Tamales* Become Mennonite Food

By and large, Mennonites did not choose the peoples and cultures of the environments in which they settled; their movements were often not voluntary, were sometimes sudden, and were directed by various external forces. Whether the interactions across cultural boundaries were positive or negative, they were certainly transformative. For immigrants, food encounters between old and new worlds help to bridge cultural barriers but may also reinforce xenophobia toward particular groups. The very notion of a fixed Mennonite identity – cultural or religious – is challenged if we consider evolving diets as part of that identity.

Scholars, myself included, frequently use the term "diaspora" to describe Mennonites, by which is meant the historic and contemporary scattering of Mennonites who maintain some connection to a "homeland" – whether a physical locale, or a set of memories and emotions attached to "place." The propensity of Mennonites to move back and forth across borders over several generations, to maintain group and familial connections across these borders, and to retain notions of homeland origins, reinforces such a diasporic identity. The notion of homeland is different for all groups of Mennonites. Swiss Mennonites maintained certain European customs – even if their memory of migration two centuries earlier had long since dissipated – that were transformed by interactions with other Germanic groups in Pennsylvania. Russian Mennonites were perhaps even more bound to an ancestral past because so many left their homes abruptly and involuntarily as revolution, civil war, and two world wars led to the disintegration or dispersal of their communities.

Their particular diaspora saw Mennonites migrate to many parts of the globe, where their Mennonite diet and their Mennonite identity were simultaneously reinforced and transformed.[10] Histories of the Mennonites in various times and places have not, I believe, given sufficient weight to the importance of the cultural changes that occurred, even while Mennonite separateness in religious ideals was maintained. While historians have emphasized Mennonites' language retention, independence in education, social separation, and economic differentiation, much less attention has been given to the Mennonites' absorption and adaption of cultures that surrounded them. Past narratives of Mennonite self-sufficiency and autonomy that predominated in written accounts and collective mythology strengthened Mennonites' sense of their uniqueness and also reinforced ethnic and class stratification vis-à-vis their neighbours. By perpetuating notions that "Mennonite food" existed as a distinct cuisine, Mennonites could maintain distance from, and a sense of superiority toward, the populations among whom they settled, be those Indigenous peoples, Ukrainian peasants, or Mexican labourers.

For Mennonites, each settlement era and locale produced modified understandings of the place of food in ethnic and religious identity. The differentiation of foodways served to connect Mennonites with the national and regional environments within which each Mennonite group found itself. Such differentiation solidified important identity markers that set Mennonites apart from each other with labels such as Russian, Swiss, or Mexican, or something else. The 1974 *Melting Pot of Mennonite Cookery*, published by the women's association of the Mennonite-founded Bethel College in Kansas, is a good example of this. Profiling the origins of ten different Mennonite ethnic cuisines, the cookbook reinforces intra-Mennonite differentiation, while yielding a new national identification by drawing on the American motif of the "melting pot."[11] *Borscht*, a soup with eastern European, Russian, and Ukrainian roots, but often identified by Mennonites as one of their traditional foods, became the symbol for both difference *and* sameness. It draws Mennonites together in their collective historical experience of Russia, Ukraine, and Eastern Europe, yet serves to define uniqueness by virtue of selective ingredients – beets or cabbage, meat or no-meat, dill or no-dill, and so on. Often including beef or chicken as a main ingredient, and with cabbage more common than beets, Mennonites implicitly understood their *borscht* as superior to the no-meat, beet-based Ukrainian variety – even though the soup's name itself evolved from the Slavic word for beet.[12]

Like *borscht*, other Russian Mennonite foods emerged from Dutch, Prussian/Polish, and Russian/Ukrainian traditions, while Swiss Mennonite foods drew from Swiss and South German influences. The foodways brought to the Russian empire beginning in the late eighteenth century had Germanic, Polish, and Dutch influences, and included such items as *portzelky* (deep-fried fritters, usually made at New Year's, similar to the Dutch *oliebollen*), *vereniki*, and *zwieback*, also possibly traceable to the Netherlands. A cold fruit soup called *plumi moos* has Scandinavian origins and may have arrived at the Mennonite table because of cultural interaction in the Baltic region. The Christmas cookies that my mother and I still make – tiny little peppernuts – have northern European origins though as a child I assumed that only Mennonites ate them! These foodstuffs then accompanied Mennonites when they migrated to Canada and the United States beginning in the late nineteenth century, as well as to Mexico and Central and South America in decades to follow.

Drawing on concepts of "food-mapping," Robert Zacharias notes "the way in which the foodways of the Russian Mennonite community in Canada quietly bear witness to the serial migrations of their past."[13] Each signature dish that is ascribed a Mennonite label is a hybrid of accumulated recipes, continually modified across households and generations. Often these foods are associated with assumptions that Mennonites are mainly rural, agricultural people with simple diets. While this is true in some historical contexts, urban Mennonites in the seventeenth and eighteenth centuries in the Netherlands and Prussia adopted "fine eating" and cultivated "exotic plants."[14] For example, in Danzig, Prussia (present-day Gdańsk, Poland), a Mennonite-founded restaurant has been a site of fine dining since the sixteenth century, still operating as the Pod Łososiem/Under the Salmon restaurant in 2022.[15] This was also where a Mennonite distiller developed and became renowned across Europe for the liqueur *Danziger Goldwasser*.

In a similar way, Mennonites who identified ethnically as Swiss engaged in food exchange in the Alsace and Palatinate regions of Europe and again after migration to Pennsylvania, with other British and European newcomers, beginning in the late seventeenth century.

As Mennonites in America interacted with a range of settler cultures with Germanic roots, an ethno-cultural fusion in language, craft, art, and foodways emerged, known as "Pennsylvania German." William Woys Weaver suggests that the process of borrowing and adapting certain foods and recipes is one of the most interesting aspects of Pennsylvania German cooking, an evolving cuisine that reflects the blending of diverse religious and national origins.[16] A Swiss Mennonite table, as well as an Amish one, was often ordered by the adage "seven sweets and seven sours" because of the culture's preference for just about anything pickled – eggs, cherries, watermelon, pig's feet, corn – and the tendency to include multiple desserts – especially pie – with a meal. Sociologist John Hostetler called the "seven sweets and seven sours" description an invention by the tourism industry, thus underscoring the role of public stereotypes regarding Mennonite and Amish cuisine.[17]

Perhaps even more important than pickles and pies is meat, especially sausage, in the Swiss Mennonite diet.[18] Today, that *wurstkultur* (sausage culture) is evident in the popularity of sausage often labelled as "Mennonite" or bearing the producer's recognizably Mennonite name. For the Swiss ethnic stream of Mennonites in North America, shoofly pie also became a signature dish – a unique molasses and sugar pie that required shooing the flies away because of its stickiness. Sauerkraut is another staple Pennsylvania German/Swiss Mennonite and Amish foodstuff, but is well known within Germanic cuisine more broadly. Indeed, Weaver proposes that sauerkraut is the "one unifying element and the key dish that made the [Pennsylvania Germans] different from all the other American groups ... and a cornerstone that holds up the entire cuisine."[19]

Swiss/Pennsylvania German food culture endured as a regular part of a Mennonite diet through the eighteenth century and was brought to Upper Canada (present-day Ontario) when Mennonites migrated there in the early nineteenth century. The Amish who migrated directly from Europe to Canada beginning in 1822 brought comparable foodways. Over the course of the twentieth century, certain cultural hallmarks of Swiss Mennonites and

Amish – *fraktur* calligraphy, charming as a healing art, hex signs on barns, the Pennsylvania German dialect – began to disappear. Yet, food customs were maintained and even strengthened in the context of farmers' markets and theme restaurants that cater to tourists interested mainly in the horse and buggy Mennonite and Amish version of the Swiss diaspora. In Waterloo Region, where I live, the close identification of Mennonites with pie is rather ironic, given that this method of combining fruit and pastry and sugar has origins going back centuries, and was brought to North America by Dutch, Swedish, and British immigrants. Pie-making is a culinary practice that Mennonites and Amish acquired over time, learning from the ethnic environments in which they lived. The strong association of pie with Mennonite culture in certain regions demonstrates how everyday foods can become cultural symbols, providing an identity marker that is reinforced by the community's own embrace of the symbolism and their association with it by outsiders.

Since women prepared the meals for their household, they were the ones who were introduced to pie and, in the case of the Russian/Ukrainian experience, to *borsch* and *vereniki* by the Ukrainians who worked for them as domestic and farm labourers. Mennonites acquired Ukrainian techniques for pickling cucumbers and watermelon, as well as the (now somewhat notorious) pastime of visiting while cracking and spitting sunflower seeds.[20] Indeed, it was Ukrainians who introduced Mennonites to watermelon, which then became one of their favourite foods.[21] One memoir describes the Mennonite adoption, from Russian culture, of the *samovar* to make tea, and the custom of placing a lump of sugar between one's teeth in order to sweeten the tea while sipping it.[22] At an early twentieth-century Mennonite wedding in Russia, a mother and daughter agreed that they would serve "Borscht, and all the other side dishes the Mennonites had made their own under the influence of their Russian cooks."[23] Here, the appropriation of foodways across an ethnic and class hierarchy to create a "Mennonite cuisine" is obvious. While Mennonites view such appropriation nostalgically, people of Ukrainian descent, such as Canadian writer Myrna Kostash, are

1.2 Swiss Mennonite woman Selina Frey preparing pies for Mennonite Relief Sale, Ontario, 1970.

more critical, pointing out the exploitative relationship that existed between Mennonite landowners and Ukrainian labourers, even in the midst of food adoptions on the part of Mennonites.[24]

The patterns of encounter, exchange, and borrowing continued in the experience of Russian Mennonites from Canada who settled in Mexico in the early twentieth century, followed by additional migrations and relocations to countries in Central and South America. As one poignant story of Mennonites arriving in Mexico in 1922 reveals, food is often at the centre of first encounters between groups with vastly different language and culture; indeed, it is often a food exchange that allows for an encounter at all. Told from the Mexican perspective, the story recounts that Mennonites "gave out jars of fresh milk" when they first disembarked from the train. For one twelve year-old Mexican girl, the jar of warm milk became symbolic of "an encounter between two cultures."[25] Mennonites migrating south from Canada brought with them the Dutch-Russian recipes that had changed little during their four decades on the Canadian prairies; one description noted that they "are a religious group that has preserved its cultural identity nearly intact since ... the end of the 16th century."[26] Even while they lived in fairly closed communities and transplanted most of their Germanic-Mennonite customs and institutions to dedicated colonies in Mexico, foodways did allow for the incorporation of some Hispanic culture and vice versa. In fact, while rigid cultural and social boundaries were maintained between Mennonites and Mexicans, eating across borders was permitted, and perhaps even encouraged. Maria Martens, owner of Mennomex, said that Mennonites were told to "stay away from everything else in Mexico, but the food was so good; we just loved it; every time Dad went to town we got a taco, we just loved it."[27]

The nature of the landscape and climate meant that Mennonites had to modify their diets in this setting. With the production of beans, chilies, corn, and tomatillos on their farms, Mennonites began to incorporate such items into their own recipes. Thus, the "hearty European soups ... of Mennonite gastronomy" took on "depth of flavor and a pleasant warmth" with the addition of chilies, for instance.[28] Aganetha Bueckert, living in southern Mexico, prepared one such hybrid recipe, described as a "mélange of 'corn, meat, green beans, potatoes, chilies, and salt,'" and considered "distinctively Mennonite" even while adapted to the environment in which she lived.[29] Mennonites in Mexico experienced perhaps the sharpest contrast between the food of past homelands and the food of their host country – bland versus spicy, wheat versus corn, potatoes versus chilies.

The cultural fusion expressed in food hybridity continued for Mennonites who began "returning" to Canada from Mexico and South America in the latter twentieth century. Maria Martens' mother-in-law specialized in corn-wrapped *tamales* – one of the

Mennomex's most popular items. On the day I visited the store some years ago, the woman – who spoke Low German and wore a head covering according to the dictates of her Mennonite church group – had just made and sold a record 1,000 *tamales* in one day. Maria herself prefers the Mexican cuisine of her childhood but tried to introduce "traditional" Mennonite recipes such as *vereniki* and chicken noodle soup to her children.[30] The cuisine of her Mennonite cultural group provides "a combination of foods not available in any one country but in the networks that linked them."[31]

Within this particular community, the ongoing back and forth migratory journeys that witness families spending part of the year in Mexico and part in Canada makes those food networks that much more active. Their food networks also include the sharing of recipes in the *Mennonitische Post*, a newspaper that connects Low German-speaking people in North and South America. Robyn Sneath, in analyzing these recipes, observes, "The sharing of food traditionally has been an integral fact of Mennonite community and while these people physically are unable to sit at a table and pass the potatoes, the sharing of recipes represents this communion" and serves to obliterate geographic boundaries.[32] Mennonites from Mexico and Central and South America have a sense of multiple homelands – Russia and Ukraine, Canada, Mexico – all imagined initially as utopias yet none of which lived up to those promises. For this group, diaspora is a present reality, as families migrate north or south, depending on their circumstances and leanings, or develop transnational identities as temporary migrants.

Indigenous Encounters

In almost every era, Mennonite migrations were part of larger movements promoting white colonial settlement to expand empires and displace or eliminate non-white, non-Christian Indigenous peoples.[33] These Mennonite settlers did not consider themselves part of a colonial project but rather viewed their land grants and purchases as God-given for them as unique people seeking freedom from religious persecution. They did not understand displacement as wrong, even if they fully understood that they were settling on land lived on and cared for by Indigenous peoples. Furthermore, they viewed Indigenous people as the Other – non-white, non-Christian, uncivilized, and not in God's favour. Later, Mennonites would view Indigenous people as a mission field to be converted and educated.

When Mennonite migrants settled on lands inhabited by Indigenous peoples, food encounters often occurred because Mennonites experienced food scarcity and/or unfamiliarity. In such cases, Mennonites relied on food exchanges with Indigenous peoples or their knowledge of the soil, plants, and animals in new environments. Yet, as food writer Corey Mintz notes, "the exchange between the diets of early settlers and Indigenous peoples were largely one-sided."[34] Elaine Enns, who explored Mennonite-Indigenous encounters on the Saskatchewan prairie at the turn of the twentieth century, has stated, "Mennonites, like so many other pioneer Settlers, survived initially *only* because of the aid, compassion and knowledge of their Indigenous neighbors."[35] Given the paucity of sources, it is almost impossible to discern the full extent of these encounters. Information is mainly anecdotal, found in memoirs, community histories, and in stories passed along orally.

Enns recounts the story of Emilia Wieler, who immigrated to Saskatchewan from Prussia via the United States in 1894: "Her husband died shortly after their arrival, leaving Emilia to raise a family of nine children. Soon there was nothing to eat, and in desperation Emilia sent two of her sons to a nearby Cree chief for help. The ice across the South Saskatchewan River was already breaking up, and it would soon be impossible to cross to the store in Duck Lake. Hearing of their desperate plight, the chief risked his life by jumping across the perilous river on the ice-floes to get to the store, then re-crossing it with much needed supplies for the widow and her children."[36] Another version of this story describes how Emilia also provided food to the chief, named Almighty Voice, when he was fleeing police.[37]

Similarly, Janis Brass, whose ancestry is both Indigenous and Mennonite, recounted the story of her Mennonite great-grandmother who, during their first difficult winter in Manitoba in the 1870s, received milk "and other necessities" from Indigenous people. Given what she concluded was Mennonite "dependence" on Indigenous peoples, Brass was disturbed by descriptions of those neighbours as lazy and hostile.[38] In the 1820s in Ontario, Amish migrants from Europe began settling on land where the Mississauga peoples lived and harvested crops. According to several accounts, the Amish and Mississauga traded staples and "sometimes shared food and meals." However, development of present-day Wilmot Township led to the collapse of the Indigenous economy and the Mississauga were forced to move elsewhere.[39] One could argue that Mennonites and Amish exploited their relationships with Indigenous peoples to enhance their own settlement success at the expense of the Indigenous inhabitants.

Some encounters evolved into ongoing friendships. Maria Campbell, a Cree woman from Saskatchewan, describes the relationship between her Kookoom (grandmother) Mariah and the "Mrs," a Mennonite woman who was presumably a neighbour. The two women, both midwife-healers, made medicines together and attended births together. According to Campbell, the two elderly women loved and respected each other. About their food sharing she said, "I see them in the garden exchanging wild ginger and dill. In the summer kitchens making headcheese, cooking moosenose."[40] When Maria accompanied the women to pick blueberries, she recalled their lunch was headcheese (Mennonite) and bannock (Indigenous). Their experiences also included mutual surprise as each encountered food practices unfamiliar to the other: the Cree woman was startled to see a pig head boiling on the stove of the Mennonite Mrs, while the latter was similarly taken aback to see a moose nose boiling on the stove of Kookoom Mariah.[41]

Eating encounters were not only about the exchange of food knowledge and foodstuffs. As Susan J. Fisher demonstrates, they also occurred when Mennonites brought seeds of fruits, vegetables, grains, and vegetation from their homeland to their new homes in order to recreate their food cultures in new environments and to transform those environments themselves. Today, we might call these invasive species. By and large, settlers were oblivious to the food cultures of the Indigenous people on whose land they settled, even though Métis people showed Mennonite settlers where to find "chokecherries, plums, blueberries, saskatoons, and cranberries." Fisher states, "while Mennonite community memory has historically held the legend that the plains of Manitoba were uninhabited before the arrival of Europeans, entire generations of Mennonites failed to connect their community's intimate knowledge of the Manitoba landscape to the [Indigenous peoples]."[42] That collective memory has more often portrayed Indigenous people as beggars for food at Mennonite doors.[43] Fisher references an anecdote by Joe Braun: his mother "always opened the door to Louise (an Indigenous woman), never knowing when she would arrive." Joe suspects that the main reason his mother invited Louise in for dinner was the fact that his mother had experienced food shortages growing up in Ukraine.[44] In historical writings by Mennonites, they often portray themselves as the primary benefactors in anecdotes that emphasize food insecurity of Indigenous peoples who are "fed" by settler women.[45]

Similar histories of food encounters, accompanied by memory erasure of those exchanges in official narratives, occurred in many parts of the Mennonite world. When my grandmother's family moved to a village in the North Caucasus region of the Russian Empire in the early 1900s, their cattle died soon after they arrived. Desperately needing milk, they procured a "daily supply of buffalo milk" from the nearby Tatar families; Tatar is an umbrella term for originally nomadic peoples with shared ethnicity, many of whom were converted to Islam. In the first year, before building a permanent home, my ancestors built a shelter in the Tatar style.[46] Once their community of Mennonites began growing different varieties of fruit in the fertile soil, they sold "fresh fruit, especially apricots" to the Tatars.[47] When the family was forced to leave their home in 1918, they found refuge along the way in Tatar homes; reportedly, my great-grandmother Anna Duerksen Enns taught the Tatar women how to "bake bread and cook Mennonite chicken soup."[48] Whether that teaching was requested or imposed, we don't know.

Mennonites in the Ufa region of Russia interacted with the Bashkir peoples in the first decades of the twentieth century, with whom one source states they "enjoyed friendliest relations." The Bashkirs were "most hospitable" and served them "Kumys, a refreshing drink of fermented mares' milk."[49] The same was true of the nearby Tatars: one Mennonite recollection notes that "generous quantities of mutton" were served in a Tatar home along with mares' milk. The latter, because of its "nourishing qualities," was used to treat tuberculosis and helped to cure at least one Mennonite.[50] Mennonites purchased beef and mutton from the Tatars because the latter, being Muslims, did not eat pork. The Tatars helped Mennonites with threshing their crops and the two groups drank tea together in the fields. One Mennonite recollection noted that for the Muslim Tatars, threshing season could be "sometimes tortuous" because of their fasting during Ramadan.[51] It is notable that, in these sources, food exchanges and food shared are recalled without cultural or spiritual judgment but as a matter of fact.

An account by Mennonite Gerhard Fast praises the Indigenous peoples of Siberia, even while implying that they were inferior. According to Fast, "These people helped the new settlers overcome the difficulties associated with the early years of settlement by generously contributing towards their daily needs. The settlers received assistance with low-cost agricultural products such as grain, flour, potatoes, meat, eggs, etc." Fast describes the "friendly and growing relationship of trust" between "the native group and the Mennonites" but also seems surprised that Indigenous people were "unfamiliar with evil behaviors such as theft, cheating, suspicion and trickery."[52] Mennonite stories of food exchange generally focus more on what the Mennonites brought to Indigenous peoples, rather than their dependence on Indigenous knowledge. Most Mennonite migration and settlement narratives, rooted in assumptions about God's leading them to freedom from persecution, do not question the violence and unequal relationships created by colonialism. Although Mennonite settlers received food-related "help" from Indigenous peoples, the reception of that assistance was accompanied by an assumption that the newcomers had the right to the land on which they settled and were not indebted to the people on the land.

Food encounters with Indigenous people were not just about amicable or equitable exchanges of foodstuffs and knowledge. Ben Nobbs-Thiessen describes the efforts of Paraguayan Mennonites to convert Indigenous Enlhet peoples to Christianity in the 1930s. Those efforts went beyond the spiritual to include dietary conversion as the Mennonite colonists attempted to turn Indigenous peoples away from alcohol consumption and food-foraging in the bush and toward Mennonite practices of wheat cultivation.[53] The patronizing suggestion that the lives of Indigenous peoples improved with the arrival of Mennonites appears in various sources. In his memoir, a film-maker who recorded the stories of Mennonites and Indigenous peoples in Paraguay states that Indigenous peoples "learned [from the "white man"] to cultivate the land and were able to enjoy a more secure food source."[54] However, other research counters colonizer narratives that suggest Indigenous peoples were saved from starvation by Mennonite food charity. Ethnographic accounts from Enlhet elders indicate that Mennonite settlement practices and road placement interfered with Indigenous sweet potato plantings and the movement of their goat herds to the point that some Mennonites whipped goat owners when the animals wandered into their fields.[55]

Food exchanges continued long after Mennonite migration and initial settlement. Menno Wiebe recalled that when his family moved to British Columbia (probably in the 1940s), his mother exchanged her "freshly butchered chicken with equally fresh salmon" offered by a Salish man who lived further up the Fraser River. When his mother was reminded that it was illegal to purchase fish from the Indigenous people, she replied that "We only traded. They have fish and we have chickens. So shouldn't we exchange?"[56] More recent is the example of Lance Cote, a First Nations man raised in a Mennonite foster home in the 1990s. Having always "appreciated a good, hearty Mennonite meal," he decided to celebrate the recipes of his foster mother in a blog titled *MennoNeechie Kitchen*. The recipes for Russian Mennonite foods like *borscht*, *paska*, and cracklings (bits of pork that are strained from rendered pig fat) are accompanied by stories that are "good, bad, or just plain funny."[57] Some of his stories reveal the clashes across cultures that occur when encountering unfamiliar foods. When Lance, aged eighteen months, arrived at the Mennonite home with his older sisters, his foster mother considered them malnourished and so served traditional chicken soup. Unfamiliar with the homemade noodles, the children began screaming because they thought she was serving them worms.[58]

Indigenous children like Lance, who were fostered by or adopted into Mennonite homes, may have grown up with appreciation for so-called Mennonite foods, but with little knowledge of their own Indigenous food ancestry. Lance embraces both. Understanding food histories, including processes of sharing and exchange across cultural boundaries, brings to light some of the complexities in Mennonite encounters with the Other: how Mennonites had contact with their Indigenous neighbours and, when in need, might literally eat their food; and yet, at the same time, how the concept of "Mennonite food" was a way of reinforcing difference. As Elaine Enns demonstrated in workshops held to explore reconciliation between settlers and Indigenous peoples in Saskatchewan, food could also serve as a metaphor for divides between these groups. As one of her participants said, "Between Tiefengrund, where I grew up, and Duck Lake there was a solid curtain made of bannock on one side and *Roll Kuchen* on the other side."[59] It was a strange contact zone where unequal power relations, colonial intentions, and racism were accompanied by food curiosity and need for sustenance on both sides.

Familiar and Unfamiliar Foods

In relocating to new cultural environments, Mennonites encountered unfamiliar foodstuffs and foodways even while the familiar was reinforced. Although migration is a disruptive experience, a community's food customs are frequently *enhanced* through the process, as individuals and families cling to familiar patterns in unfamiliar environments, a phenomenon that historian Donna R. Gabaccia calls "culinary conservatism."[60] For Mennonites, who attempted to recreate many aspects of their pre-migration community and church life, culinary preservation reinforced their desire to live as separately as possible from the societies within which they settled.

Reflecting on her Mennonite neighbourhood in Clearbrook, British Columbia, Anne Konrad writes, "It dawned on me that here in BC, families in our village shared a heritage, a language, a culture, a code of conduct and faith – it was like the whole street did things in ways my parents knew from 'back in Russia' ... We ate the same traditional foods ... it was an enclosing Mennonite world."[61] Konrad describes the typical food fare in her household and community, which included customary Russian Mennonite foods: "*Zwiebach* were indispensable for a *Faspa* meal [light evening meal usually on Sunday] ... A roasted chicken was reserved for a Sunday noon dinner, as might be a ham or beef roast. When relatives or friends came for a main meal, but not on a Sunday, my mother might serve any one of a large variety of soups, often cabbage *borscht*, hambone or green bean soup or chicken soup (the prize winner). Sometimes she also made *Varenicke* (cottage-cheese-filled dumplings) or Mennonite meatballs called *Kotletten*. Once in a while we fried our home-cured ham or occasionally made cabbage rolls (called *Hallopse*)."[62]

The routine of traditional foods not only reinforced the boundaries of community; it also created comfort and stability in new environments that demanded adaptation or assimilation at many levels. Tina Klassen Kauffman describes at length the traditional Russian Mennonite foods her family ate after settling in rural Saskatchewan in the late 1920s. Since dried fruit was considered "a necessity" for preparing certain dishes, her family purchased it at the store, despite their poverty, and stored autumn eggs through the winter in order to maintain their diet of noodles and *vereniki*. Tina observed that "food changes were made very slowly" but gradually they learned to enjoy "Canadian foods" such as peanut butter, Roger's Golden

Syrup, and Jell-O brought home from school by her sisters – "What do we do with it? It sounded like jelly but we could not spread it on bread. It was dessert."[63]

Immigrants also construct an "imagined culinary tradition" as a way of preserving an attachment to their homeland when confronted with strange foodways.[64] The preparation of so-called ethnic foods is one means for newcomers to "survive psychologically"[65] as they make other difficult transitions in climate, language, and host society environments. For some immigrant groups, when faced with assimilative pressures from the outside and concern about cultural disintegration on the inside, particular foodstuffs became powerful public and private symbols of identity. Indeed, some so-called traditional foodways experienced a renaissance in new world settings as producers and consumers of those foods sought "authenticity" in a context where a group's cultural identity appeared fragile or threatened. For Icelandic immigrants in North America in the late 1800s, and for South Asians in Toronto a century later, the cake *vínarterta* and the bread *roti* became respective food items that took on new meaning and value.[66]

This was also true for Mennonites immigrating to the Americas, although one could debate which foodstuff became a symbol of authenticity. For Swiss Mennonites, it might be sauerkraut or shoofly pie. For Russian Mennonites it might be *zwieback*, the iconic double-layered white flour buns. One woman maintained that the *zwieback* she made in North America "never lived up to" the ones baked in an outdoor brick oven in Russia. In this example, authenticity may be attached less to the actual taste of the bun than to romanticized memories of pre-migration times.[67] Competition in one Canadian community over which group from different settlements in Russia or Ukraine made the best *zwieback* suggests a yearning for the most authentic Mennonite baking.[68] Inter-Mennonite tensions over authentic foodways is not limited to Swiss-German or Dutch-Russian traditions. At a 1972 cross-cultural Mennonite youth convention in the United States, attended by African-American, Latino, Native American, and white youth, among the most popular workshops were "how to make a piñata, cook ethnic foods, arts and crafts, and tie-dying."[69] Yet conflict arose when Puerto Rican Mennonite youth claimed their ethnic foods, prepared at the convention, were disparaged by African-American youth and "butchered" by the cooks; a "hunger strike" was averted when an apology was issued.[70] This incident demonstrates how close cultural foodways are to identity maintenance. In this case, they may have been a self-conscious gesture of challenge and resistance, by minority youth, toward a predominantly white denomination.

For some Mennonites, ethnic foodways helped to separate them from their neighbours. Tina Klassen Kauffman, whose family moved from Saskatchewan to Manitoba in the late 1930s, recalled discomfort about hosting her non-Mennonite teachers at her home "because we were ethnic and they would not be familiar with our foods."[71] Debates over so-called authentic representations of traditional Mennonite foods may be increasing in an era when other tangible aspects of the past are ephemeral. This idea was reinforced for me in early January 2021 when, on social media platforms, I saw more posts of *portzelky* than ever before. The photos were accompanied by comment threads about which methods and results were closest – most authentic – to how *portzelky should* be prepared. Not only was this another example of a home-baking craze, but it suggests that the insecurity of the Covid-19 pandemic was offset by grounding oneself in cultural food roots.

It is also true that immigrant foodways are transformed in small or large measure because of the interaction of multiple food cultures in settings where different cultural groups are mingling together and molding new societies. Not only is food "an extraordinary vehicle of self-representation," according to Massimo Montanari; it is "also the first way of entering into contact with a different culture."[72] When Swiss Mennonites settled in Volhynia (a region that overlaps present-day Poland and Ukraine) in the late eighteenth century, they encountered other Mennonites – of Dutch descent – as well as German Catholics and Lutherans, and Polish, Russian, and Ukrainian peoples. This was described as an "exciting time" in part because of the new foods that were introduced and old foods that evolved; these included such foodstuffs as poppy seed rolls, *bohne beroggi* (mashed beans inside buns), and thin pancakes with a variety of fillings.[73]

Conversely, the foodways of the "host" society and its residents will incorporate ingredients, recipes, and tastes from newcomer cultures. For example, histories of food customs in West Prussia note the influence of Dutch Mennonite foodstuffs, such as noodles, peppernuts, *portzelky*, and possibly *zwieback*. It has been suggested, though not verified, that potatoes were not known in Ukraine until Mennonites arrived in the late eighteenth century.[74] Although Mennonite narratives speak triumphantly about this food import, Ukrainian-Canadian memoirist Myrna Kostash argues that Mennonites razed the former settlements and burial grounds of displaced Cossacks and Tatars in order to plant their beloved potatoes.[75] Mennonites purportedly brought Turkey Red wheat and poppy seeds to Kansas in the nineteenth century and transformed the foodscape there.[76] And the *queso menonita* produced by Mennonites is renowned throughout Mexico (and elsewhere), considered part of that nation's "gastronomic identity" and no longer thought of as "'foreign' or 'international.'"[77] Mennonite cheese has also become an "ethnic signifier" in Bolivia.[78] This is to say that Mennonites introduced and became associated with particular foodstuffs in new national contexts.

Of course, narratives that focus on how Mennonites enhanced the foodscapes of the places they colonized serve a collective memory that situates Mennonites as superior to the peoples and cultures onto which they imposed themselves. As Ben Nobbs-Thiessen and Susan J. Fisher have both noted, the Mennonite desire to transplant specific food and plant products during the settlement process in the Americas aligned with the agenda of settler colonialism that sought to civilize – especially in the case of wheat production and consumption – what was perceived as a "fugitive landscape."[79] Triumphal descriptions of the success of Turkey Wheat in the American Midwest attest to this. An unattributed anecdote in Norma Jost Voth's *Mennonite Foods and Folkways* states, "An observer at the time wrote: 'Day after day, through all the fall and winter, the Mennonites came in with wheat.

The native American stands on the corner and complains but the Mennonites come in with the wheat.'"[80] This narrative perpetuates the racist discourse of the productive, hardworking Mennonite and the failed Indigenous farmer. Furthermore, Mennonites were able to preserve traditional foodways in part because of their white privilege; the foodways of racialized immigrants were suppressed or were sites of xenophobia.

Migration also meant that Mennonites encountered the unfamiliar – climate, agricultural methods, plant varieties, and animals – requiring them to adapt or, in some cases, completely transform, their traditional diets. Some new foodways were appropriated eagerly while others were incorporated reluctantly, usually by necessity. This duality can be found in just about every setting. For instance, Mennonites in Ukraine acquired a taste for certain Middle Eastern foods that came across the Black Sea, such as *halvah* (sesame paste dessert) and Turkish shish-kabobs. Soviet Mennonite immigrants to Canada in the 1920s were thus delighted to find *halvah* in Jewish groceries in north Winnipeg.[81] In the same context, during times of famine in the early twentieth century, Mennonites learned from their Ukrainian neighbours which mushrooms could be collected and eaten and that coarse rye bread could be substituted for white wheat bread.

Encounters with the unfamiliar were particularly profound for Mennonites who migrated to Central and South America in the twentieth century. Some of these moved from Canada to Mexico and Paraguay in the 1920s, seeking greater autonomy over their religious practices and the education of their children. In 1930, several thousand Mennonites who escaped the Soviet Union created a colony in Paraguay. Later, about 4,000 Mennonite refugees from Eastern Europe and the Soviet Union were sent to South America after the Second World War. Still other communities of Mennonites in such places as Belize, Honduras, and Bolivia were established by southward relocations from Mexico in the latter part of the twentieth century.

In her memoir, Wera Teichroeb recalled that, en route to Paraguay in 1947, the ship stopped at the Canary Islands where passengers could barter for goods with the residents. This was her first opportunity to taste tropical fruit – oranges and bananas. On arrival in Paraguay, she encountered mandarin oranges that fell from the trees and "cover[ed] the ground by the thousands."[82] She went on to describe new foods encountered as they established the Volendam colony in Paraguay: "Oma bakes some kind of flan consisting of grated cassava roots. We don't have shortening of any kind, so she shapes little cakes out of this grated mass and dries them on a piece of tin on an open fire. We have no oil, no frying pan, no flour or eggs to make it taste a little better." Cassava roots proved to be multipurpose starch plants, standing in for potatoes, that could be boiled, fried, made into salad, or put into bread, and fed to livestock. Eventually Mennonite settlers learned how to use cassava water or whey in baking bread, which helped it to last longer. When wheat flour and yeast were available, they baked bread in mud ovens, but without refrigeration it spoiled quickly in the hot and humid climate. With no butter or jam to put on the bread, they often spread it with lard and a bit of salt or sugar to taste. Eventually they learned how to harvest wild bee honey in the forest.

The first plants they cultivated were sorghum, corn, sweet potatoes, cassava, and sugar cane. They planted fruit trees – orange, mandarin, grapefruit, mango, and papaya – which helped to improve a sparse, vitamin-deficient diet. A treat was mango compote cooked with sugar if available. Wera describes the planting of peanuts and the making of peanut butter, and producing syrup from sugar cane – "a laborious and prickly task which takes all day, often longer."[83] The settlers longed for a fried or cooked egg, but eggs were taken to the cooperative to exchange for salt, sugar, meat, flour, and kerosene. Wera also recalls that in the Paraguayan jungle, they found themselves eating "exotically" when her uncles, as "fierce hunters," brought back "wild ducks, geese, pink flamingos, parrots, wild boars, turkeys and even crocodile."[84]

Encounters with the unfamiliar could sometimes lead to what Ben Nobbs-Thiessen describes as "a struggle over foodways [that] lay at the heart of Mennonite place-making in the Chaco," a region of Paraguay where Mennonites from the Soviet Union settled in 1930.[85]

1.3   Helena Harms Hiebert (left) grinding sorghum, with woman and children, Paraguay, c1948–50.

Unlike the jungle-like Volendam Colony – described as a "green hell" – where Wera Teichroeb settled, the Chaco was dry and difficult for farmers. Coming from an agricultural environment in which Mennonite foodways were based on such crops as wheat and fruit trees, in South America their diet was altered in significant ways. As Nobbs-Thiessen notes, new foodstuffs "included sweet potatoes, manioc, peanuts, rice and sorghum. In the absence of fruit trees, Mennonite women used a variety of hibiscus to produce juice and jam. They replaced the abundant potatoes of the 'old homeland' with the yam and yucca of the 'new homeland.'"[86] Similarly, Margaret Siemens Braun described new foodways as "soup from red beans. Stew without meat. We had yams, mandioca, [and] peanuts for oil."[87]

Mennonites also embraced *yerba maté*, the staple Paraguayan caffeinated beverage. The dried leaves of the yerba plant are steeped in boiling water poured into a *guampa* (hollow gourd) and drunk with a common metal straw called a *bombilla*. Otto Klassen, who migrated to Paraguay after the Second World War, at first resisted *maté* until he came to understand its meaning – benefiting health and fostering "relationships and community by creating an atmosphere of peace and relaxation, acceptance and hospitality."[88] Another proponent of the beverage and ritual explained that "maté is not a drink, it is a philosophy; a habit, a reason to sit together."[89] A Paraguayan Mennonite named "Rudy" recognized that foodways encouraged cross-cultural encounters for separatist Mennonites: "We Mennonites are sometimes too stubborn to learn from others, but we have learned to drink maté."[90] In Canada, I experienced *yerba maté* at the Mennonite college I attended and began to think of it as a Paraguayan "Mennonite" custom. I am not alone in the misperception that *yerba maté* was a "Mennonite thing." Manitoba-based Andrew J. Bergman says that "sipping yerba" was "as entrenched in our Mennonite culture as adult baptism and chicken farming."[91]

Even while Mennonites adopted new foodstuffs in the process of migration, out of necessity and sometimes out of a sense of adventure, there often remained a longing for culinary "normalcy" or a sense of loss over traditional foods that were elevated as "proper" over the unfamiliar.[92] The cultivation of wheat, which Mennonites had done so successfully in Russia and Ukraine, the Canadian prairies, and the American Midwest, was less viable in the southern climates of Mexico or South America. To the extent that wheat bread was central to Mennonites' social and religious life, the absence of this foodstuff threatened their basic identity. And it also led to conflict as some Mennonites in Paraguay resisted planting more practical crops like sorghum because they were considered to be animal-feed or food for the poor[93] and represented a decline in socio-economic status. On the other hand, new approaches to bread-baking required collaboration, as did almost all tasks performed to survive. Newly married in Paraguay, Margaret Siemens Braun recalled that when making bread with sorghum flour, "You had to share with the neighbours ... because if you didn't eat all the bread, the next day it would have a slime and you couldn't eat it." She continued, "We made it every day. One day my mom made it. One day I did it. One day the neighbour. I did three balls in one pan and put it in the outdoor oven. We were sharing."[94]

The desire for familiar food often revived during times of fear and insecurity, such as might be provoked by migration, war, or political repression. Mennonites escaping the Soviet Union in 1930 had to confront dangerous crossings of the Amur River into China. On their first night in a new environment they were served *pampushky* (a Ukrainian yeast bun) that was unfamiliar, but "after the long cold trip and the oat flour bread we had been eating in Russia, this meal was a special treat for us." Jakob Unger remarked that the *pampushkies* were steamed and tasted like *zwieback*; he explained, "The reason I mentioned zwieback is because of the drastic change in food that we had been eating for the last while."[95] Comparing this unfamiliar food item to *zwieback* was a means to obtain normalcy in an unfamiliar and fear-filled setting.

Familiarity and normalcy are found by recreating homeland foods in new contexts, but also by physically returning to those places. Ethno-tourism is an important way by which Mennonites maintain their psychological and physical connections to a homeland, subscribing by the hundreds to annual heritage tours of former Mennonite settlements in Ukraine, Russia, and Europe.[96] These heritage ethno-tours facilitate the "memory of place"[97] through a sensory return to the homeland by means of food. Local tour guides cater to the nostalgia of return by serving so-called "Mennonite foods" such as cabbage rolls and *borscht* to North American tourists. For these visitors, maintenance of food traditions was a way to recapture the "golden age" of their Russian Mennonite ancestry, a time of economic prosperity and flourishing culture prior to the Bolshevik revolution in 1917 and the tumultuous events that followed. "Eating Mennonite" in places considered to be "home" reinforces, and indeed creates, identity. Writer Connie T. Braun, who visited her father's Ukrainian village during a 2005 heritage tour, where watermelon was consumed in a ritualistic pursuit of memory, recalled "how instantly taste transports us geographically, temporally, how inextricable our histories, our roots, are from the foods we have eaten. Food in our mouth, taste on our tongue, engender a narrative of our past."[98]

For historically minded Mennonites, the connection commonly drawn between eating and nostalgia reveals "the symbolic capacity of food to contain the past."[99] The fact that Mennonite tourists return to eat traditional foods in abundance in places where they or their relatives experienced severe food deprivation is not only ironic but may well serve to elevate the food memories of the pre-revolutionary era in the Russian empire above the memories of scarcity during the 1920s and 1930s. I explore experiences of severe hunger and deprivation in chapter 4. I cannot help but recall my own experience at an academic conference and heritage tour in Omsk, Siberia in 2010. Here we were eating substantial, hearty meals that represented the hybridity of Dutch-German-Russian fare considered uniquely Mennonite in the midst of Siberian forests where Mennonite women and children lived near starvation in Stalin's labour prisons. For the most part, those gathered did not dwell on the brutal deprivation that had occurred in that place, and the collective memory that imbued the tourist experience was merely tinged with sadness over the past. The conversation was more likely to turn to the inferiority of Ukrainian-made beet *borscht* when compared with the more meaty Mennonite-made *borscht*. The trauma of those decades was, and is, possible to avoid when the sense of taste prevails. Furthermore, eating traditional foods in ancestral Mennonite homelands suggests an ownership of spaces that were taken away when Mennonites underwent forced migration. In this way, the colonizer mindset pervades the eating of both familiar and unfamiliar foods.

Spring Rolls Become Mennonite Food

By the late twentieth century, North American Mennonite cuisine had evolved to include a wide range of foods brought to that continent by immigrants, most of whom were not Mennonite before their migration. Some were refugees sponsored by Mennonite churches who eventually became Mennonite themselves; others were newcomers who established Mennonite churches in response to mission outreach by Mennonite institutions. A diaspora of new Mennonite ethnicities has emerged in Waterloo region, a place that may have the greatest diversity of Mennonites in the world, although these patterns are occurring elsewhere. In addition to an already varied assortment of Mennonite types, based on historical, theological, and doctrinal differences, diversity has grown due to churches and communities made up of newcomers with or without a Mennonite ancestry from countries in Central America, Asia, and Africa.

This diversity reveals itself in the presence of as many as fifteen languages spoken in one Mennonite conference group. As I noted in the introduction, the plurality of Mennonite identities led to debates, beginning in the 1970s, about the seeming tension between religion and culture. The increase of Mennonite church participants with ethnicities that were neither Swiss nor Russian prompted some unease about the notion of "Mennonite foods." For example, for several years in the early 1980s, Mennonites in Winnipeg, Manitoba, sponsored a pavilion at Folklorama, the city's large multicultural festival. Polarized views on the pavilion emerged, as some viewed the portrayal of Mennonites as too exclusive, focusing on cultural features such as the Low German dialect and traditional foodways. One voice in the debate argued that, rather than rejecting historic ethnic attributes, the pavilion might include Mennonites of "native Indian descent, Vietnamese, Indian, Chinese, Negro, etc. and some of their foods and folkways."[100] The language used here racializes Mennonites who were not white, but decades later, reflecting on the debates, some mused whether this inclusion might have happened had the short-lived pavilion continued and evolved.

That evolution did eventually happen. Mennonite church communities with a common religious label but very different cultural backgrounds now put forward their distinctive foods in at least one shared venue – the annual Mennonite relief sale. Relief sales are volunteer-driven events, held across North America at varying times of the year, that (usually) raise funds for Mennonite Central Committee, an international relief, development, and peacebuilding agency. The main items sold are quilts and food. At the sale I attend, in New Hamburg, Ontario, the Mennonite foods are listed as Russian, Swiss, Asian, and Hispanic. Some of the Hispanic foods are prepared and sold by European-origin Mennonites from Mexico, like those who run the Mennomex store. Other cooks are Hispanics who joined the Mennonite church in Ontario when they immigrated as refugees from countries like Colombia, El Salvador, and Nicaragua in the 1980s. They were integrated into the historic First Mennonite Church in Kitchener, founded in the early nineteenth century by Pennsylvania immigrants, where summer sausage and shoofly pie would have been common food fare. Hispanic *papusas* – meat-and-vegetable-filled pastries – are sold by the multicultural youth group at that church.

Another popular Mennonite food at the sale is spring rolls – stuffed, rolled, and deep-fried – by Laotian and Hmong Mennonites, who founded their own churches after immigrating to Canada from Laos as refugees in the late 1970s and early 1980s. The Laotian-Canadian Mennonites became renowned for their annual spring roll sale, held in the parking lot of their church, at which they would sell 900 dozen spring rolls. The money raised was to pay off the church mortgage. A few weeks after their sale in spring 2012, about thirty women, men, and youth gathered again to prepare an equal number of spring rolls for the Mennonite relief sale. I joined them for that occasion, and amid mounds of chopped onions, shredded carrots, and fragrant pork, they told me about the role of food in their religious and cultural life.

I learned that when they settled in Kitchener-Waterloo, Ontario, their traditional Laotian foods had to undergo adaptation in Canada since there were so few ethnic grocery stores in town. They substituted

1.4   Members of Grace Lao Mennonite Church, Kitchener, Ontario, making spring rolls for the Mennonite Relief Sale, 2012.

Chinese vermicelli for their preferred sticky rice and thus learned to eat noodles. I learned that sticky rice was their food staple and also their food for flight – much like *zwieback* for Russian Mennonites. When they prepared to leave their homes to travel secretively through the mountains of Laos or cross the Mekong River and the border to Thailand, they packed ample sticky rice for the journey. Just like Russian Mennonites who baked, roasted, and packed dozens of *zwieback* for their migratory journeys, these Laotian immigrants knew that as long as there was still sticky rice, there was hope for survival, and for the future.[101]

The "international" foodways featured at the annual relief sale are growing in popularity. A news article on the 2018 sale in New Hamburg, Ontario, described the "ethnic Mennonite delicacies like vereneke (Russian), pupusas (Hispanic) and the popular egg/spring rolls (Southeast Asian)."[102] What is notable is the inclusion of Hispanic and Southeast Asian foodstuffs as "ethnic Mennonite" food. The article noted that the Grace Lao Mennonite and First Hmong

Mennonite churches would together make and sell 14,000 egg and spring rolls. The variety of cultural foodstuffs on the menu at these sales is increasing, a result of growth in the number of Mennonite churches with historical national and ethnic identities that are neither Swiss nor Russian. Churches with a majority of members from Ethiopia, Korea, China, or India, for example, are now part of Mennonite religious identity across North America. One former church leader, who was otherwise dismissive of the significance of family histories and ancestral culture, nevertheless astutely commented, "if you are going to talk about 'Mennonite food,' you had better start including some of my favourites, like Korean bulgogi, Laotian spring rolls, spicy Amharic dishes, or Hmong na vah."[103] This gradual incorporation into Mennonite cuisine of foodways that are neither Russian nor Swiss in ethnic origin deepens and complicates the question of Mennonite identity.

Food Encounters on the Mission Field

As a result of missionary initiatives beginning well over one hundred years ago, Mennonite churches and communities emerged in Indonesia, Ethiopia, and the Democratic Republic of Congo, to name just three global south countries with significant numbers of Mennonites in the twenty-first century. So-called "foreign" missions, embraced with enthusiasm by Mennonites from the mid-nineteenth century onward, were sites of multi-dimensional cultural encounters. Mission activity was part of global imperialism whereby land conquest and occupation went hand in hand with religious domination. Even while the primary purpose of missions was to convert people to Christianity and "plant" churches, food was often the most immediate exchange and encounter and remained at the centre of cross-cultural interaction. In an essay about their missionary mother, the children of Anne Loewen state that missionaries "often pioneer food shifts that become the norm or, at a minimum, new food options for succeeding generations."[104]

In some settings, missionaries found it easier to embrace food than other forms of culture, such as dance or dress. As Massimo Montanari proposes, "Eating the food of the 'other' is easier, it would seem, than decoding the other's language."[105] Food historian Jeffrey M. Pilcher notes that imperialist attempts to "civilize" dominated peoples included efforts to replace non-Western diets with food considered superior, such as bread. However, "culinary exchanges often reversed the direction of influence, as the British began eating Indian rice and curry," for example.[106] Borders between foodways may have been the most penetrable in the context of missions, even while other forms of cross-cultural interaction presented barriers to the spreading of Mennonite forms of Christianity. These encounters reinforce the notion that religious belief and practice are always embedded in culture.

In Indonesia, where Dutch Mennonite missionaries first arrived in the mid-nineteenth century, Dutch foods were imported by the colonizers, including the Mennonites. Thus, Dutch *oliebollen*, a deep-fried fritter that Mennonites adopted as *portzelky*,[107] came to be eaten by Indonesians. Today, Mennonites, and other Christians in Indonesia, try not to practise any food habits, customs, or rituals that will set them apart from the majority in the predominantly Muslim country.[108] Even so, Mennonites in Indonesia in the twenty-first century view the sharing and exchange of food as a "platform" for living out their religious beliefs and transforming situations of conflict across political and religious divides.[109] As the country prepared to host an international gathering of Mennonites in 2022, videos that introduced potential attendees around the world to Indonesian "Buffalo Satay" seemed to be a representational device to explain how Mennonites eat in Indonesia.[110]

At the end of the nineteenth century, several missionaries travelled to India from Ukraine in response to severe famine in India. In the first quarter of the twentieth century, Mennonites from North America followed, as India under British occupation became an active target for Christian missions. Food was one of the main adaptations made by Mennonite missionaries even as they attempted to retain a familiar Western diet. The missionaries ordered food from abroad to supplement what was available from local markets and gardens, and to maintain their white European cuisine. One organization in Canada sent them monthly supplies of yeast, so that North Americans could maintain their leavened bread habit. Gradually Western tinned food became more available.[111]

Part of the missionary enterprise included debates over what cultural traditions could be appropriately adopted by the foreigners. As a missionary in India in the early twentieth century, Anna Penner enjoyed wearing the sari, in part because she "loved its feel." She wore it regularly around her house but didn't "dare" wear it to mission conferences because "they continued to debate how much missionaries should accommodate to local customs."[112] Such debates centred on food as well. Anna and her husband, John, reportedly suggested that "since the Hindus do not eat meat, if we also abstained from eating meat, it would open the way for more friendships with them."[113] Anna seemed to develop a love of Indian foodways, favouring the "Hot Lime," which "evoked a kind of euphoria along with its spicy hotness."[114] According to her biography, Anna's children shared her food preferences. Missionary children who grew up outside of the West adapted to "foreign" food more readily than their parents. Anna and John Penner recalled that when Mennonite missionaries from Russia gathered for retreats, they ate "Zwiebach and Borscht ... along with some of their other favourite Russian Mennonite foods." Their children, however, "preferred curry and rice" over "these other strange foods."[115] Similarly, a missionary's child who was a toddler when the family arrived in India in 1938, recalled, "I quickly learned to love the spicy curries, our staple."[116]

Some missionaries expected their North American diets would not change very much in the field. American Mennonite missionaries first went to the Democratic Republic of Congo in 1912, then referred to by its colonizer name the Belgian Congo. When going into the countryside they purportedly took along "several tinned items: cheese, margarine, vegetables, meats ... and freshly baked bread and maybe some cookies."[117] A Congolese missionary account from 1947 noted that certain foods could be expected in the villages, such as "sweet potatoes, fresh corn, chickens, eggs, pineapples, and bananas." But other foods had to be transported, since they were not available; these included staples like "flour, lard, butter, tea, coffee, milk" but also "corn beef, sardines, salmon, bacon, for one gets tired of chicken at almost every meal," said one missionary.[118] As in India, but not for religious reasons, less meat was available than North American Mennonites were accustomed to. Sarah Peters, who arrived in the Belgian Congo in 1956, grew tired of eggplants, saying "They grew so well but how many different tasty meals can you make from them till you are filled to the hilt and long for real meat." She was clearly delighted when another missionary and a hunter brought them canned buffalo thighs.[119]

Dietary adaptation was an unavoidable part of the missionary experience, which soon became apparent even to those who tried to maintain their customary food practices. Anne Loewen crossed "food borders" numerous times as a missionary in Colombia, Peru, Zambia, and Togo. She found that baking with flour in the "humid jungle heat" was difficult, and learned to replace potatoes with yucca and rice. For their part, her children came to prefer tropical fruits such as bananas, papayas, and guavas, picked directly from the tree, over imported apples that seemed "dry and unappealing."[120] A fascinating source for practice in the mission field is an undated cookbook compiled by two Mennonite women called *Missionary Meals around the World*. The cookbook came into being because of the difficulty missionaries experienced in trying to "cook an American-type meal with foreign ingredients." The compilers noted, "sometimes we are inclined to come to the foreign land with the idea that our good old-fashioned Mennonite food is the best ... We need to keep an open mind to the foods of other lands and not be prejudiced against the native foods ... We have seen the hurt looks, when the missionary can't eat their food and tries to sneak it to the dog under the table." They encouraged new missionaries to learn to "tolerate" new and different fruits and vegetables and hopefully come to enjoy and appreciate them.[121] These women clearly understood that embracing or rejecting unfamiliar cultural customs could open or close doors to relationships with the people whom they wished to missionize.

The trying of new foods could either reduce or increase the space of cultural understanding. While missionaries tried to change many aspects of Indigenous cultures judged as inferior to Western ways, some were eager to embrace local foodways. Elva Landis, a nurse-midwife in Tanganyika, experienced her first *ugali* meal at a wedding just after her arrival on the mission field in 1949. *Ugali* was a starch made from ground cassava roots or corn meal and eaten with the fingers. "Elva had to learn how to take a bit of ugali, form it into a ball, press her thumb into it, dip it into the beef broth and then pop it into her mouth. It was very tasty." She also recalled with excitement a hippo butchering, finding that "hippo meat is very good."[122] Sarah Peters' first meal upon arriving at her mission station in Kikwit, Belgian Congo, in 1956, was chicken with "mango-sauce instead of applesauce." She recalled that it was so delicious she was "forever spoiled" since applesauce did not have "nearly the flavor."[123] Mary Toews, in her 1953 account *Glimpses into Congoland*, observed that in Congo, "mushrooms really come into their own" and notably "appear on the tables of both black and white." She said that a substantial meal for "a native" was a "large ball of mush, a dish of mushrooms and a bit of goat's meat seasoned with red-hot peppers." When a "white man" was "indulging" in African food, he might add a dessert of sliced pineapples, or a fruit salad of papaya, bananas, and grapefruit.[124] The racialized diet differentials are clear.

Many missionaries were forever changed by their food encounters across borders. Anne Loewen's children said that their mother's "cultural and spiritual outlook [shifted] from insular to global."[125] One of Anna and John Penner's first food experiences in India is described by their biographer: "The welcoming meal to celebrate their arrival, when compared with Russian Mennonite celebrations, was refreshingly simple. Each person sat cross-legged before a large banana leaf on which rice and curry were placed. The Indians ate with the fingers of their right hand. The left hand was considered unclean. They offered the westerners spoons. Anna and John insisted on eating like the Indians, although they had difficulty eating using only one hand."[126]

Annie Goertz describes one of her early meals upon arriving in India in 1947. This celebratory meal happened to be on Christmas Eve and was described by Annie as a "love feast." "We had rice which was good, the chapattis were very good too. The curry was made with mutton in it, which was goat's meat. We were eating with our fingers for my first time I think and I found the curry very spicy. My thoughtful senior missionary had given me a banana to eat when it got too hot. She sat next to me. Well, I could not get the meat between my fingers for it was too slippery. When I did manage, I gagged for I thought I was eating entrails. It most likely was so. The missionary quietly told me it was a 'no no' to gag on the food that the Christians had prepared so graciously."[127]

Missionaries sometimes described the food traditions of nationals or Indigenous peoples as slightly barbaric, yet curious oddities. James Bertsche described the way Congolese children captured the *tusua*, a much-liked insect that was plentiful at certain times of the year. With this abundant food source, "the protein content in the African diet is higher than usual." The way in which children then ate the insect reminded him of threshing days on the farm, with the *tusua* going in one side of the mouth and wings coming out the other.[128] Even if not viewed as uncivilized, some food-related practices and methods of preparation were simply difficult for missionaries to adopt. According to his daughter, Mennonite missionary Daniel Bergthold did not like his food prepared over a cow-chip fire as was customary in rural central India where they worked, so the family carried its own fuel during its travels between villages.[129] Other food adaptations resulted in misunderstanding about meaning attached to certain foods. One account described two single female missionaries who drank lime juice every morning since oranges were unavailable. They came to understand that their failure to establish a church was due, in part, to the fact that lime juice was thought to have contraceptive qualities and thus the unmarried women's morals were questioned.[130]

Whether they adapted to new foodways with reluctance or enthusiasm, it was often missionaries who paved the way toward change in North American Mennonite diets, well before "eating ethnic" was a commonplace thing to do. Margaret Suderman was a career missionary to India from 1929 until 1962. Her nephew, recalling her furlough visits to the United States, said that on "extra special occasions" she would bring home the "rare and precious gift of real Indian curry powder" which introduced their whole family to a "lifelong love for curry."[131] For individuals who spent the better part of their lives in mission settings, an embrace of "foreign" foodways was symbolic of their sense of where "home" had become. Helen Kornelsen, who spent nearly forty years in India, exclaimed, "We're home!" after returning from a leave in North America. She said, "What the first hamburger means to the wayfaring American after a long absence, so a good rice and curry meal touches our palates with a sweet sensation of satisfaction."[132] Another missionary woman chose to compile a small cookbook titled *Spices of India* to "benefit new workers going to India." The compiler, named as "Mrs Paul Toews," developed the recipes after "time was spent observing and cooking with Indian Women."[133] For most missionaries, after the initial phase of facing the unfamiliar had passed, foodways of the mission field culture were gradually embraced. While missionaries attempted to alter the religious beliefs of people they met, and measured their success by conversions to Christianity, it was the missionaries themselves who underwent change, oftentimes more so, as they learned from and adopted the daily food diet of the so-called "heathen."

In the mission context, most missionaries had househelp to assist with the laborious daily tasks of food preparation, laundry, and general housekeeping. It is difficult to discern to what extent local people were compelled to adopt the housekeeping methods that their employers were accustomed to, rather than doing that which was familiar. This challenge may have been especially true in the kitchen. One missionary family had their cook prepare the Russian Mennonite *vereniki*, filled with cottage cheese, in India.[134] Similarly, Agnes Harder Wiens's cook, Elahi Baksh, learned "the intricacies of Russian Mennonite cooking," and "his zwieback and peppernuts, his borscht and rai-rai rivaled any produced by a Kansas cook."[135] Cooks who worked for missionary families were essential parts of the household, whatever a family's preferred cuisine. When one missionary family, preparing to leave India and return to the United States, divided their belongings to leave behind, their cook was considered "the most highly prized of what we claim ownership to."[136] Such a statement reinforced the colonial mindset that missionaries brought with them, but also underlined their dependence on the population they wished to convert.

Since Indian cooks in missionary households were frequently male, gender assumptions in Mennonite families may have been upset. Some missionary wives expected that their central role would be domestic – cooking and keeping house for their missionary husbands – and were dismayed to learn that not only were they not wanted in the kitchen but their suggestions for food preparation and kitchen order went unheeded. In her history of Mennonite missions in India beginning in 1900, Ruth Unrau offers the following analysis of the relationship between missionaries and househelp: "some people become unexpectedly psychotic about their servants. Intelligent women can be made to feel like fools by their cooks. An American or Canadian housewife coming from a carefully controlled, sanitized, pasteurized kitchen, from a routine of shopping that pays attention to cents per ounce, can be thrown into an economic depression for which the only cure is Hershey bars. Eventually she may come to realize that no good comes from hankering after hygiene."[137] This homemaking identity crisis actually allowed missionary women to embark on activity that was disallowed them in their North American churches, such as leading Bible studies, teaching, and nursing. Jeanette Martig Thiessen worked full time as a nurse in India and so a cook for her household was a necessity. And while she insisted that they could "get along very well on Indian types of menus," her cook knew "only Western dishes."[138]

I had my own experience of eating encounters, and associated unfamiliarity, when I travelled to the Democratic Republic of Congo in 2012 to join Congolese Mennonites as they celebrated their centennial – one hundred years since the first mission was established in 1912. This offered me the opportunity to do research

1.5   Mennonite women preparing *foufou* at church gathering, Mbuji-Mayi, Democratic Republic of Congo, 2012.

on two of my favourite topics – women and food. In the context of an organized small tour group, I visited three cities in which I was able to arrange conversations with groups of women. I wanted to explore possible links between Mennonites and food in their context and to know what food meant religiously and culturally for Congolese Mennonite women.

   I was surprised by many things. I was reminded that food hospitality is universal but actually often more prominent in settings where resources are lacking. Two women, Sidonie Swana and Beatrice Kadi, whom I hosted for dinner at my home in Canada years earlier, took the bus carrying pails of food to share a meal with me at the guest house where I stayed. When women learned that I was interested in food, a spread of dishes – special and everyday – was laid out for me; I realized that these gatherings also created opportunities for poor women to eat better than they normally did.

My first conversation was with a dozen women who sang for me and then waited for my instructional lecture on nutrition. I was at a loss for words when asked, "how do I feed my children so they are not always sick?" Other women were eager to tell me about the many burdens they carried in a country with high unemployment and poverty, and where just carrying out the tasks of the day was so difficult. They also did not hesitate to speak emphatically about their frustration with patriarchal households and churches. During my visits, I learned to eat caterpillars, a delicacy. And most importantly, I ate *foufou* three times a day. *Foufou*, a spongy starch, made from maize and cassava, is akin to *zwieback* or sticky rice – the food of survival, the food of hope, the food of life. I learned that while there may not be Congolese Mennonite foods, their foodways are differentiated by ancestral tribal origins, something the women still consider important even though the missionaries tried to eliminate such allegiances.

Mennonites have changed through food encounters in varied ways. By eating across borders in the process of migration, ethnicity is performed, imitated, or practised. In fact, the hybridity, fusion, and cultural exchange that is central to understanding the evolution of ethnicity and foodways makes borders and boundaries transitory and ephemeral. Even while food differences may create conflict between groups, for Mennonites it has perhaps reduced their historical separation from the world, while other practices – dress, language, political engagement, religious stances – were more solid points of nonconformity and differentiation. Indeed, cuisines that emerged in varying geographic contexts connected Mennonites to those so-called "foreign" environments while they served to separate Mennonite subgroups as culturally distinct from each other. The phenomenon to "eat like a Mennonite" emerged as Mennonites encountered other cultures across time and place, where they embraced, imposed, appropriated, and modified foodways to create a continuously evolving cuisine. That women were often at the forefront of food exchanges points to their centrality in the resilience and transformation of foodstuffs and foodways marked as Mennonite. The act of "eating like a Mennonite" is a gendered one – the topic of the next chapter.

Zwieback

Recipe by Mrs A. Rempel, Chortitz, Manitoba

This is the recipe I use on the rare occasions I make *zwieback*. It is taken from *The Mennonite Treasury of Recipes*, which was compiled by a committee of Mennonite women and first published in 1962. In early versions of the cookbook, the women were identified by their marital status and husband's name. Phrases lacking in specific instructions, such as "beat in enough flour" and "make a smooth soft dough," recognize the baking expertise that emerges from experience and sensory knowledge.

2 cups milk
1 cup butter, room temp.
1 package yeast
½ cup lukewarm water
1 tsp. sugar
1 tsp. salt
6 cups flour

Dissolve 1 package of yeast in the lukewarm water, and 1 tsp. sugar and let rise. Scald milk and cool. Put milk, butter, yeast and salt in large bowl. Beat in enough flour to make stiff batter. Add more flour to make smooth soft dough. Knead well, cover and let rise until double in bulk. Now form buns the size of a large walnut placing a smaller bun on top of a larger one on a greased pan, pressing down firmly with one finger. Let rise till double in bulk. Bake in oven 350 degrees for approx. 15–20 min.

2

Mennonite Women Can Cook

Gendered Notions of Foodways

In the mid-1950s, a prominent American sociologist, John Hostetler, whose work focused on Mennonites, wrote a popular booklet about Mennonite beliefs and customs. In a section devoted to "Things Feminine," he said this about Mennonite women: "Not being afraid of hard work, they eat well. They cook, can, stock their whitewashed fruit cellars, and provide well for their household. They probably pay less attention to their waistline than do most American women, and they find the needed creative satisfaction to free them from much worry."[1] One wonders, with some concern, at the research methodology that led Hostetler to draw conclusions about women's eating habits and their waistlines. Another example of generalization is found in the *Food That Really Schmecks* series of cookbooks by Canadian cookbook icon Edna Staebler. Even while focusing on the foodways of the smaller, culturally conservative Mennonite subgroups in Ontario, Staebler gave a broad portrayal of Mennonite women with descriptors such as "plump," "placid," and "well-rounded."[2] Elsewhere, Staebler provides a detailed description of a traditional Mennonite meal that includes numerous references to the plumpness of the cook and those who eat her food.[3] While these appear to be complimentary portrayals, they have the effect of stereotyping not only the foodways but also the bodily natures of Mennonite women. In this, they can be compared to Doukhobor women, whose bodies, described by the media as strong, large, and nude, came to symbolize and define both their gender and their religious group.[4]

If one thinks such linkages between women, food, and bodies are the stuff of history or antiquated frameworks, one need only probe more recent allusions. For example, in *The Amish Cook at Home* (2008), Lovina Eicher, the cook, is described as "calm" with a "round face, a ready smile, and the ability to 'multitask.'" Her "ingenuity, stoicism, and sense of purpose" are linked to her Amish ancestors' escape from persecution in Europe centuries earlier.[5] In her 2021 creative memoir, Carla Funk describes *Glums*, the cottage cheese filling for "Wareniki … our Mennonite perogies." Funk compares these to "the pitted, cleft flesh of a woman's thigh and buttocks, as if Mennonite aunts and grandmas and moms had given themselves and their cellulite to the making of the food."[6] Funk pays tribute to the food-related artistry of her female ancestors, yet in describing her difficulty swallowing the *vereniki* (my spelling), she may be signalling Mennonite discomfort with things of the body. This example suggests that eating certain foods elicited memories imbued with emotions both positive and negative.

Another observation subtly decries those women who may have departed from what was and is deemed their essential nature. A non-Mennonite doctor, visiting the Steinbach Heritage Village (a Mennonite-themed village museum in Manitoba) in 1971, described his experience with *vereniki*: "Oh yes, those vereniki were something else: big, excruciatingly delicious, soaked in real cream from a cow … there isn't room on this page, nor was there room in my stomach, to fully savor the flavor. One can only be thankful that there are still Mennonite women who haven't been taken in by modern 'convenience foods.'"[7]

These brief examples speak volumes about both insider and outsider perceptions and expectations of Mennonite femininity and Mennonite ethnicity. Mennonite women have often been stereotyped by their associations with food, whether they are preparing it, eating it, or cleaning up after its consumption. The linkages are

2.1 *Vereniki* (perogies), farmer sausage, and *plumi moos* (fruit soup) served at Mennonite Heritage Village, Steinbach, Manitoba, 2018.

common in popular portrayals for tourists, or in media reports about Mennonite relief sales, where various foodstuffs abound, or in the cookbook publishing industry, which has thrived on the public's interest in Mennonite and Amish foodways. These observations create connections between Mennonite women and food abundance, wholesomeness, and culinary prowess. Frequently, such sources offer a blanket generalization about women's food skills. The presumptive truism of Mennonite women as "good cooks" can be found in numerous observations, well before the 2011 *Mennonite Girls Can Cook* cookbook phenomenon – the inspiration for the title of this chapter. For example, early Canadian feminist and agricultural journalist E. Cora Hind visited rural Manitoba Mennonite homes in the late nineteenth century and observed, "Let me tell you that no bread can surpass that of the Mennonite housewife, baked in these ovens ... I doubt very much if many Canadian or American housekeepers could show such creditable housekeeping at a moment's notice."[8]

Similarly, journalist Victoria Hayward, who published a travelogue of the peoples of Canada in 1922, commented, "All of the Mennonite women are good cooks."[9] In the face of such statements, any Mennonite woman who wasn't keen about cooking, or didn't excel at it, could easily feel inadequate as both a Mennonite and a woman.

The gendered nature of food and its practices, and the corresponding perceptions of women, is also prominent in Mennonite academic and community histories and in auto/biography and other memory sources. Speaking about the conservative Old Colony Mennonites, historian Royden Loewen observes, "As in most peasant societies, women's identities are indelibly wrapped into their roles as producers of food."[10] One woman from that community, Margaret Reimer, joked that "Mennonite women can cook chicken soup from a rooster," suggesting a collective ability to prepare something from nothing.[11] In her memoir, writer Katie Funk Wiebe noted that in her understanding, growing up and becoming a Mennonite woman "in essence meant learning to cook."[12] By contrast, Ted Friesen's recollection of his mother's homemaking skills implies there was nothing to be learned since "Mother was a natural cook, who used no recipe books, or measuring utensils."[13] Anne Loewen's children said their mother had "all the characteristics of a Mennonite mother," including that she "cooked and made borscht, varenike, and zwiebach from memory."[14] In her creative memoir, Carla Funk describes her female ancestors as "a long line of women praised for flaky pie crusts, bountiful gardens, covered heads, held tongues, sharpened knives, and bread dough that baked into risen golden loaves."[15] These descriptors are mainly food related. Mennonite foodways expert Norma Jost Voth included the activity of preparing traditional foods in her tribute to the "courage, stamina and faith" of "our mothers and grandmothers."[16] In her autobiography, Tena Friesen describes her mother as a "virtuous woman" according to the criteria of Proverbs 31:15, which includes providing food for the family. Friesen devotes an entire chapter to this theme, detailing her mother's gardening and food preservation practices in a narrative that clearly exhibits the relationship between food and gender. She says very simply, "Mom was very creative in cooking, baking, and running the household. She often made something very tasty out of leftovers or a limited supply of groceries."[17] Such tributes are, of course, commendable and welcome, given that domestic activity, and women's lives generally, have received limited attention in Mennonite historical writing.

All of the above examples reinforce the stereotypical notion that Mennonite women "can cook," and convey understandings of female labour, physicality, and personality. While one might argue that this is a generational idea, no longer applicable in the twenty-first century, even in an era when men also cook, and many Mennonite cooks are non-gender binary, food activity remains intertwined with assumptions about gender roles and identity in varying ways across the Mennonite spectrum. This chapter explores the complex terrain of food and gender in a Mennonite context.

Women and Food

Mennonite women are not the only people typecast by their relationship to food. As sociologist Sherrie Inness, a leading theorist of food and gender, bluntly puts it, "if we are to study women's gender roles ... we need to study food."[18] There are many stereotyped notions of food and gender, including dichotomies constructed to reinforce gender distinctions at historical moments when these were becoming blurred. The contrast between maleness and femaleness is sometimes illustrated and reinforced with socially constructed food preferences – for example, men like meat while women like salads.[19] Rebecca Sharpless suggests that the ephemerality of cooking – meals preceded by long hours of preparation are consumed within minutes – contributes to the invisibility of women's labour. It is fleeting and lacks permanency, unlike the visible legacy of men's labour.[20]

There is a large body of literature that both celebrates and bemoans the essentializing of women as producers and preparers of food. Some feminist food studies theorists suggest that the linkages between women's roles in the kitchen and patriarchal oppression have been so strong as to make historians of women "recoil" from food-focused research for "fear of associating themselves too closely with the domestic drudgery of the kitchen."[21] Warren Belasco submits that the traditional "separate spheres" model of gender relations reinforces the connection between women's historic food-related labour and ideas of "patriarchal oppression and women's domestic 'enslavement.'"[22] Much of the historical work on women and food has centred, and rightly so, on dysfunction and deviance. And women's relationship with food and its attendant tasks has been depicted as one of oppression and drudgery, even while women are ironically praised for serving as the drudges.

In keeping with an interest in exploring agency and empowerment in women's traditionally gendered activity, late twentieth-century scholarship offered more positive perspectives on women and foodways. In a review essay about cookbooks, Hélène Le Dantec-Lowry observes that "the kitchen can be seen as a place of oppression, but it is also described as a space for solidarity and creativity."[23] Arlene Avakian similarly argues that "the work of cooking is more complex than mere victimization"; cooking is "a vehicle for artistic expression, a source of sensual pleasure, an opportunity for resistance and even power."[24]

I would add that this assessment is ultimately predicated on whether one (whatever gender) actually enjoys preparing food. I, a self-identified woman, have my moments of foodways enjoyment, but, as noted earlier, it is my male partner and male children who find boundless interest and enjoyment in preparing a meal for friends and family. As a family unit, we turn the stereotypes about food and gender upside down, as do many other twenty-first century households I know. That this re-ordering continues to elicit remarks, indeed occasional surprise, is a reminder of the prevalence of the assumption that all women are at home in the kitchen. Women themselves can't seem to win either way. One woman, commenting on her struggles with food, said, "In contemporary women's struggle to live our feminism, we have consistently been made to feel ashamed of our love to cook; just as prefeminist pressures shamed the women who did not enjoy this activity."[25] Folklorist Diane Tye's mother was like many women for whom "baking was obligatory, a response to family and community needs rather than an activity that gave her personal enjoyment."[26]

As Tye and others have noted, domestic labour, including that which is food-related, is part of an ethic of care that women have alternately embraced and rejected, but have certainly been socialized into.[27] Sonia Cancian, writing about two generations of Italian households in Montreal, observes that despite the influence of second-wave feminism, she "came to understand that a woman's primary responsibilities – whether she was employed full-time or not – were anchored in the domestic sphere as she adopted the roles of nurturer, feeder, and caregiver of her family."[28] The socialization embedded in feeding the family meant that the kitchen was a site where girls and young women not only learned the skills of food preparation but also internalized their obligatory caring roles. Such roles mutually reinforced ideas and feelings about care and comfort.

In discussing how people become "enclave eaters" – consuming foods that bring together "food, identity, and community" – Donna R. Gabaccia argues that "comfort foods are usually heavily associated with women as food preparers and organizers of the family's emotional life."[29] *Zwieback* is one Mennonite food item described as a "comfort food" because of its associations with family history, memory, and security.[30] The ethic of care, as it relates to food, means offering comfort to family and community during times of stress and uncertainty, or during everyday life. In Hutterite colonies in the past, there were specific guidelines about what women should receive after each childbirth; in 1929 this included "¼ pound of tea; 3 pounds of sugar; 1½ pounds coffee; 1 cup flannel leaves; 9 boiled eggs; 2 bushels *Rascha Zwieboch* (roasted zwieback); 4 ounces cinnamon sticks; 1 cup of cream or ice cream daily; 2 quarts whiskey and 1 quart wine for toasts."[31] I am struck by the relatively modest amount of some foods – nine boiled eggs – but the large quantity of *zwieback* – two bushels! – pointing to the centrality of this foodstuff as a feature of care. The Covid-19 pandemic beginning in 2020, in addition to highlighting a desire for comfort food, reminded us of the persistence of gendered relations of labour, as women assumed much of the labour of care, including meal preparation, which increased during this unique stay-at-home crisis.[32]

The relative absence of food in published institutional and academic histories about Mennonites is commensurate with the invisibility of women and gender-related topics until the late twentieth century. Official Mennonite church and community histories often left women out altogether and rarely discussed women as food producers or preparers. A poem about the first Mennonite settlers in Yarrow, British Columbia, in the late 1920s does not mention women, even though it celebrates "Twelve stalwart men from a Prairie Town" who ate "Borscht, beans, bacon and corn" when they arrived home "all tired and forlorn."[33] Surely the women who prepared those foods were also tired in light of the extensive indoor and outdoor labour to build a new community, but perhaps their fatigue is just taken for granted rather than lauded.

While the female relationship with food is stereotypical, it is true that women played – and continue to play – crucial roles with respect to the maintenance and/or transformation of their communities' foodways. As the primary purveyors of food and food-related customs in families and religious organizations, women carried special power to shape identity both internally held by Mennonite communities and as perceived from the outside. They were ultimately responsible for what it meant to "eat like a Mennonite." Furthermore, because women's roles were so closely tied to foodways historically, their own sense of self emerged from that. The polarity of food labour as oppressive or enlivening shaped their personal identity and the way in which they were described and remembered by others.

Food Identity as Power

The descriptors linking Mennonite women and food have ambiguous meaning. On the one hand, such characterizations gave women pride in culinary abilities that were publicly recognized as markers of who Mennonites are. On the other hand, stereotypes that exalted the intrinsic nature of women's activity in the kitchen minimized the drudgery of that labour and undermined their potential capacity in other sectors of community and societal life. Religious studies scholar Pamela Klassen stated it well when she observed that "Because of the Mennonite romance with food, women's roles as the traditional makers of shoofly pie, varenike, portzelky, zwiebach, and all the other relishes, breads, and sweets clustered on the table have been a source of power used by women and against them."[34] For Mennonite migrant communities, women as food producers were, as Nadia Jones-Gailani states about Iraqi women, "in a position of power as facilitators of stability, offering some reassurance that not everything in life has changed immeasurably because of their dislocation."[35] Similarly, a 2021 study on foodways, migration, and mothering observes that "mothers ... retain the power of food as a major pathway for negotiating membership to kin groups, communities, and nations."[36] Women's capacity (and challenge) to create food security and familiarity in new environments was pivotal to settler success, even if rarely acknowledged as such.

For women who enjoyed food-related tasks and received praise for their ability in the garden or kitchen, their labour elicited positive self-esteem and pride, and even offered a sense of power over the domestic realm. Serving a meal to a large group of family and friends presented a Mennonite woman with an opportunity to display her skill at a task that was perhaps second only to childbearing in its place as an intrinsic aspect of being a Mennonite woman. For many generations in the past, and in traditionalist groups today, women simply understood, whether eagerly or grudgingly, that their destiny was to marry, bear and raise children, and carry out domestic labour, a large portion of which was food-related. Margaret Heinrichs Groening recalled that her goals as a wife were to be "kind, cheerful, a good cook ... to be neat, have the house clean, meals on time."[37] When Tena Friesen married in 1962, she felt good about the lack of "cultural or language barriers" between her and her new husband, including the fact that "Carl didn't even have to adjust to a different style of cooking." This was due, in part, to the fact that "our mothers were both excellent cooks, cooking all the Mennonite dishes from the page-worn recipes that have passed the test through the ages."[38] Agatha Fast was remembered by her children for her food-related identity even in retirement years: "Mother, as had been the case her whole life ... was still often busy cooking and baking ... She always got much satisfaction from people's enjoyment and appreciation of her cooking and baking."[39]

How closely women were tied to the kitchen in reality and in memory is indicated by a special Mennonite heritage event in the year 2000 devoted to the Mennonite woman's apron as a symbol. In a newspaper article reporting on this event, the writer reminisced: "Definitely one of my clearest memories of my mom when I was a child is of her stirring a pot of soup or kneading bread on the kitchen cabinet ... wearing a turquoise blue checkered apron with cross-stitch along the bottom."[40] I remember compulsory, female-only home economics classes in the early 1970s in which my first sewing project was an apron! Perhaps an easy garment to make, but also an implicit suggestion about a fundamental need that I would have because of my gender. Such assumptions about roles exist today in gender-stratified Mennonite subgroups.

While Mennonites disdained many forms of entertainment and cultural endeavour as being "worldly" – that which hindered separateness from modern society – food production and consumption, as an activity closely related to the land and necessary for sustenance, did not come under scrutiny as something that would induce pridefulness or excess. Especially in eras when "sinful" was a descriptor attached to most forms of extravagance, the kitchen was exempt. In fact, in the Kansas-based *Centennial Treasury of Recipes,* the foreword says this: "It was a sin to be lavish in clothing, in home furnishings, in entertainment, and in other areas but the Swiss Mennonites felt that money and energy spent on food was a necessity."[41] On the jacket cover of Darcie Friesen Hossack's collection of short stories *Mennonites Don't Dance,* the author is described as "introduc[ing] a culture in which dancing is *verboten* [forbidden] but the sensual pleasures of food are celebrated with artery-clogging abandon."[42] In Mennonite sources, there are allusions here and there to the idea that while talk about sex (or even the act itself) was discouraged or suppressed, cooking and eating were sensory activities that were unrestrained. For example, one writer of Mennonite descent speaks about taboos on sex, among other vices: "Maybe I couldn't follow the dirty jokes at school, but, by gum, I could fry up some succulent rollkuchen!"[43] The idea that the suppression of sexuality, whether talking about it or even acknowledging it, could prompt some groups to channel libido into food, is intriguing but largely untested. Nevertheless, one cultural commentator suggests that, in an age where everyone is a foodie, food is the new sex.[44]

In a context where non-functional artistic expression was suspect,[45] women could receive much affirmation and encouragement as, in essence, culinary artists. In fact, the *Centennial Treasury of Recipes* begins with the words of compiler Alice Kaufman's mother: "Cooking is an art and don't you ever forget it."[46] Food can empower women when they love it and imbue it with a sense of creativity and beauty, as many cooks do. Eleanor Martens observed that her mother's artistry was evident in food preservation: "the way she lined up the fruit – apricots, cherries and plums ... the jars stood there gleaming on the basement shelves, straight and sparkling in their newly-preserved perfection, pleasing to the eye as well as to the palate."[47] In her memoir, Maria Martens Klassen Loepp states in large bold letters, "Cooking and Company is my Delight,"[48] proclaiming rather than apologizing for her food artistry. Women themselves found small and subtle ways to exhibit pride in their food production. Maria Reimer Martens stamped her initial M in her butter, sought out by people who were "particular in their tastes for butter."[49] The Amish too had a tradition of molding butter into forms such as lambs for special occasions.

Female self-worth was often tied to food preparation and presentation, whether it was the amount a woman could "put away" – preserve – at the end of harvest, or the size and symmetry of her *zwieback*, or how quickly her *vereniki* were snapped up at the church fundraiser, or how fast her dish was emptied at the church potluck.

2.2 Food artistry is displayed in this carved "butter lamb," traditionally made for Amish weddings. This one was made by Rosella Leis, Ontario, in 2022.

My mother-in-law, whose childhood in the Soviet Union saw her malnourished and lacking school education, was renowned for her *zwieback* in her Canadian church community. Elfrieda Schroeder, who also experienced food insecurity during her childhood in Paraguay, became known as the "Zwiebach Lady" in her church in Manitoba.[50] Competition could easily develop between women as they judged among themselves and were judged by their menfolk on such pivotal things as whose pie crust was flakiest and whose *zwieback* were the shapeliest and fluffiest. Esther Wiebe recalled that in the Bolivian Mennonite context of her childhood, a woman was judged by "three earmarks" – number one was the "texture of her buns (light, fluffy, and with just the right amount of crustiness)."[51] Writer Connie T. Braun, in reflecting on the food traditions of her British Columbia immigrant family, said, "women wanted to know of their husbands, whose *borscht* tasted better, whose *rollkuchen* crisper – your mother's or mine?"[52]

While this might be viewed as a dynamic no longer operative in the twenty-first century, writer Melissa Miller reflects on her feelings of inadequacy at a 2012 church potluck – a meal to which everyone contributes a dish. She was dismayed when her pie – "sublime apple maple syrup custard and the delicate lemon sponge (from the *Mennonite Community Cookbook*)" – went untouched at a Mennonite church where food prepared by "grandmothers and aunties and long-term friends" was eagerly eaten, placing Miller, from a different Mennonite tradition, as an "outsider." For her, potlucks represented a "500-year ancestry of mothers who groom their children in the unwritten rules of potluck etiquette."[53] Here, the church potluck is not only a positive depiction of commensality – eating together in community – but a site for the politics of pride or inadequacy.

One community history plainly states that "the culinary reputation of every housewife on the threshing circuit was at stake each season."[54] This was harvest time on farms, when women were required to serve large meals at the exact appointed time to teams of hired farm workers. As threshing teams moved from one farm to the next, each cook tried to outdo the one who came before her.[55] One Mennonite cookbook devotes two descriptive pages to "Cooking for Threshes," a season when "especially women were extraordinarily busy" from dawn until midnight preparing meals and snacks for up to twenty-five men.[56] L. Marie Enns recalled that her mother was the last to eat at the end of a long day of constant food preparation for the team of men harvesting their crop in northern Saskatchewan in the 1940s. The day's menu included the following: fried potatoes, bacon, and eggs for breakfast; freshly baked cake with coffee for mid-morning break; roasted chicken with dressing, vegetables and potatoes, and homemade pudding for dinner at noon; cookies straight from the oven in mid-afternoon; and for supper, fried ham, potatoes with cream gravy, canned corn and dill pickles, bread and buns, and blueberry pie baked that day. Of course, everything was home-grown and home-preserved. According to Enns's children, "It was late when the men had eaten, later when we had eaten, and even later when Mom had everything under control and could go to bed … This frenzy of harvest work and cooking would continue until the threshing was done."[57] Community pig-butchering bees also placed pressure on the hosting homemaker. Marlene Plett, within a lengthy description of those day-long events, said the "special faspa at the end of the afternoon consisted of the lightest buns, the freshest butter, pickles, cheese, and jam, and a whole host of cakes and pies." Plett also noted that the "farm wife would try to outdo the faspa served at the previous butchering bee."[58]

These examples demonstrate the pressure of food performance – offering food that would be praised for both its quality and quantity. In eras when ingredients were few, cuisines were simple, and food insecurity was a recent memory, quantity was often the hallmark of a successful meal. In her overview of Pennsylvania German household life, Lorna Shantz Bergey observed that a woman's "reputation as a cook and good homemaker among her peers in the community was at stake if she was caught unprepared with second helpings."[59]

Yet cooking and baking were not only sites of competition between women; they created opportunities for cooperation. Especially in eras when church buildings had no kitchens or limited cooking capacity, food preparation for weddings and funerals was spread across households. Within some communities, in advance of a wedding, the mother of the bride would prepare a large amount of bread dough that was then distributed to village women to form into buns and bake – a shared contribution to the wedding meal. In cases where up to 500 *zwieback* were served over several days, the sharing of ingredients and labour among community members was "as traditional and natural as attending the wedding."[60] In Maria Klassen Braun's memory, aproned women would gather at the bride's home, each contributing ingredients other than flour, such as milk, cream, or butter, and together they would mix and knead the dough. Then, each woman would take home a portion of the dough to bake the buns. One can only imagine that these gatherings were not only necessary activity to prepare food for a large group, but also times for social bonding around a significant community event.[61] Marlene Plett recalls that for her 1952 wedding, thirty chickens were prepared by "neighbourhood women," and baked in the ovens of several homes.[62] Collective food

2.3 Women preparing food at the Mennonite Church General Conference, Waterloo County, Ontario, 1953.

preparation also occurred for the numerous church events, weekly and annually, that women were called on to serve. While this activity limited and stereotyped their roles within church life, it nevertheless brought them together and validated their gender-based capacities.

Furthermore, gifts of food were, and are, the most common way to support people in need. There are many examples. According to her granddaughter, Margareta Sawatsky Peters' chicken noodle soup was "the stuff of legends" in her southern Manitoba community. Not only did she send soup to people who were sick or had experienced "some family tragedy," she participated in a ritual whereby the women of her village all sent a jar of soup to a new mother. "In this way the women of the village showed solidarity and support to the new mother, so she didn't have to cook too much while she was regaining her strength."[63] The ethic of food care performed by Mennonite women went well beyond their own households.

Food preservation was another activity whereby a woman measured her skills and those of others. At her grandmother Linie Krahn Friesen's funeral, Erika Friesen recalled the food production of both her grandmothers (called Oma), whom she described as "my Ontario fruit farming, canning, baking, pickling and singing Oma and my Manitoba organizing, travelling, canning, baking, pickling and singing Oma." One of Erika's favourite things was being sent to the pantry or freezer for some item of food that was "put away": "these freezers were ALWAYS full to the brim – shuttable only due to the sheer weight of the lid!" Food preserved in abundance was not just to feed the family, but was women's art, given as gifts. Erika recalled that after a visit, her grandmother Linie "would select precious jars to send home with you – jars of jam – strawberry – strawberry rhubarb – apricot – plum ... and pickles – baby dills, spears and pearl onions. She always made it seem like your choice, but she always chose, and it was always your favourite."[64]

Particularly for rural-living Mennonites, and during times of food hardship such as the Depression of the 1930s (and Covid-19 in the 2020s), and in eras when food self-sufficiency was a mainstream assumption and not a fringe activity, preserving food consumed an enormous portion of female labour. The children of Agatha Fast recalled that their cellar was a "wonderful delight!" in autumn, with shelves "loaded with well over a hundred two-quart jars filled with a wide variety of canned goods; jams, jellies, fruit preserves, pickles, dills, and even some meat, such as chicken and fish." The family also stored a "large cache of potatoes, carrots, beets, watermelon, and other vegetables."[65] Another woman's cellar contained crocks with "pickled pig's feet, tongue, heart, zillchees (head cheese), dill pickles and sauerkraut."[66] Anne Konrad too recalled the extent of her mother's food preservation labour when their only purchased groceries were staples like flour, sugar, salt, vinegar, baking powder, yeast, and vanilla. In her words, there were the root vegetables to be dug out: potatoes, carrots, parsnips, red beets and turnips. Carrots, beets and potatoes could be stored in the root cellar in our basement. Parsnips were dried, as were onions. Cabbage was shredded for sauerkraut and dill and garlic were used to pickle cucumbers. Most families had a crock of dill pickles sitting in the cellar. Beans and peas were particular. To prevent botulism, they had to be canned in glass sealers in a water bath in a large canner. [There was] plum, gooseberry, raspberry and strawberry jam. Jars of peaches, pears and other fruits were cooked in light syrup for winter desserts. Plums were dried into prunes and apples schnitzed and dried into apple pieces.[67]

The capacity of women to adopt as normative food practices that in the twenty-first century we might describe as sustainable is notable. Tena Friesen's comment in her autobiography is exemplary in this regard: "Food was never wasted. Mom saved all the fat drippings and used it to bake bread. She saved water from cooking noodles to starch clothes. When this wasn't available, she cooked a starch by adding a flour mixture to boiling water … Mom used the whey from making cottage cheese to pickle the pig's feet and other meat."[68] Similarly, Esther Wiebe recalled this about her mother: "A notable characteristic of hers was her no-waste attitude towards everything. Stale bread was turned into bread pudding, too much cabbage became sauerkraut. Table scraps, vegetable peelings, and unusable leftovers went to either the dogs, chickens, or pigs. There wasn't a fruit that she couldn't turn into jam. Even watermelon rinds were pickled."[69] Of course, in the twenty-first century, some sustainable practices that emerged from necessity and poverty are now a hobby; during Covid-19, my husband revived his mother's traditional Russian Mennonite art of pickling watermelon.

The art and practice of food sustainability, including preservation, is not a thing of history for Mennonite women in conservative groups, who also apprentice their daughters into the skills of canning, drying, pickling, and salting. One observer of Old Order Mennonite culture said the "cellar looks like a store" because of its extensive holdings.[70]

A memoir describing a conservative family's life in northern Alberta recalled that "fall was more demanding than any other season. No refrigeration meant canning the summer bounty. Buckets upon buckets of peas were picked, shelled, and canned for winter. Hundreds of jars of peas, pickled cucumbers, beets, and wild Saskatoon berries were preserved. Then, all these jars, along with the potatoes, carrots, and onions, were carried down into the cellar ... When the weather turned cold enough to keep meat safely, the pig, cow and chickens were butchered."[71] Amish writer Marianne Jantzi also described autumn as the "picture-perfect" time in her basement: "The shelves are beautifully loaded with jars of gold, auburn, shades of green, cherry, orange, and ruby red. The potato bin is heaped with dull-red orbs. The carrots sleep beneath their layers of newspaper. Cabbages are piled crisp and green. The onions hang in their mesh bags."[72] Here again, food production and preservation are not only a functional activity, but reflect a woman's artistry and creativity.

Food preservation on the scale described above was, and is, possible only because of the large gardens overseen by Mennonite women. While men helped with heavier garden tasks such as tilling the soil, "the women of the Mennonite household were the chief gardeners."[73] In eras of rural self-sufficiency, gardening was far more than a hobby, as it is for many modern families. Maria Klassen Braun recalled a "huge" vegetable garden planted with enough "potatoes, carrots, cabbage, beets, etc." to feed her family through the winter. Watermelons and cantaloupes were eaten fresh in summer, while numerous other fruits, vegetables, and herbs were grown in abundance to be preserved for the year ahead. Her mother's grocery list, Maria observed, was small.[74] Like the cellar, gardens were sites of both artistry and sustainability. Roland M. Sawatzky describes historic Mennonite gardens as evolving "landscapes of beauty and pride" that were settings for social activities.[75] Pride resulted from a sense that certain standards had to be met in a Mennonite garden, described as "neat and free of weeds."[76] Furthermore, gardens were adapted over time through the process of migration. As museum curator Jenna Klassen notes, not only were gardens "vital source[s] of food," but they were also exhibits of "cultural change" as settlers in new locales adapted their produce, and diets, to unfamiliar soil and climate.[77]

Women's empowerment through foodways also occurred in the passing of domestic skills to their daughters, whose accomplishments in the kitchen reflected the teaching of their mothers and grandmothers. In conservative communities where formal schooling ends in early adolescence, ongoing education occurs, for females, in the spaces where cooking, sewing, cleaning, and childcare take place. Esther Wiebe, recalling her childhood in Bolivia, said, "Girls watched and learned from their mothers. After turning twelve, a girl stopped going to school to fully learn every aspect of homemaking – baking, cooking, canning, milking, cheese-making, cleaning, sewing, gardening, and childrearing."[78] Esther's published memoir is replete with stories about the food-related knowledge and skill she obtained from her mother.

The linkage between Mennonite women and food is reinforced in the memories, oral and written, of Mennonites about their mothers and grandmothers. As Nadia Jones-Gailani puts it, "Through food, women become the connection that links the family from the past to the present."[79] Even though the "past" for Mennonites includes many experiences of food deprivation and insecurity, as I explore in chapter 4, in memory sources it is more likely that women are remembered for the quantity and capacity of their food production, rather than the limits. Elaine Enns, within an analysis of Mennonite memories of trauma in the Soviet Union in the 1920s, nevertheless recalls her own grandmother as a "wonderful cook," retaining mental images of her "rolling and cutting long noodles for delicious chicken noodle soup."[80] Edward Giesbrecht recalls the mammoth task his mother had in baking weekly for eleven people: "On Saturday she bakes six pans of zwieback, 12 loaves of bread, butterhorns, cinnamon buns, and pies. Except for the bread, most of these are consumed by Sunday night. Often she bakes biscuits on Monday and pancakes on Tuesday to tide us over until Wednesday, when she bakes another eight loaves of bread. Her baking requires over 200 pounds of flour every month."[81] Anne Konrad's family memoir echoes this: "Imagine keeping eleven persons clean and fed. Mother cooked many soups and baked brown and white bread every week. On Saturdays she baked *Zwieback* buns and perhaps (if she anticipated guests) raisin bread (*Stretzel*) or *Pljushky,* a sweet roll brushed with egg white to a shiny brown top ... Saturday suppers always consisted of fresh *Zwieback* buns, boiled eggs and tea."[82]

Though my own mother has on occasion avowed her dislike of kitchen labour, among my sharpest childhood memories is the aroma of the curly butterhorn rolls that she baked on Saturday afternoons. I did not meet my paternal grandmother but like other women of her generation, she is remembered mainly for her domestic production, especially with regard to food. In the words of her daughter, one of thirteen children, "What stirs up family memories more than our favourite foods? Mom in the kitchen, leaning over a huge *Teigschuessel* dough bowl, hands sticky as she reaches into the large flour bin beside her and adds another saucer of flour to the weekly batch of bread dough. I still see her kneading that massive ball, punching and finally letting it rest. The bits and pieces of dough clinging to her hands were rubbed into the dough. Coming home from school to the wonderful aroma of freshly baked bread is a vivid memory."[83]

Specific traditional foods are remembered in sensory and relational ways, as described in this memory of eating a fresh *zwieback* bun: "There would be a puff of steam as you pulled off the top of a double-decker bun and as you bit into it you could feel the love of a grandmother or great grandmother, or great-great grandmother, and be part of a primordial Mennonite home."[84] Of her Mennonite background, Connie T. Braun says, "Food is our family story, but a story without words. It is the language my grandmother spoke, but without speech."[85] In many sources, the language is the scent of the baking foodstuff which evokes memories and understandings.

Women's foodwork functioned to preserve historical memory in both sensory and practical ways. In their socially assigned roles as feeders of the family, Mennonite women had a clear purpose and sense of self, and when their productivity in the kitchen was praised, they felt empowered.

Food Identity as Fear

While some women were empowered by cooking, others experienced it as oppressive. For those who were critiqued or felt inadequate in the kitchen or simply didn't enjoy cooking, the daily meal might prompt feelings of dread or even fear. Jennifer Evans, who studied women and food in northern Ontario after 1945, observed that "food and its related activities became a critical site for identity formation and a sense of belonging but also a source of fear, loneliness, exclusion and discrimination."[86] This point of analysis applies to Mennonite women as well. Especially in past eras, because a woman's self-identity was closely tied to her skill in the garden and kitchen, any sense of inadequacy in that domain dealt a blow to self-worth. For example, the children of Elizabeth Wiebe compiled a collection of her beloved recipes, but noted their mother "never really believed that her food was any good, let alone worth replicating."[87] Women's roles as feeders of the family could be a site for fear, or self-doubt, or pain.

In reminiscing about their mother, the children of Susanna Kehler Wiebe all gave much space to their mother's culinary abilities, describing fondly the Russian Mennonite foods she prepared for her husband and ten children, but also noting that she often cried while she cooked, and was always the one to eat last and to take the smallest helping. Her son Henry recalled, "At mealtimes she was the last to sit down, and constantly up again – to bring things from stove to table, to put more *gereischtit Brot* (toasted bread) on the plate, or potatoes, or to re-fill our bowls with *Borscht*, or our coffee cups." Susanna's daughter Tina echoed her brother: "Mother serves everyone before she herself sits down to eat her own small helping, half-crying because she is thinking of the children who are no longer at home, and whom she misses very much."[88] Did she also cry because she disliked cooking, or because she felt inadequate to the task, or for other reasons? While the meaning goes unanalyzed in the source, it is possible that the rituals of feeding her family kept deep depression over her losses at bay. Indeed, food could be both symbolic of and a concrete way to respond to emotion, and may have functioned as a panacea for difficult times. For example, when

David Klassen arrived with his family by oxcart to their new home on the banks of the Scratching River in southern Manitoba in 1873, the (unnamed) women reportedly wept. He permitted them to cry for twenty minutes, then said it was time to make waffles.[89] One wonders if the women may have taken comfort in sitting together with their sadness – thinking of homes left behind in Ukraine and fearing the unknown future in a new land – but were compelled to meet the eating demands of their menfolk.

Similar behaviour was remembered by individuals interviewed by Elaine Enns for a study examining the trauma carried by Russian Mennonite immigrants of the 1920s. One man recalled that his mother sat at the table during meals with "tears streaming down her cheeks."[90] I think of my maternal grandmother, whose experiences of violence during the post-revolutionary years in the Soviet Union caused significant mental illness, and while she was mostly vacant after electroconvulsive therapy in the years that I knew her, she nevertheless always pushed me to eat more, in order that the sun would shine the next day, as she said in German. I, in turn, wondered, if I ate more, could I make her happy? The complex and contradictory connections between food labour and mental health are alluded to in Julia Kasdorf's poem "When Our Women Go Crazy," in which she says, "When our women go crazy, they're scared there won't be / enough meat in the house. They keep asking / but how will we eat? Who will cook? Will there be enough?" The poem describes the abundant food production of women who "are sane," whose "refrigerators are always immaculate and full, / which is also the case when our women are crazy."[91]

The compulsion to please others was another fear-ful side of women's food labour. Katie Funk Wiebe offers a telling anecdote about her Aunt Neta:

> For a time, as a young woman in her late teens, she was helping out temporarily in the home of a close relative. Near Christmas she and her kinswoman were baking cookies. She mixed the cookie dough and the other woman baked them, for she

feared the youthful, less experienced Neta might burn them. Unfortunately, the first pan of cookies, under her own watchful eye, burned to a crisp. Wood and straw-burning ovens in those days were not always easily controlled. The woman burst into tears and shook visibly. Why? She feared her husband's anger. How could they remedy the situation? "Why we'll simply toss the burnt cookies into the oven and no one will know anything about them," was Neta's quick response. "But that's impossible," said her terrified relative. Young Neta lifted a stove lid, picked up the pan, and scraped the offensive charred remains into the fire. Not a moral issue. She felt sorry for this dear woman to have such intense fear of her husband.[92]

This recollection only hints at the fear and pain that may have been attached to a woman's kitchen tasks, as she struggled to feed a demanding husband whose wrath exploded when she did not meet his expectations of a good wife. Cooking to please one's husband was not uncommon. While the kind of fear displayed in the story above may have been extreme, many women in the past were like Diane Tye's mother, who "measured her success as a wife" by catering to her husband's tastes.[93] The fear of not meeting male expectations was not an imagined consequence of personal insecurity or even societal norms. Cookbook publishers and other food industries, especially during mid-twentieth century, frequently included advice and instructions for women on how to cook to please their husbands.[94]

Women who were unable or unwilling to "cook Mennonite" and who feared food expectations placed on them experienced challenges to their self-identity as women and mothers. During difficult economic times, as in the years of early settlement on the Canadian prairies or American plains or Paraguayan Chaco or jungle, or during the 1930s Depression, women were tested severely in feeding their families according to Mennonite custom and expectation. For instance, during the Depression years, with six children to feed and clothe, Mary Neufeld offered meals consisting mainly of "bread with lard (or shortening) with a sprinkling of sugar and for dessert, bread dunked in the juice of preserves."[95] One family's memories cited a "bread-rich" menu as the only "viable diet" during this period.[96] Tina Klassen Kauffman, whose family immigrated from the Soviet Union to rural Saskatchewan in 1925, recalled her mother had a "hard time cooking like she had cooked in Russia" because the land was "too dry to produce well" and "money was almost nonexistent."[97]

Helen Janzen, who bore and raised nine children in rural Saskatchewan, reflects often on her fear and inadequacy as a mother when food scarcity was a constant reality in the 1930s and 1940s. Things improved once she was able to sustain a garden, and despite there being "usually no meat," she remembers "cooking up beans, potatoes, carrots, and onions." Much of her self-worth was related to her capacity to feed her family in the midst of hardship: "I guess I was a pretty good cook; everyone seemed to like the food. In fact, one of my sons once said, 'Mama could make shoe leather taste good.'"[98] Even when farms produced sufficient foodstuffs and there was income to purchase other staples, food preparation was laborious and time-consuming in the era prior to kitchen modernization, when women were often cooking for large families and farm hands as well. My aunt, one of thirteen children, recalls her mother's experience in the mid-1940s: "The food preparation alone was daunting for any woman. Mom rarely had less than ten places set around the table. She had no mixer or food processer; dishes were washed the old-fashioned way. There was no refrigerator until 1957."[99]

The role of mothers as food providers was tested especially during times of starvation and severe food insecurity. During the years of famine in 1932–33 in Ukraine, Helene Dueck's mother had gone out to try to procure food for her children, her husband being in prison and she thus not allowed to work. She had left the baby in the care of a three-year-old sister with the door locked. When Helene came home from school, she heard the two little girls crying in the house, but the older child was unable to reach the latch to open the door. Helene then too sat down and cried. Their mother had stayed out longer than planned because she had difficulty finding food. Helene recalls, "With the baby in her arm and the other little one hanging on to her apron she cooked a soup with the three potatoes and the beans she had brought. Gerhard had two more beans than I and I complained. Mother, without a word took two beans out of her dish and gave them to me."[100] Understandings about gender differences may have also created priorities when it came to distributing limited food. Justina Neufeld recalled that when she was four or five years old in Ukraine in the mid-1930s, there was often a shortage of food and she often felt "the gnawing feeling of hunger." On one occasion, her two older brothers received a second slice of bread, while she was told by her mother, "No, you are smaller and a girl ... You don't need as much as the boys."[101] Food shortages compelled women to make difficult choices, beyond limiting their own nutrition, which challenged their self-worth as mothers and went to the heart of gender identity.

Women who arrived in Canada as refugees from Ukraine and eastern Europe after the Second World War, many of whom came to adulthood during years of food shortages and famine, felt inadequate when their abilities to "cook Mennonite" were found wanting. The Mennonite identity of "Katja and Agatha," whose life stories are told by Pamela E. Klassen, included the "foods they cook and eat" despite the fact that they learned to prepare "traditional Mennonite meals only upon coming to Canada" after the war.[102] As a refugee during the Second World War, Helene Dueck worked for a pastor in Germany. There she was taught how to wash lettuce and how to boil an egg. But she recalled, "fortunately I did not have to do much cooking because, having grown up in Russia during Stalin's reign, I had not learned to cook since there was little available to cook with. Anyone could cook a thin potato soup with a few beans or carrots added."[103] When some of these women arrived in Canada and worked as domestic help in wealthy homes, they frequently learned to cook English, or cook kosher, long before they cooked Mennonite.

Working as domestic help in non-Mennonite and Mennonite homes was common for earlier waves of immigrants, and also for women from conservative groups who were not married and had limited choices in terms of education or vocation. In many cases, this meant leaving their rural communities to live in Canadian cities such as Winnipeg, Saskatoon, or Vancouver, where Mennonite church bodies established "girls" homes as places of temporary residence or gathering places for women on their days off. These women upset the social and economic orders in their families and communities in a variety of ways, not least of which was family reliance on their wages to support struggling immigrant households. The acquisition, in non-Mennonite homes, of knowledge regarding household practices, including foodways, brought subtle change to isolated Mennonite communities that resisted interaction with people viewed as outsiders. As one woman recalled, "I'd never even heard of hors d'oeuvres before, let alone made them. And a cucumber sandwich! What kind of thing was that to eat?"[104] Tina Klassen Kauffman, like many Mennonite domestics, was introduced to new foods such as root beer, celery, and avocado.[105] Women who worked for orthodox Jewish families learned to cook kosher, while others learned to serve cocktails (though they preferred positions in which serving alcohol was not required).

In a fictional study of a Mennonite woman in domestic service, Dora Dueck addresses the encounter with unfamiliar foods through a letter written by the protagonist to her family: "There are some foods in this house I am not used to. I wish I could let you taste them. I think you would find them interesting or else you would laugh."[106] This fictional character brought a box of Corn Flakes home to her family, who "marveled at the crunchy orange petals."[107] In some cases, employers did not provide adequate nutritious food to the women who prepared and served them their meals. One young woman sneaked dry cereal between meals to supplement her inadequate diet, but did not dare to eat any bread or milk, fearing her employer's retribution.[108] In other cases, women helped out their own impoverished families by sending home bread crusts or cooking fat.[109]

Mennonite women working as domestic help was a pattern common in many parts of the world. Mabel (Yoder) King worked as a live-in cook for a Norwegian family in 1930s Pennsylvania; her experience taught her how to follow a recipe and she incorporated at least one newly learned dish into holiday rituals in her own home – a Christmas cookie called a "pig-tail" because the dough was twisted in a particular way, a detail about which her employer was "very fussy."[110] As Julia Spicher Kasdorf suggests in her study of Amish Mennonite women who "worked out," these women represented a "cultural vanguard" by bringing dress, décor, and food from the "outside world" into their homes and communities, and thus had a significant impact on group identity.[111] One family memoir attributes their grandmother's "reputation as a fine cook and baker" to her time spent working for others when newly arrived in Canada.[112] The domestic work of young women in the cities also enhanced food security for their families, who depended on the wages of their daughters. One woman wrote to her daughter working in Winnipeg: "If only I could hold you to my heart and kiss you for all that you have done for us. Often you have saved us from death by starvation."[113]

The women who felt the fear of inadequacy at cooking and baking, or those who struggled to feed their families during food shortages, or those who learned new foodways to keep poverty at bay, were at odds with the assumption that Mennonite women "can cook."

Modernity as Opportunity and Challenge

The modernization of kitchen labour, which included the advent of electricity, indoor plumbing, and appliances such as stoves, refrigerators, freezers, and eventually microwave ovens, had a transformative effect on women's lives. Given that most Mennonites, at least in North America, were living in rural areas longer than the general population, some of these utility and technological innovations came later. Yet, they arrived to almost all households by the mid-twentieth century, other than to very remote communities or to conservative groups who were explicitly anti-modern and would not allow electric appliances into the house.

Modern appliances had a significant impact on food preparation. Deep freezers may have exemplified the dual impact of modernity in the kitchen. One the one hand, increased capacity to freeze any kind of food over longer periods of time made food preservation easier and safer. On the other, that ease also then placed greater expectations on women to "put away" more food and more types of food. By the mid-1970s, as the women's liberation movement was influencing even Mennonites, women were questioning and challenging rigid and unequal gender roles in all spheres of activity, including assumptions about intrinsic food-related skills and labour. LaVerna Klippenstein, columnist in a Mennonite periodical, questioned the way in which female self-worth was tied to domestic tasks. She noted that in previous generations, a woman who did not fulfill domestic expectations was considered an "enigma. Unchristian almost." Even today, she said, in many rural communities, the woman who does not plant a garden and bake her own bread, is looked upon as lazy, queer, or both." Even in an era of modern appliances that lessened household labour, Klippenstein critiqued women who persisted in "baking calorie-rich dainties for dieting friends, and sewing yet another garment to add to bulging closets. Mennonite women, in particular, have clung almost desperately to domesticity as though there were intrinsic virtue in zwieback and home sewn house dresses."[114]

The postwar decades also saw a rise in convenience foods, which today are viewed with scorn, and yet which dramatically altered the labour-intensive food-work of women. They also represented what Sandra M. Gilbert calls "gastronomic relief" in the aftermath of the food insecurity of the Depression and wartime rationing.[115] In *Baking as Biography*, Diane Tye reports that her mother didn't really like baking and her fairly plain, unexotic, economical foods were indicative of an era when women who didn't especially like cooking could now "whip up" dishes rather quickly.[116] While today we condemn convenience or processed foods, they were an important aspect of liberation from the kitchen for some homemakers of the 1950s, 60s, and 70s. The children of Anne Loewen observed that in the late 1950s into the 1960s their "working mother ... appreciated the time-saving help" of foods like Dream Whip and canned peaches.[117] For a generation of women like my mother, easy to prepare processed foods represented emancipation from the tedium of a task she was not especially fond of. And so we delighted in canned soup and beans, fish sticks, pasta in a box, and even TV dinners (actually eaten in front of the television) when our father was away. Many food scholars decry the corporation-driven turn to convenience foods as diminishing women's culinary independence; however, as Sherrie A. Inness suggests, cookbooks that included convenience foods "played a positive part in freeing women from countless hours of kitchen work."[118]

Other aspects of modern cooking were similarly ambiguous in their impact on women. One of these was the replacement of communal cooking traditions with individual accomplishment in a modern kitchen. In a 2020 blog on cooking during the Covid-19 pandemic, a Muslim woman reflected with sadness on the household-only daily *Iftar* dinner that broke the Ramadan fast, and the absence of a community food celebration that marked *Eid*, the end of the month-long food and faith tradition. Arwa Hussain, a member of the Dawoodi Bohra community, a sect of Shi'te Islam found across the globe, described the loss experienced by women who, because of physical distancing restrictions, continued making daily meals for their household, rather than joining the traditional communal meal preparations. "This was quite a blow for women," she said, "as it meant that most would have to continue cooking daily meals on their own. There would be no sense of community, which is essential to this period, and no break from their daily routines and the labour that entails."[119]

I am reminded of times and places where Mennonite women also benefited from communal food activity and the loss of shared labour and sociability that resulted from a shift to individualism in the kitchen. In traditionalist Mennonite and Amish communities today, such collaborative food work at weddings and funerals remains common. In communities where modernity diminished communal food preparation but was not accompanied by the opening of other spaces for female leadership in churches, women were left without a clear role to play in the life of their congregations.

Food Spaces in Kitchen, Business, and Church

Preparating food together was an important way for women to build and maintain social networks. Yet, the spaces in which food was and is prepared are imbued with contradictory gendered meaning. Even while the phrase "relegated to the kitchen" reinforces the notion that foodspaces are oppressive, in contexts where women's roles are narrowly defined, the kitchen was women's domain – the space in the household over which, in most cases, she had full control. Helen Barolini, in coming to terms with her Italian-American food identity, said she wanted to "turn the so-called woman's room (the kitchen) from a holding pen into what it really is – an embassy of cultural tradition."[120] Gloria Wade-Gayles says the kitchen in her African-American ancestry was where women went "to work, to serve, to think, to meditate, and to bond with one another,"[121] a statement that may apply to the Mennonite kitchen as well. It was where women gathered for talk and where female relationships across generations and extended families were negotiated. It was where they shared comfort in times of personal crisis, or discussed the business of church meetings where they were not allowed to speak. In her book on "the flower women" of Mexico – Low German-speaking Mennonites – photographer Eunice Adorno says, "The houses, and in particular the kitchens, constituted a kind of secret on the horizon where the Mennonites take refuge, for hours on end, among objects and trinkets full of personal meaning."[122] Kitchens were emotive spaces and elicited sensory memory. In her memoir, Anne Konrad reflected that "Nothing defined any Mennonite kitchen along Clearbrook Road on a Saturday afternoon more than the smell of fresh *Zwieback* just out of the oven."[123]

The kitchen was the space in which girls learned gendered roles from their mothers, aunts, and grandmothers.[124] This was true for Esther Wiebe, who recalled the centrality of the kitchen table to her education about domestic skills during her childhood in Bolivia: "When it wasn't filled with people eating, the table became our workspace. Vats of dough turned into loaves, buns rose in layers, and ultimately, warm golden bread was piled high on it to cool, filling the whole house with the smell of yeasty goodness. I had spent countless hours watching Mam and my older sisters rolling out the dough for cinnamon rolls, pies, perogies, and noodles, and mountains of chopped cabbage become borscht and sauerkraut on it. Tomato canning, pickling, jam-making, and churning butter all had happened on this table."[125] In many generations of Mennonite families, the kitchen was the "hub of activities" for everyone, young and old, female and male. According to Lorna Shantz Bergey, in Swiss Mennonite households, mealtime was "an anticipated experience as the family gathered around the tantalizing aromas rising from the entire meal already set on the table."[126] For plain Mennonite and Amish groups, the kitchen is still "the primary room of the house."[127]

The cooking space itself changed dramatically over time. In early settlement eras, or at times of the year when cooking outdoors prevented adding heat to indoor spaces, women learned to build and cook in clay ovens. Such ovens, common in Russia and Ukraine and later in South America, required an intuitive approach to baking that became akin to artistry: "women knew their ovens, how to feed them, what fuel worked best. They became skilled, not always by choice, but out of necessity, baking day after day."[128] Rural families frequently had a summer kitchen as well – a vestige of practices in Europe and Russia – attached to the main house. Women would cook there seasonally in order to keep the main house cooler, and sometimes families would eat there as well. The amount and intensity of food labour in the summer also meant that, if carried out in an alternate space, the main house required less cleaning.[129] The summer kitchen's further practicality was to store frozen meat and other food items in the winter.[130]

The existence of two kitchens in a household reinforced the significance and labour intensity of food preparation and preservation. When my parents-in-law built a sprawling ranch house on their farm in the 1970s, two large kitchens were included. The kitchen in the walk-out basement was used almost exclusively for the abundant canning that my mother-in-law did every year. Adjacent to the kitchen was a bedroom-sized pantry always full of jams and pickles, and with several huge freezers filled with baking and meat. As a post-Second World War refugee from the Soviet Union, she experienced severe food insecurity until adulthood, and remained fearful of not having "enough."

While women may have held a certain kind of power in the kitchen, if only symbolic,[131] other forms of gendered power relations may have existed at the table where food was served. In various times and places, particularly if a large group was gathered, it was not uncommon for men to be served first, then women. Children were sometimes last. According to Andrea Pető, in a patriarchal context "power is manifested in who is being served and who is serving the food."[132] Such a hierarchy is confirmed in Eleanor Hildebrand Chornoboy's compendium of stories, in which she describes eating at family gatherings that saw men eat first, after which "each woman sat in the same warm seat that her husband had just vacated"; sometimes they would get clean cutlery but usually used their husbands' unwashed plates.[133] According to Katie Funk Wiebe's memoir, in the Old Colony of Chortitza in Ukraine, it was the custom for children to eat from the unwashed dishes of the adults who had eaten first.[134] Today in India, it is customary for women (many of whom have jobs outside the home) to first serve food to their husbands, in-laws, and children and then eat what is left over.[135] While women held power over their kitchen spaces and the food preparation that occurred there, gendered power hierarchies in the household overall meant that women and children deferred to the eating needs and preferences of their menfolk, at least historically.

The kitchen was a space for women to exercise their influence in families and in community. Yet, the productive output of the kitchen had broader influence in terms of household financial security, as numerous Mennonite women used their kitchens as a base for food businesses. Mennonite women as food entrepreneurs is a topic barely studied. In part because food is tied to female identity, one of the few non-homemaking vocations for women, especially in conservative groups, has been as owners and operators of food-related businesses. Maria Martens, founder of the food store Mennomex profiled at the beginning of chapter 1, is a good example. At the age of fifteen, with the help of her father, Maria had already opened her own store in Tamaulipas state, Mexico, unusual for women but also for Mennonites generally, she recalled. It was a convenience store selling pop and snack foods, and served Mennonites and Mexicans in a rural area far from town. Maria had to give up her business after her father died and, with no brothers or other menfolk in the household, it became unsafe for her to operate the store. When she had the opportunity to purchase an existing food store after immigrating to Canada in 1996, she jumped at the chance because "I just love retail. I love buying and selling."[136] Over twenty years, she built a very popular food enterprise and in 2019 opened a second store in southwest Ontario.

In Mennonite groups for whom agriculture-related vocations are prioritized, but where the potential and need for income beyond farming itself is a reality, food businesses are an acceptable vocation for women to undertake. Sometimes this occurred of necessity, as for Lydia Bauman Martin who began a market gardening business during the 1930s Depression years since her husband was an unpaid church worker. In addition to selling fruits and vegetables at the local farmer's market, she baked up to 200 dozen cookies and eighty loaves of bread weekly.[137] Similarly, Lorna Shantz Bergey headed up the family cheese business after her husband was disabled following a farm accident in 1954. With significant hospital bills to pay, but with "no business experience," she nevertheless managed the business for several decades, selling cheese at markets throughout southern Ontario.[138] This scenario saw Bergey and her husband shift gender roles as he cared for their children and undertook household tasks while she administered the family business. According to Bergey, this led to some "awkward situations," such as when her husband answered a knock at the door with a tea towel in his hand![139]

Especially in the twenty-first century, as the demand for local and non-processed foodstuffs increased in the general population, opportunities for female entrepreneurship in Mennonite communities increased accordingly. Food businesses were also places where single women could achieve financial independence. One such business is Kitchen Kuttings in Elmira, Ontario, founded in 1989 by Old Order Mennonite sisters Lydia and Elmeda Wideman and friend

Nancy. A thriving business with a storefront, website, social media, and a booth at the local farmers' market, the business specializes in cheese, summer sausage, preserves, baking, and "home-cooked" take-out meals, as well as other food items. The need to use a car and computer for the business meant that the women had to leave the Old Order church, where these technologies are disallowed.[140] The business continued to expand, adding a café in 2019, and catering to modern foodies by, for example, selling Halloumi cheese from Cyprus alongside their homemade cheese curds as well as gourmet vinegars and charcuterie boards. The Facebook page includes videos of conservative Mennonite women preparing their specialty foods – almost like a television cooking show. Kitchen Kuttings responded nimbly to the challenges of the Covid-19 pandemic by swiftly installing necessary safety equipment, offering curbside pickup and home deliveries, and keeping their social media active with daily comfort food specials.

In the rural areas north and west of Waterloo region, I regularly frequent food stores owned and operated by conservative Mennonite women. They have become adept at using the technology required to run a successful business, within the limits allowed by their particular church group. Some of their stores sell only food products, frequently homemade or from farms within their community, while others are akin to general stores with an array of items geared toward conservative church communities. The success of these businesses reflects, in part, a desire of the general public for unprocessed, local foodstuffs. They offer a message of health and wholesomeness that is appealing in an age of food industrialization, and contribute to the linkages between Mennonites and food outlined in the introduction. It is also women's business acumen that brings economic stability to their households and allows them to stretch their gender-defined realm of activity, even while the business of selling food can be understood as an extension of their care-giving domestic roles.[141]

The evidence of female entrepreneurship in conservative Mennonite communities shows that the separate spheres analysis often applied to understandings of these groups must be nuanced. Women are

2.4 Shelves of baked goods and preserves at Sunnycrest Home Baking, operated by Old Order Mennonite women, Hawkesville, Ontario, 2022.

not active only in the private sphere of family and household, while men are in the public sphere of workplace and societal interaction. Even while conservative groups as a whole do not fit this paradigm neatly, since their collective outlook overall is one of separation from the public realm, within these groups women business owners often engage with the public more than men. The idea that "work" and "home" exist separately does not hold for modern-day traditionalist women.[142]

Masculinity and Food

Female food entrepreneurship may seem like an anomaly in a community where men are normally viewed as the owners of businesses. Analysis of Mennonite women and food of necessity also implies meaning about men and food and about non-binary individuals and food. About the former there are few Mennonite sources that allow one to draw conclusions or even offer speculative thoughts. About the latter – individuals for whom neither masculine nor feminine is an accurate descriptor – there are even fewer.

Food historian Jeffrey M. Pilcher proposed that in patriarchal societies, women are assigned the task of "everyday feeding," while men "usually prepare high status dishes, large cuts of roast meat, elaborate haute cuisine, or ritual food for the gods."[143] A similar oft-held gender dichotomy, explained by Michelle Szabo, is that while women cook to please and care for others – their caring labour described earlier – men's cooking is generally "self-oriented leisure."[144] Some sources suggest that modern Mennonite men, like others, have entered into kitchen roles as a form of leisure. Stanley Kropf, who grew up in a community where on Sundays "the women cooked dinner and washed the dishes [while] the men sat around talking and napping," assumed cooking responsibility at first because his wife had a more demanding job. Later, however, he joined a men's cooking club for the "sheer pleasure of cooking and eating."[145] Another man, an academic administrator and professor, described his cooking and baking activity as a "diversion" that even qualified as "Sabbath rest."[146] This is a very different motivation than for women whose food work was a requisite and feminized form of labour.

Other research points to the close association of men with outdoor cooking, particularly as barbeque chef.[147] Certainly Mennonite men barbeque like other men. In a 2003 reflective tribute to the food labour of women, Henry Neufeld acknowledged that meal preparation was traditionally women's work. Yet, he remarked, "in recent years men have become more involved in preparation of meals, though this is often limited to standing around and watching meat (prepared by women) burn on the barbeque."[148] I experienced a reversal of gendered food roles on a visit to Mennonite communities in India in 2015 and 2016, during which I was a participant at several large church gatherings of women. At these events, which always included eating together, it was often men who performed the work of cooking and cleaning up after the meal.

2.5 Mennonite men preparing rice at a women's church gathering, Balodgahan, India, 2016.

Another Mennonite tradition that warrants gender analysis is the community practice of pig butchering, a ritual with defined and separate roles for men, women, and children. While men's work took place mainly at the outset of a butchering event – the animal slaughter and cutting up of the carcass – women carried the multiple tasks of preparing meat for preservation or eating fresh. On top of this, they had to feed the several households undertaking the work on site. One detailed description of community pig butchering ends by saying, "I always thought the women worked harder than the men this day."[149] Animal butchering, discussed in greater detail in chapter 5, was central to Mennonite community life, in various places and times, because meat itself was central to a Mennonite diet.

Many food theorists have identified linkages between masculinity and meat eating. According to Massimo Montanari, meat, the "perfect food for increasing robustness and body strength," was thought to empower and strengthen warriors and thus had militaristic meaning.[150] The twentieth-century nonviolent activist Mohandas

K. Gandhi, whose Hindu beliefs included vegetarianism, was sometimes viewed as effeminate because he eschewed meat consumption. Mennonites, as pacifists, may have made meat central to their diets as a way to bolster their self-identity as muscular, not weak, and thus capable of being warriors, even if their beliefs rejected that role. Perhaps this was one reason Mennonites in Russia and Ukraine added plentiful quantities of meat to their *borscht*: it fortified their masculinity. Even if not connected to militarism, hearty meat and potatoes meals, like those served at an Amish-themed restaurant in Ohio, evoke "nostalgia for the kind of productive labor that brings sweat to the brow and makes one's muscles ache," according to Susan L. Trollinger. The "substantive replenishment" offered by such simple meals reinforces a masculinity that contrasts with the femininity of those who prepare and serve the food.[151]

Clearly, more work needs to be done to consider the intersection of masculinity and food in a Mennonite context. This is challenging when so few sources put these categories together, mainly because foodstuffs and foodways, at least within the household, are coded as feminine in so many ways. In the twenty-first century, gender identities are multiple, complex, and fluid. And Mennonite men are inserting themselves into activities and ideas surrounding food, exemplified in the 2015 recipe collection *Mennonite Men Can Cook Too*. The cookbook, perhaps the most prolific genre of Mennonite writing, signifies meaning about gender and identity at many levels and is the focus of the next chapter.

Tamales

Recipe by Eva Friesen Vogt

This recipe is striking for its minimalist measurements and instructions, and also because it is multicultural, with ingredients for a Mexican dish listed in English and German. The recipe assumes knowledge of amounts (meat, cornmeal) and the steps involved in making the dish. It appears in a Mennonite cookbook published in Mexico in 2011, *Kommt Essen: Mit den Mennonitischen Frauen von Durango, Mexiko (Come and eat with the Mennonite ladies from Durango Mexico)*. There is no authorship attached to the cookbook, which begins with the statement "Food unites."

1 Teel Oregano (tsp. oregano)
½ Teel Comino (tsp. cumin)
5 Knoblauchzähne (garlic cloves)
Sabroseador (complete seasoning)
23 rote Chiles (red peppers)
2 grosse Löffel Schmalz (tbsp. lard)

Koche dieses mit dem Fleisch zusammen (Cook together with meat.)

Teig: (dough)
Kornmehl (cornmeal)
1 Essl. B. pulver (tbsp. B powder)
Fleischsuppe (bouillon)
1 Essl. Schmalz (tbsp. lard)

3

Recipes and Beyond

The Cookbook Phenomenon

In 2009, I received a cookbook, *Food for the Journey*, as a thank-you gift for talks on food I had given at a Mennonite church. The book was created by Mike Lee-Poy and Thomas Brown, who love cooking, as a gift to attendees at their wedding two years earlier.[1] Mike and Thom's marriage was perhaps the first celebration of a same sex union in a Mennonite church in Canada. Subtitled *Recipes and Quotations from Our Community*, the collection includes favourite recipes submitted by friends and family of the couple. It thus both reinforces and topples the stereotypical notions of what a cookbook is. As may be obvious, the cookbook's authorship topples gendered assumptions about who produces cookbooks and why. While the creators were two gay men, the book otherwise follows a conventional structure with three sections on appetizers and starters ("Starting the Journey"), entrées ("Trekking Along"), and desserts ("Journey's End"). Recipes derive from a wide range of ethnic and national cuisines and represent both tradition and innovation; there is no recipe that I would say represents an identifiable and particular Mennonite food tradition.

Like most other Mennonite cookbooks (Lee-Poy and Brown might not categorize their book this way), *Food for the Journey* demonstrates both "attachment to the familiar and the appeal of novelty."[2] For me, the cookbook denotes love of food, the importance of food in community, and that recipe compilations can be political statements.

These characteristics are found in most Mennonite cookbooks. For the purpose of definition, I consider "Mennonite cookbooks" to be recipe collections compiled by Mennonite churches or organizations; or recipe books that focus, at least in part, on food traditions that some Mennonite individuals and groups carry as part of their historic experience in varied times and places; or compilations produced by individuals whose stated identity as Mennonite is integral to their cookbook. The specific cookbooks I discuss are mainly Canadian in origin, but are representative of a genre that includes hundreds, perhaps thousands, of varied recipe collections produced by individuals, families, churches, and organizations around the world.

One could argue that Mennonite cookbooks have conveyed more knowledge about Mennonites than any other written work. Certainly some cookbooks, as Amy Harris-Aber observes, are explicitly outward-looking and function as "souvenirs" to educate "people unfamiliar with the Mennonites."[3] Nadia Jones-Gailani's observation about Iraqi women in North America can be applied to Mennonites as well, in that the "cookbooks they publish make them cultural public ambassadors for the entire community."[4] I argue that they are also "religious" ambassadors. In fact, in his book *The Naked Anabaptist*, Stuart Murray says that when he asked newcomers to Anabaptism (a religious label that is sometimes preferred over Mennonite) what books they had read that drew them to the church, most listed *The Politics of Jesus* by John Howard Yoder and the *More-with-Less Cookbook* by Doris Janzen Longacre.[5] With sales of close to two million copies in multiple editions, the *More-with-Less Cookbook* has likely reached more readers than the writings of Yoder.[6]

In a journal on theology and culture, an American Mennonite church leader states that her "conversion to the Mennonite church began with a cookbook" – specifically *More-with-Less* – which she discovered while teaching in the Dominican Republic.[7] This particular cookbook is perhaps the most widely known, even internationally, yet there are numerous other bestsellers that have introduced Mennonites to mainstream society by way of foodstuffs and foodways. This chapter will analyze Mennonite cookbooks with attention to a number of themes: the role of women in fundraising for Mennonite institutions; the connections between foodways and ethno-religious identity; the evolution of identity in the midst of modernization and acculturation; and the possibility of diet as political statement.

Cookbooks as Textual Artifact

Cookbooks, as possibly the bestselling genre of books, were (and are) produced in abundance by Mennonites, mainly women, as a means to build community, raise funds, reinforce identity, and celebrate a long history of food production. Yet cookbooks, associated with the mundane, with the material, and with women's work, have rarely been regarded "as having any serious historical value"[8] beyond providing instructions on preparing a particular dish. Food scholar Sherrie A. Inness suggests that society considers cookbooks "culturally unimportant" because they are part of a female domestic realm marginalized as trivial and insignificant when compared to the interests of men.[9] Certainly it is true that, historically, cookbooks both reflected and reinforced women's domestic roles and indeed, notions of their inherent natures.[10]

Scholars in many fields have examined cookbooks as a type of source – textual artifact, anthropological document, everyday autobiography – that reveals much more than how many teaspoons of salt to put in a good bun dough. Janet Theophano, in *Eat My Words*, states, "There is much to be learned from reading a cookbook besides how to prepare food ... The cookbook, like the diary and journal, evokes a universe inhabited by women both in harmony and in tension with their families, their communities, and the larger social world."[11] Canadian cookbook bibliographer Elizabeth Driver comprehensively claims, "No other category of book evokes such an emotional response across generations and genders and is freighted with so much cultural and historical meaning."[12] Carol Gold, in her study of Danish cookbooks over three centuries, observes, "Cookbooks tell stories, as do all books. Perhaps the stories are not linear; they do not have a beginning, a middle, and an end, but they are stories nonetheless."[13] Cookbooks are also performative in that they deliberately or subconsciously create a story about the subject, in this case Mennonites, although I include Amish here because of the significant number of recipe collections by and about that group. A cookbook can be read simply as instructions for producing a particular culinary dish, but it can also be studied as a gauge for cultural change, as an indicator of gender roles, as a treatise of ideas and beliefs, and as a statement of political advocacy.

Although many Mennonite women did keep journals and write letters, for those who were not comfortable with or were disinclined toward that form of reflective expression or daily recording of events, writing down and making public their favourite recipes was a way of "making themselves visible."[14] In eras or contexts in which women's words were not accepted into institutional or collective understandings of what constituted publishable writing – the tomes of history, theology, and doctrine, for example – recipe-writing was a means for women to record their ideas, values, and knowledge. While cookbooks do not explicitly reveal the events and circumstances of a woman's life, as does the memoir or diary, they do capture and illuminate an aspect of her domestic life that is "evanescent and often unnoticed,"[15] yet consumes so much of her labour activity. According to Sharon L. Jansen, recipe-writing was a composition form acceptable for women, not unlike letter-writing. Jansen's mother's recipes were "recipes in narration, description, analysis, even argument."[16] Cookbooks have been described as everyday autobiography,[17] as texts that present what is commonly eaten within the households and collective gatherings of a community and reflect food preferences, food aspirations, and what might be considered culinary trademarks of the group that compiles the cookbook. We can even obtain glimpses into the lives of women who were users, if not creators, of cookbooks through the "marginalia" – the handwritten comments, corrections, as well as the spills and stains – on frequently used pages.[18]

Mennonite women's recipe-writing was, and is, a form of self-expression that professionalized and gave credence to the material and artistic act of food preparation. The creation of community cookbooks brought the food-related labour of women in the so-called private sphere of home to the public sphere of church, community, and in the case of some best sellers, to wider sectors of society. One Mennonite cookbook author understood the significance of her undertaking, noting that "food has played a leading role as a force behind many great events ... where important decisions have been made."[19] In compiling and making public their recipes, women put forward the value of their food labour to the institutions in which they often had little voice. The business and clerical aspects of cookbook production also allowed women to exhibit and hone their organizational and administrative abilities. Ken Albala, in describing the emergence of "recipes as scientific procedures" with explicit instructions for measurements, methods, and cooking times, noted that women's roles thus obtained "a certain dignity and seriousness of purpose."[20] In the very writing down of instructions to create dishes for both everyday and extraordinary occasions, women were indicating that their food labour required knowledge and skill, and that these were not intrinsic to their sex. The cookbook served to professionalize the everyday act of cooking, especially at a time when historic recipes were disappearing from memory.

Cookbooks also play a role in processes of cultural transformation, especially for immigrants or others within distinctive cultures. Women in ethnic communities were often viewed as cultural carriers, with responsibility for maintaining traditions, customs, language, and other group characteristics across generations. Cookbooks are historical documents, linking people to their past and gifted across generations. Thus, one can view cookbooks as a feminine culinary genealogy of sorts and "one means by which women can commune with earlier female kin."[21] A good example of this is Andrea Eidinger's textual and social historical analysis of a popular Jewish cookbook, *A Treasure for My Daughter: A Reference Book of Jewish Festivals with Menus and Recipes*.[22] Originally published in the 1950s in Montreal, it holds a place of honour in the home of many Canadian Jewish women. Eidinger's research provides a valuable analysis of how cookbooks are tools whereby a group shapes its community ethnic identity through the efforts of women. She demonstrates how, by promoting food customs through a cookbook, women were actively involved in shaping the ethno-religious identity of their community and doing so by training their daughters. The text itself goes well beyond the culinary: the carefully constructed conversational exchanges and reflections by a mother and daughter on the cookbook pages reveal much about prescribed gender roles as well.

Some Mennonite cookbooks can similarly be viewed as immigrant documents illuminating the cultural transformation through food that occurred as Mennonites crossed borders and settled in new environments.[23] The hybrid food, and other, identities that emerged over time as Mennonites moved into new cultural spaces are clearly written into recipe collections.

Cookbooks are also examples of how food practices are preserved in memory. Cookbooks, as Janet Theophanos remarks, "served as a place for readers to remember a way of life no longer in existence or to enter a nostalgic recreation of a past culture that persists mostly in memory."[24] This may have been especially the case for migrant groups who left their homelands abruptly and involuntarily and with a sense of loss and displacement. For people who were wrenched from places in which rich cultural traditions and memories had been formed, the collections of recipes representative of those traditions are described by Carol Bardenstein as "nostalgia cookbooks" or "collective memory cookbooks."[25] The proliferation of Mennonite cookbooks with an ethnic character allows Mennonites, and even more so their children and grandchildren, to reproduce food memories in concrete, edible form. By reading the recipes for meaning beyond culinary instruction, and by analyzing the intent and presentation of the volume itself, I suggest that the cookbook is a significant source by which immigrant groups maintain a public connection with homeland culture, reinforce ethnic identity, integrate into a new culture, and form new hybrid identities.

Cookbooks also have a prescriptive function and offer evidence of aspirations and expectations of how Mennonites view themselves, through the lens of foodways, in various times and places.[26] As Malinda E. Berry notes in her essay about Mennonite Central Committee's World Community Cookbooks, "cookbooks help subgroups define themselves within and even over-and-against dominant culture."[27] They reveal how Mennonites wanted to present themselves to others, whether in cultural, religious, or political terms. In such volumes, women tell of their "lives and beliefs" and "present their values."[28] To the extent that many Mennonite cookbooks included religious poems, sayings, or prayers, they also functioned to link women's work in the kitchen to their informal roles as religious teachers.

From Notebook to Cookbook

Despite the strong association of Mennonites with food and eating, I am not aware of any Mennonite cookbooks formally published before mid-twentieth century. Handwritten recipe books were, however, prevalent in Mennonite homes, as was the practice of remembering or being in the habit of performing a recipe – what Donna R. Gabaccia calls an "unwritten form of female art."[29] Norma Jost Voth notes that "few, if any" printed cookbooks accompanied families across the ocean from Europe or Ukraine or Russia to North and South America.[30] Handwritten collections of recipes were brought by some immigrants, but mostly women carried cooking knowledge in their heads or even in their hands. Recipes were recorded, Voth suggests, in order to retain memory of how to prepare a dish eaten at another's home, or for foods made only at certain times of the year, not for regularly eaten items such as the Russian Mennonite *zwieback* or *borscht*. As common as handwritten compilations, and before or alongside published cookbooks, were recipes on file cards in small boxes, or scrapbooks filled with recipes cut from magazines or written out by friends. My own grandmother, Maria Driedger Dick, who immigrated to Canada from the Soviet Union in 1924, had a collection of handwritten recipes that unfortunately was not preserved. Maria Klassen Braun, whose parents settled in southern

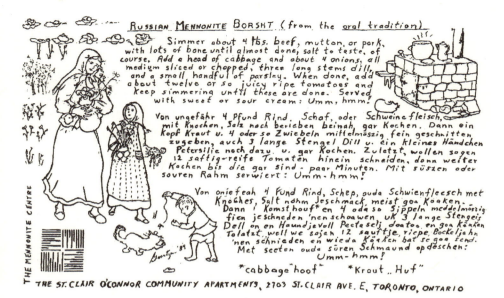

3.1   Sketch by Marta Goertzen-Armin of a recipe for Russian Mennonite *Borscht*, 1984. In English, German, and Low German languages.

Manitoba, recalled that her mother had a "brownish covered small note book" with handwritten recipes mainly for specialty foods, not for every day, as well as instructions for pickling, preserving, and medicinal remedies. The "Mennonite every day foods" – her "real culinary arts" – were stored in memory.[31]

Only a few of these immigrant documents are preserved in archives. One example is that of Margarethe Kroeger. She married Abram Regier in 1920 and together they had nine children. They immigrated from the Soviet Union to Canada in 1923, first settling in the bushland of northern Alberta, later farming in Saskatchewan, and finally settling on the Niagara Peninsula in Ontario where she died at the age of ninety-two. When Margarethe immigrated, she brought with her a notebook, now housed in the Mennonite Archives of Ontario, which is in three languages – Russian, German, and English. At first glance, the archivist and I thought the whole book was a collection of recipes. Soon we learned that the Russian section, presumably written when Margarethe was a schoolgirl, was likely her arithmetic homework, as it consisted of sums and number calculations. The second section of the notebook, in German gothic script, contains mainly recipes for traditional dishes made by Mennonites in Russia – *rollkuchen*, peppernuts, *platz* (coffee cake).[32] Margarethe's cookbook is a transnational document of women's writing – a way for her to inscribe her daily activities as a student and homemaker and indeed professionalize those endeavours. It is a testament to her education and learning. That she would carry this book across borders, oceans, and continents suggests her desire to hold on to her Russian Mennonite community and culture through the process of migration. Everything else might change – language and climate, for example – but she could bring along her recipes, her words. In the absence of other documentation about Margarethe's life, the recipe book functions as "autobiography explaining who she was and where she went."[33]

The informal personal recipe collection was not just an immigrant artifact, but rather characterized a past era when everyday cooking was plain and repetitive and did not require specialized instructions. For many Mennonite and related groups, recipes continue to be passed along in oral tradition and by example. Mary-Ann Kirkby observes that the passing along of recipes fits within the Hutterite "rich oral tradition" that preserves history, songs, and stories.[34] Younger cooks look to older cooks to demonstrate and provide verbal guidance in cooking traditional foods, although one head cook uses many sticky notes, according to Kirkby. Edna Staebler, who popularized Pennsylvania German Mennonite cooking in Ontario, said the unique cuisine was based on "recipes that have passed from generation to generation of Mennonite housewives without being printed in a cookbook."[35] Indeed, many informally published cookbooks were compiled by families who wanted to preserve recipes that existed only in oral form.

Even while cooking by memory and example continues in some households and predominates in some Mennonite groups, an explosion in cookbook publication of all types occurred in North America in the latter half of the twentieth century. Mennonites followed the trend. Few libraries and archives that specialize in Mennonite studies make a concerted effort to collect cookbooks in the same way they might accumulate church histories or theological writings. The library at Conrad Grebel University College, where I taught for over twenty years, is an exception, as the librarians embraced my enthusiasm for cookbooks as text and artifact. I was repeatedly astonished at the quantity of new cookbooks that arrived in the library, despite the perception that no one used hard copy cookbooks anymore, instead turning to the internet for recipe advice. These Mennonite cookbooks vary from typewriter-written and staple-bound manuscripts circulated within a small area as projects to raise funds or celebrate family history, to glossy and professionally published collections that in a few cases have become bestsellers.[36]

By the 1950s, the creation of an assembled cookbook as a source for recipes was symptomatic of a new generation of cooks that were thought to require the scientific and professionalized instructions offered by tried and tested cookbooks. The postwar era in Canada, as in the United States, represented a time when female domesticity and vocational homemaking were called to new standards of perfection even while homemakers themselves were searching for ways to make their jobs easier. While many, particularly urban, Mennonites were part of these trends, they also resisted the modernizing patterns of the mainstream. Thus, another justification for Mennonites to publish cookbooks was to stave off their own acculturation. The foreword to one early 1970s American collection noted that foodways had undergone a "drastic change" due to the introduction of "prepackaged foods and the supermarket ... A consequence of this acculturation is that many of the old dishes are already forgotten and others will die unless this [cookbook] revives interest in them."[37] Reviving historic food traditions was one means for Mennonites to resist assimilation and maintain their separateness.

Possibly the first example of the above impulses was *Mennonite Community Cookbook: Favourite Family Recipes*, by Mary Emma Showalter, first published in 1950. It is described as the "'mother' or 'grandmother' of all Mennonite cookbooks."[38] A professor in home economics at a Mennonite college in Virginia, Showalter compiled the cookbook in an effort to preserve the recipes contained either in "worn and soiled" handwritten booklets or in the memories of the Mennonite women of her mother's generation.[39] According to one account, Showalter was first inspired to undertake the cookbook project after visiting work camps for conscientious objectors, many of whom were Mennonite, during the Second World War. She found that "wherever she went ... Mennonite cooking was much the same" and that men "hankered" for dishes from their "home communities."[40] Indeed, the popularity of cookbooks like Showalter's in the postwar era may, as Jessamyn Neuhaus proposes, reflects a longing to eat "abundant, rich food," or "comfort food" in the aftermath of wartime anxieties and food rationing and in the midst of growing fears of nuclear destruction.[41] Certainly, rich and abundant would describe recipes in *Mennonite Community Cookbook*.

In 1947, Showalter wrote to the "wives of Mennonite pastors" in Canada and the United States, asking them to solicit "favourite family recipes" from within their communities. Of the over 5,000 recipes she received, about 1,150 went into the published book.[42] The cookbook, Showalter said, "is an attempt to preserve for posterity our own peculiar type of cookery that has been handed down for many generations."[43] A Mennonite church publisher rejected her cookbook proposal, saying they were not in the business of printing cookbooks. Two decades later that publisher "snatched up" the chance to take over the cookbook from a secular company after the book sold "exceedingly well."[44] Showalter later remarked, understatedly, "I had no idea it would be such a success."[45] A report on Showalter's retirement from teaching in 1972 noted that the *Community Cookbook* had gone through sixteen printings and sold about 200,000 copies.[46] In 2008, close to 500,000 had been printed, with 4,000 copies continuing to sell annually, and the cookbook was on the publisher's bestseller list.[47] When Showalter died in 2003, it was said that the *Community Cookbook* was "the parent of a whole family of Mennonite and Amish related cookbooks which came along in the half century since its first publication."[48]

The influence of Showalter's book is revealed most strikingly in a 2021 publication, *The Vegan Mennonite Kitchen: Old Recipes for a Changing World*. Dedicating the cookbook to her Mennonite grandmothers, creator Jo Snyder chose to adapt recipes from *Mennonite Community Cookbook* for a vegan diet. Indeed, the book commences with a photo of the tattered, clearly well-used 1950 cookbook as well as an original illustration of Showalter herself. In the *Vegan Mennonite Kitchen*'s foreword, writer Jan Braun astutely describes it as "a work of reverence as much as it is rebellion."[49] Snyder reveres the traditions of her Mennonite and family heritage, and the women who maintained them, but rebels against what she considers an unsustainable and environmentally destructive diet. Showalter's and Snyder's cookbooks bookend an evolving genre of published Mennonite writing that feature both nods to the past and signposts of the future.

The Community Cookbook

Mary Emma Showalter's book title included the word "community," suggesting the recipe contributors were part of an explicit community – Mennonite – but also implicitly proposing that the recipes would help to build community for those who cooked and ate them together. The category of community cookbooks is often put forward as the first and predominant genre of recipe collections. These include cookbooks created by and for churches, schools, associations, neighbourhoods, institutions, towns, and other localized entities, with multiple goals such as raising funds, celebrating anniversaries, building profile, and simply drawing groups of people together around food. My own cookbook shelf has an abundance of these. Lee-Poy and Brown's *Food for the Journey*, described earlier, is one example. A highly specific and localized community is found in *Friendly Favourites: A Collection of Favourite Recipes from the Markham Waterloo Mennonite Girls Born in the Year of 1995*. In this case, twenty young women from the same church community and born in the same year compiled a cookbook with no obvious goal other than to share their love of cooking and friendship.[50] Community cookbooks often have an end goal that is well apart from providing instructions for food preparation. As such, according to Emily Weiskopf-Ball, they "seldom clarify their editorial direction or introduce their contributors and, being more concerned with including, not selecting, contributors, often provide multiple versions of a recipe."[51]

This was certainly true of the following publication.

Ten years after Showalter's *Community Cookbook* appeared, a comparable and ambitious cookbook project was launched in Manitoba. The simple, spiral-bound 1,000-recipe *Mennonite Treasury of Recipes*, compiled by a committee of women, would become a bestseller among Mennonite books in Canada. First published in 1961, by the mid-1980s the book had gone through thirteen printings and sold 42,000 copies. By 2020, nearly 400,000 had been printed.[52] The inspiration for the book came at the 1960 annual Conference of Mennonites in Canada sessions at Steinbach, Manitoba, when, after cooking meals that resulted in 5,000 plates for several hundred delegates over six days, a group of women agreed that it would be a good idea to write down recipes for mass cooking for future reference. The introduction to the cookbook points out that "the delightful Mennonite custom of gathering in large numbers and dining together" was gaining in popularity as travel increased, and thus "a sheet" to explain how to cook popular Mennonite recipes for large groups was necessary. Many of the recipes, the compilers noted, hailed from "days of want and austerity," but they felt future generations might find them interesting.[53]

The *Treasury* is situated within the genre of community cookbooks – localized projects undertaken usually by a group of women for the purpose of recording and sharing favourite recipes, often to raise funds, and frequently with a collective or unnamed authorship. Even while community cookbooks appeared anti-feminist in their praise of food-related domesticity, their very nature signified feminist goals. According to Kennan Ferguson, these include "a politics of celebrating women getting together, creating collectively, feeding and nurturing others, valuing women and women's work."[54] Some analyses even refer to community cookbooks as acts of resistance,[55] though it is unlikely that Mennonite women, conditioned in humility and self-denial, would have described their undertakings in that way. They more likely situated their cookbook production within the framework of gender-specific church volunteerism and service to which they were accustomed.

The project became a joint initiative of the women's societies at a number of southern Manitoba churches with the Ebenezer Verein (society) of Steinbach Mennonite Church taking the lead.[56] The self-deprecating approach to their work was typical of Mennonite women's groups: a 1968 report reflecting on challenges and difficulties in their work stated, "When sometimes the way seemed dark, we knelt down, questioned our motives, repented, and then the Lord always gave the victory."[57] Though the women considered their work questionable and unworthy, and were unable to take credit for their own ability and energy – and possibly not given credit either – they did seem to recognize the *Treasury of Recipes* as among their greatest accomplishments. In the words of the Ebenezer Verein, "It required much, much time and energy from a number of women to organize and see it through to the first printing." In the end, they recalled, the cookbook "was well received and grew into a tall tree which today is still living and still growing."[58]

One of the *Treasury*'s organizers, Anna (Derksen) Rosenfeld, recalled that despite a consensus among the women that "yes it would be nice" to produce a cookbook, "nobody thought we would go ahead as we had no money." She summoned "all [her] courage" and approached her brother, who operated Derksen Printers. When the project committee learned that the printer wanted to produce 3,000 copies to start, one woman expressed deep skepticism that such an amount would ever be sold, stating, "you will never get rid of them."[59] Derksen Printers agreed to print the book interest free, even if it took five years to pay for it. The "enormity" of the project became clear to Rosenfeld when she realized that the women's group was carrying a debt of $3,750.00.[60] At times, she recalled, she wanted to "throw up my hands in despair."[61]

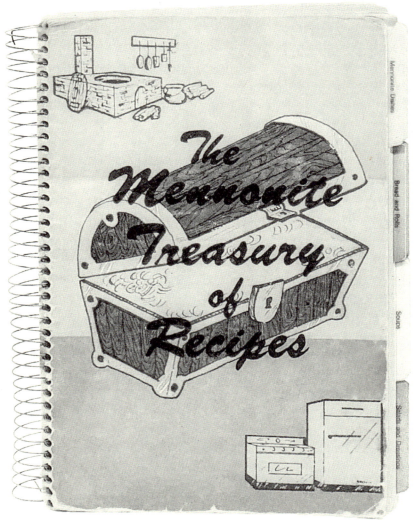

3.2 *The Mennonite Treasury of Recipes*, 1962 edition.

The creation of the cookbook involved many hours of "considerable asking, writing, and begging" women across the country to contribute recipes. The submissions then had to be sorted, translated, and organized into categories, and were typed "days and evenings" by Rosenfeld's daughter Marion. The time demands of the project prompted the committee to go to a cottage by the lake for two weeks in order to better concentrate on their work, and so their husbands were "left to shift for themselves."[62] When the first books came off the press in December 1961, Rosenfeld recalled, "I was humbled and so thankful; it was a beautiful book. All the work had finally paid off! So often we had been discouraged, and now it was a reality!"[63] Her 1990 obituary noted that her greatest success lay in the publication of *The Mennonite Treasury of Recipes*.[64]

The announcement of the *Treasury*'s publication in the national English-language Mennonite newspaper, the *Canadian Mennonite*, in February 1962, noted that the book sold for $2.25 and was compiled by "a committee of ladies" from Steinbach, Manitoba. Hedy Durksen, who wrote a regular column titled "Just around the House," stated she was "very well pleased" with the new cookbook, which was "also very handsomely assembled" and "attractive as well as useful." She reported that proceeds from the sales of the *Treasury* were to be used "in the interest of missions."[65] In 1977, the Ebenezer Verein reported that 50,000 books had been printed and distributed in "all the Lord's lands."[66]

The 1962 edition that I possess begins with a poem, "The Housewife," that exalts the "small affairs," "trifling worries," and "little cares" that consume the life of a homemaker, among which was "A hungry husband to be fed." Reflective of its particular social era, the cookbook's individual recipe authors are named according to their husbands, as in "Mrs John Rempel," or "Mrs F.E. Reimer," while the single women contributors are labelled as "Miss." Diane Tye sees this identification practice as highlighting women's "social successes" as married, or not, and their authority as homemakers.[67] The 1982 edition (the one sold by the printer in 2020) maintains the same naming system. Although I did not change my name when I married, I did get the *Treasury* for a wedding shower gift, as did many Canadian Mennonite women. Poet and memoirist Connie Braun said, "my grandmother gave me a copy of *The Mennonite Treasury* for my wedding shower in 1982 just before I married at twenty. I suppose, like a good Mennonite wife in the new world, I would, she assumed, bake, boil, and fry dough for my husband and children like the frugal Mennonite women of the Old World in Poland and Russia in the years of farming and famine; create from it our sustenance, preserve our heritage, and thus, our identity."[68] Literary critic Magdalene Redekop, of Russian Mennonite background, declared that, while Amish and Swiss Mennonite couples might receive a compendium of Anabaptist martyr stories for a wedding gift, she received the *Mennonite Treasury*.[69] Acclaimed author Miriam Toews said, probably sarcastically, that "for Mennonites [the *Mennonite Treasury*] is second in importance only to the Bible."[70]

The implication here is that the cookbook was an essential item, almost akin to a religious text, as a guide for a Mennonite "housewife" in a newly formed household, providing instructions in proper Christian womanhood as much as in cookery. Yet, even while cookbooks of the 1950s and onward, such as the *Treasury*, appear to exalt an ideology of domesticity, they also reveal a growing tension and ambiguity around women's roles in the kitchen. To the extent that they incorporated convenient ingredients like canned soups, mid-twentieth century cookbooks were acknowledging that some women wanted to reduce the time and effort required for food preparation, whether because they were not fond of cooking or because of work demands outside the home.

Fundraising was an important purpose of producing local community or church compilations of recipes. Indeed, one historian notes that the "ubiquitous community fund-raising cookbook" dates back to Europe in the 1600s.[71] The cookbook as a "tried and true fundraising tool"[72] for churches remains a phenomenon today, even more so because of the low cost of self-publishing. While *The Mennonite Treasury of Recipes* was not initiated with explicit fundraising goals in mind, sales of the *Treasury* quickly reached a level that allowed the creators to recoup their costs, pay their debt, and start contributing funds toward various church and mission projects. Indeed, they repaid their debt less than three months after the books were printed, and at the same time were able to deposit $108.09 in the bank. In the decades that followed, tens of thousands of dollars earned from cookbook sales went to a wide range of projects, such as financial support for missionaries working overseas and within North America. It is clear that the project was a money-maker that undergirded improvements made to the local church – facilities and equipment – and also the community and international work of service and mission organizations. The example set by the *Treasury* was followed by many other cookbooks, including the popular 2011 *Mennonite Girls Can Cook*, proceeds of which funded nutritional programs for children in Ukraine, and other causes.[73]

Community cookbooks provide evidence for the significance of women's organizational work and economic labour to the successful functioning of local churches, larger denominational institutions, and Mennonite charitable work more broadly.

Cookbooks and Cultural Identity

If Mennonite women's culinary labour, and the formal expression of that labour through the production of cookbooks, furthered the financial goals of their community, perhaps of equal or greater import was the preservation of ethnocultural identity. One of the main characteristics of many Mennonite cookbooks was their inclusion of a section on "ethnic foods" – recipes for what were considered traditional Mennonite dishes. Especially by mid-twentieth century, when the routine preparation of Mennonite ethnic foods began to decline in the midst of modernization and acculturation (although not among all Mennonite groups), reproducing such recipes in published cookbooks served to reinvigorate collective cultural identity.

Historian Donna R. Gabaccia reports that by the 1980s Americans were devouring cookbooks, especially those that described ethnic foodways or cooking techniques from other cultures.[74] Cookbooks served as a medium for individuals and communities to nostalgically re-create a past culture that existed mainly in memory. Cookbooks thus have often served to maintain historical memory or solidify cultural identity. While *Mennonite Community Cookbook* did not isolate ethnic recipes in a separate section, the entire book is imbued with the sense that there exists a distinctive Mennonite cookery. For their part, the women who compiled *The Mennonite Treasury of Recipes* included a "Mennonite section" when the printer suggested they do "something different with a lot of sales appeal."[75]

The *Canadian Mennonite Cookbook*, first published in 1965 as the *Altona* (Manitoba) *Women's Institute Cookbook*, had a section on "Mennonite Recipes," referred to in one edition oddly as "foreign dishes."[76] By 1980, the book was in its twenty-third printing and had sold over 125,000 copies.[77] Virtually all Mennonite cookbooks that contained a section on ethnic or traditional foods from the Russian ethnic stream included a recipe for *zwieback*, considered the "hallmark of Mennonite baking," with origins that go back to sixteenth-century Netherlands.[78] The *Treasury* also included several sections of text to illuminate other food-related customs that were passing into history. One of these was butchering, discussed in chapter 5, a highly communal activity that was described as more "exciting" than anything "except, perhaps, Christmas."[79]

That an interest in writing down and publishing Mennonite recipes appeared at mid-century and in the decades that followed is not coincidental. While the preparation and consumption of such traditional Mennonite foods as the laborious *vereniki* may have begun to decline by the 1950s and 60s, the inclusion of recipes for such foods in Mennonite cookbooks was a means to prevent their disappearance from historical memory. For latter twentieth-century Canadian Mennonites, with several or many generations of migration behind them, foodways became part of what historian Royden Loewen has characterized as a "symbolic ethnicity" that "easily complemented Canadian middle-class values and identities" as well as the nation's policy of official multiculturalism, which came into effect in 1971.[80] Even while most Mennonites were increasingly assimilating into Canadian middle-class society – something evident in their cookbooks – the retention of traditional foods was a relatively benign way to signify an identity that made them not completely mainstream, and indeed allowed them to reach outward to society around them. This was not only a Canadian phenomenon. Amy Harris-Aber analyzes eight Mennonite cookbooks published in Kansas between 1964 and 2009 and detects in the content and format evidence of "integration" into "secular" society as Mennonites moved "from farm to town and took measure of their agrarian history and immigrant heritage."[81] Cookbooks with an explicit ethnic focus were also a common way to mark anniversaries of migration and settlement and served to coalesce collective memory through food.

Perhaps the epitome of the ethnic food celebration is found in the 1990 two-volume collection *Mennonite Foods and Folkways from South Russia*, by Norma Jost Voth. Published by the former Mennonite-owned publisher Good Books in Pennsylvania, *Foods and Folkways* is part recipe collection and part anthropological-historical analysis of Mennonite foods with origins in the Netherlands, Prussia, Russia, and Ukraine from the seventeenth through the early twentieth centuries.[82] The two volumes are a veritable feast of reflections and information that portray a community whose cultural and religious identity is closely tied to its foodways. The particularity of eating goes so far as to encompass "Mennonite Seasonings for Soup" or "Eating Watermelon – Mennonite Style," as I discussed in the introduction. Furthermore, quotations scattered throughout the book in which women give their advice on the best techniques for success in particular recipes – how long to knead the bread dough or what kind of fire produces the best smoked sausage – affirm their place as experts in a daily and oft-considered mundane regimen of women's labour.

Mennonite Ethnic Cooking, a 2006 Canadian publication, follows the intent of *Mennonite Foods and Folkways*, stating as its purpose "to honour the ingenuity of Mennonite women of past decades, which we want to remember and preserve."[83] In this case, the author-compiler is both reviving the foodways aspect of Mennonite identity and valorizing the historical culinary labour of women. Another example of the retrieval, in a modern context, of ethnic recipes of the past is Selma Willms Turner's *From Oma's Kitchen: From Russia to Canada with Love, Courage & Gratitude*, a glossy book containing recipes of traditional Russian Mennonite dishes interlaced with reflections from the author's family history. The book includes stunning colour photos of the prepared foods, and reproductions of historic family photos, and comes with a DVD containing instructions on how to follow certain recipes.[84]

Yet another example that hit the foodie world by storm was published by Herald Press (later called Menno Media) and amusingly titled *Mennonite Girls Can Cook*. The 2011 book was preceded by an online blog of the same name, begun by ten women who wanted to share their favourite recipes and thoughts about cooking, eating, and life. The title could be viewed as problematic for the way in which it essentializes women's nature – some Mennonite women can't cook or don't want to. Not surprisingly, in an era when household cooking is no longer primarily a feminine role, a cookbook with the title *Mennonite Men Can Cook Too* was published in 2015.[85] The popularity of *Mennonite Girls Can Cook* led to a 2016 musical production by the same name, described as "full of excitement, confusion, and just plain frantic fun when a small town cable TV cooking show, hosted by two Mennonite women, attracts the attention of a Hollywood producer."[86] The idea for this undoubtedly sprouted from the significant media coverage of the blog and cookbook, revealing the extent to which the general public is drawn to the connection between Mennonites and food.

The women of *Mennonite Girls Can Cook* acknowledge that they were brought together by their "ethnic roots, common love for cooking, and … faith."[87] Although the recipes on the blog are varied, the women often post stories and recipes from their Russian Mennonite heritage, paying tribute to their mothers and grandmothers, who taught them the "joy of cooking and serving."[88] Furthermore, the compilers note, there were stories "behind" the recipes that were reluctantly shared because they were associated with "painful memories."[89] In this way, the cookbook serves as a device to create and preserve a collective memory that is difficult to express in straightforward historical narrative. Cookbooks with an ethnic focus can also demonstrate the "dangerous power of nostalgia," noted by Lila Kelting in an analysis of Southern US cookbooks that celebrate a culture while erasing its traumatic past, in this case the trauma of slavery.[90] For Mennonites, decades of hardship that began in 1918 rarely surface in nostalgia cookbooks exhibiting rose-tinted memories of the Russian Mennonite "golden" era of cultural and economic prosperity at the turn of the twentieth century.

The popularity of the *Mennonite Girls Can Cook* blog led to the 200-page hardcover book with glossy pages and numerous colour photographs. The collection includes traditional foods such as *paska* (a decorative Easter bread of Ukrainian origin), *platz, zwieback*, and *holubschi* (cabbage rolls). While its identity as a "Mennonite" cookbook is clear in the title, the collection is modernized to include many gluten-free options. The cookbook has an explicitly religious message, imbued with an evangelical flavour that situates the authors' Christian faith at the core of their cookbook project. The preface states, "though it is recipes for food that we share, we acknowledge that Jesus Christ is our inspiration to share the joy of hospitality."[91] Scattered throughout are brief religious testimonies by the women, called "Bread for the Journey." Similarly, the online blog is viewed as a site where recipes are shared, but also where the authors can "freely share" their faith.[92] Here we see the cookbook as a faith treatise alongside its function to preserve cultural memory.

A comparable book in the United States is *Hope's Table: Everyday Recipes from a Mennonite Kitchen*, published in 2019. The 300 pages of recipes, with beautiful photos of food and family, was created by Hope Helmuth, a conservative Mennonite woman (indicated by her dress) from the Swiss ethnic stream. She has a "passion for cooking, creating recipes, and entertaining guests." Her message, while drawing on her farm-based traditionalist upbringing, is very twenty-first century with its emphasis on local, non-processed foods, gardening, wholesome eating, and commensality (eating together). An important purpose of the book, she notes, is to preserve her Mennonite "heritage of cooking [that is] slowly being lost."[93] Even with an emphasis on ethnic foodways, such cookbooks are popular outside of Mennonite/Amish circles because they suggest a simpler time, characterized by families and friends consuming comfort foods together at the table – a hope and reality enhanced during the Covid-19 pandemic.[94] Although appearing seventy years later, *Hope's Table* is not unlike Mary Emma Schowalter's *Mennonite Community Cookbook*, with its emphasis on food preparation as both artistic and functional, and as the primary realm for women.

The preceding examples are mainly those which celebrate and reinvigorate the Russian Mennonite tradition. But similar cookbook patterns can be noted with respect to the Swiss/Pennsylvania German food traditions. In Canada, this culinary stream was popularized by journalist and author Edna Staebler in *Food That Really Schmecks* (1968), followed by *More Food That Really Schmecks* (1979), and then *Schmecks Appeal* (1987). Staebler lived with an Old Order Mennonite family in Waterloo County where she learned about their culture and cooking, which she then brought to public attention through magazine articles and her nationally acclaimed cookbooks.[95] In the United States, the Swiss/Pennsylvania German tradition is the focus in a seemingly endless series of publications about Mennonite and Amish foodways, many published by the former Good Books in Pennsylvania.[96]

In a more folksy style is a series of themed cookbooks compiled by an Old Order Mennonite man under the overall title *Mennonite Girl Presents ... Doughnuts, Soups, Potatoes, Bread*, etc. Perhaps *Girl* was inserted in the title because it wasn't deemed appropriate for a man to author a cookbook. Isaac Horst, part of the horse-and-buggy variety in Ontario, wrote extensively about the beliefs and practices of the Old Order Mennonites.[97] He also compiled numerous cookbooks with quaint titles like *Just Loafin*, *Potato Potential*, and the *High, Healthy and Happy Cookbook*.[98] In *Conestogo Mennonite Cook Book* (1981) Horst admits that he is not a cook, and even says that not all Mennonite women are good cooks either, hence the need for the recipe collection. I am amused when I think about Horst undoing both gender and cultural essentialism.[99]

While some would dispute the usefulness of ethnicity as a feature with which to identify Mennonites, to the extent that shared cultural markers enhance the cohesion of a community, then the public acknowledgment of distinctive Mennonite foodways in cookbooks has played a key role in creating community identity. Of course, prior to the twentieth century, Mennonites around the world were almost exclusively of white European descent. As noted in previous chapters, their foodways reflected these ethnic and racial identity markers, as did their cookbooks. Cookbooks published in North America in the twentieth century largely reflected and reinforced white, middle-class values, and some food and critical race theorists argue that the cookbook itself is a white artifact.[100] Mennonites in North America historically differentiated themselves from "English" society – essentially everyone but them! – but this common self-characterization functioned to veil their own white privilege and racial ignorance.

As Mennonite ethnicities expand and pluralize, foodways may provide the most meaningful medium through which ethnic and racial diversity is embraced. As such, Mennonite cookbooks are emerging that incorporate both hybridity and plurality of culinary identities. *Be Present at Our Table* is a cookbook produced for the one hundred and fiftieth anniversary of the Erb Street Mennonite Church in Waterloo, Ontario.[101] It includes a section titled "The Table of Our Mennonite Past" with recipes from Swiss, Amish, and Russian traditions – the once dominant historic ethnic ancestries of Mennonites in Waterloo Region. The second section is titled "The Table of Other Cultures." While this may seem to "other" the others, it is nevertheless not only a nod to the Mennonite appreciation for foods from other lands, but also a recognition of the many ethnic backgrounds in most Mennonite churches by the 1980s and 90s.

A 2013 example of this evolution is *The Cookbook Project*, produced by two women to mark the seventy-fifth anniversary of their congregation, Niagara United Mennonite Church in Virgil, Ontario. Even more intentional in broadening notions of Mennonite cuisine, compilers Ellery Penner and Rachael Peters found commonality in the historical experiences of individuals in their congregation, noting in the preface, "We as a church body are a community heavily focused upon food. Many of us know the pangs of hunger as we journeyed as refugees from Russia, Vietnam, Iraq, Colombia, and other countries."[102] The section "Reflecting on Heritage" includes a recipe for spring rolls with peanut sauce, and a family story, by Dung Manh Do. Dung and his family fled Vietnam and were sponsored as refugees by Niagara United Mennonite and arrived in Canada in 1979. Similarly, in the American context, the inclusion of *sopapillas* (a fried pastry) in a Kansas Mennonite church cookbook is explained as an indication of changing demographics in the state, which saw an increase in the Hispanic population, a late twentieth century shift seen in Mennonite churches as well.[103]

An especially interesting example of Mennonite ethnic hybridity is displayed in a growing genre of cookbooks about Mennonites from and in Mexico. For the most part, these represent Mennonites of European descent who migrated to Mexico beginning in the 1920s but are often described as transnational because of their ongoing migratory journeys both south and north. While the language of this complex group is primarily a Low German dialect, their foodways represent both inherited Dutch-Russian traditions and adopted Hispanic cuisine. The Mexican government itself, in a series of cookbooks about the ethnic culinary styles in the country, published a Spanish-language Mennonite cookbook in 2000 – *Recetario Menonita de Chihauhau*. Most of the recipes derive from the Russian Mennonite tradition, so that *paska* becomes *Pan de Pascua*, and *rollkuchen* is *Sopapillas*.[104] Recipe books produced by Mennonites themselves include *Mama's Kochbuch*, published in 2005 in Chihauhau, Mexico, a fundraising project on a school's thirtieth anniversary. Though the informal compilation is entirely in High German, many of the recipes are for Mexican foods.[105] A 2010 recipe collection, *Farmer's Kochbuch*, also printed in Mexico, was produced by the women of El Valle Colony to raise money for their mission projects, such as "helping the poor and so on."[106] This rationale is in keeping with the theme identified earlier whereby women's cookbook labour provides a foundation for community outreach.

In 2011, a bilingual – German and Spanish – cookbook was printed in Mexico that again included a mix of Mexican, traditional Dutch-Russian Mennonite, and miscellaneous foods.[107] The German title is translated as *Come and Eat with the Mennonite Ladies from Durango Mexico*, while the Spanish is *Enjoy Delicious Mennonite Recipes among Others*. The shift to a full Spanish translation points to the increased acceptability and absorption of Hispanic culture into the historically separatist Mennonite communities. While the early Mennonite settlements in Mexico were isolated and their members discouraged from interaction with the Mexican people, language, and culture, that separatism has changed over one hundred years. It may be at the culinary table where such evolution and adaptation occur most benignly, even while people cling to tradition and separation in other areas of daily life. The co-existence of foodways representative of cultures that in other respects remain very distant, and within a cookbook, is indicative of the transformative role of food in bridging cultural divides.

With Helen in the Kitchen (*Met Helen en de Kjäakj*) is another good example of cookbooks directed toward a transnational population. In 2007 Helen Funk, a Manitoba-based radio personality, published a collection of her radio recipes, aimed at Low German-speaking Mennonites in Canada and Latin America[108] – in a language that is historically oral, not written. According to Funk, it is the only Low German-language cookbook in the world.[109] I purchased it at a social service office in Aylmer, Ontario, where I learned that one purpose of the cookbook was to enhance literacy among Low German-speaking women. With numerous photos of Funk cooking with her grandchildren, the cookbook was also meant to strengthen the bonds between mothers and daughters.[110] For this diasporic population of Mennonites, newspapers also provide a way to stay connected with family and community across national borders, and sharing recipes is part of that. In her analysis of the *Mennonitische Post*, a newspaper serving Low German-speaking Mennonites across North and South America, Robyn Sneath observes that published recipes are a means to connect families and communities separated by vast distances. "The sharing of food traditionally has been an integral fact of Mennonite community," she says, "and while these people physically are unable to sit at a table and pass the potatoes, the sharing of recipes represents this communion ... The recipes do not appear to hail from any particular geographic region, but come from all over, further obliterating geographic boundaries." Sneath notes there are no recipes for "traditional Mennonite dishes," presumably because readers would have known how to prepare them.[111]

Cookbooks and Modernization

Even while Mennonite cookbooks possessed a character and included ethnic recipes that made their particularity recognizable, such cookbooks also reflected wider societal interests and emphases. As Anne L. Bower has noted, cookbooks tell the story of women's lives at a particular point in history and are signposts of the changes underway in a community in a given era.[112] Indeed, all cookbooks can be read for indicators about social and economic conditions of their era, and reflect "contemporary anxieties and aspirations."[113] They identify the historic moment and context in which women's culinary labour was situated. Among many latter twentieth-century anxieties was the concern that traditional gender norms were under threat and thus, as some have argued, cookbooks helped to reinforce female domesticity.[114] *The Mennonite Treasury of Recipes* portrayed the labour of newly or almost urban women who were subconsciously professionalizing their work in the kitchens of both home and church. Befitting the professionalized homemaker, such skilled labour required instructions, whether for traditional Mennonite fare – prepared from memory by previous generations – or for modern "English" recipes, or for many other aspects of middle-class homemaking. Cookbooks that appeared at mid-twentieth century and after also incorporated ingredients and instructions that revealed the prevalence of convenience or processed foods such as canned soups, jellied powders, and flavour packets. Jell-O was perhaps the quintessential convenience food that wasn't really very time-saving at all when mixed with a sometimes-strange combination of ingredients to create awe-inspiring salads and desserts. Among the odder blends in the *Treasury* is a recipe for Ham Salad Loaf that includes: lemon jelly powder, HP sauce, prepared mustard, pepper, cinnamon, onion juice, diced ham, mayonnaise, whipping cream, pickle, and celery.[115]

That cooking and baking were part of the overall vocation of homemaking is indicated by the inclusion, in many Mennonite cookbooks like the *Treasury*, of a section devoted to a range of non-culinary "household hints." For instance, the *Treasury* offers advice on how to hang pictures, how to clean bathroom fixtures and shower curtains, how to pick up slivers of broken glass off a rug, and how to re-cover an ironing board.[116] *Mennonite Community Cookbook* offers counsel on whitening yellowed piano keys, using ice-cream containers for houseplants, and preventing clothes from sticking to an outdoor laundry line on a cold winter day.[117] While these may seem trivial, indeed comical, to twenty-first century feminists, such hints were indicative of an ethos of domesticity that placed a great deal of emphasis on perfectionism in homemaking on the part of women, Mennonites not excepted. Standards of exactitude increased as the time and effort associated with the labour of homemaking eased with the wider availability of hydro, plumbing, and household appliances. The cookbooks echoed the content of the women's columns that were appearing in Mennonite newspapers, as well as radio shows such as southern Manitoba's CFAM's "Homemaker's Chat," "Hints for the Homemaker," or the American "Heart to Heart."

The cookbooks pointed to the fact that women's domestic labour was in transition in the last half of the twentieth century. This was true for their presentation of homemaking ideals and also for the culinary recipes and food practices they contained. For example, the *Treasury* illuminated the changing foodways of a generation of women who were cooking traditional rural ethnic foods alongside modern urban and partly processed dishes. So in the *Treasury* one finds ancestral dishes like *plumi moos* (cold fruit soup) and *rollkuchen* (deep-fried fritters) together with recipes for "Cheerios Cocktail Snacks" and "Quick Chinese Supper Dish," the latter containing celery, cooked rice, canned mushrooms, soy sauce, and leftover chicken. Similarly, the *Community Cookbook* had a recipe for traditional Russian Mennonite *borscht* in the same section as a recipe for French Onion Soup. The wider array of recipes and ingredients also reflected greater postwar economic prosperity in many Mennonite households, allowing cooks to purchase items to supplement what was preserved in their cellars or the inexpensive staples that were the foundation for traditional recipes.

Certain latter twentieth-century cookbooks had a character that celebrated the ancestral and ethnic aspects of Mennonite cooking while also exhibiting interest in the commercial and modern aspects of society at large. These might be labelled crossover cookbooks. For instance, a small 1980 publication titled *New Bergthal: Heritage & Cookbook*, includes text on the history of New Bergthal, a pioneer village in southern Manitoba which is today a National Historic Site, interspersed with recipes and commercial advertising. Indicative of its era, the third and fourth pages of the book offer guidelines on converting to the metric system. Most of the recipes are for dishes one might categorize as ethnic Mennonite, yet there is also a section designated "hors d'oeuvres" that contains only one recipe, for dill pickles, and a back page with detail on "Fillings for Fancy Sandwiches."[118] Cookbooks at the crossroads of modernity, like this one, also contained recipes that reflected the growing interest in ethnic foods not from a Mennonite tradition. As Franca Iacovetta and Valerie J. Korinek describe the trend, it was a "new twist on economical eating, the most common being Italian, Chinese, and Spanish" recipes.[119]

The New Bergthal book offered "a message of history, of modernity, of social change, and of culinary inventiveness,"[120] even while it celebrated the past. Reinforcing the juxtaposition of tradition and innovation, the 2006 *Mennonite Ethnic Cooking* included a recipe for homemade laundry soap (hearkening back to pioneer settlement) on the same page as a recipe for a Hot Toddy that contained wine or rum.[121] For its part, *The Mennonite Treasury of Recipes* had, in its 1982 edition, a section on low calorie cooking that didn't exist when the book first appeared. Undoubtedly, cookbooks that included both old and new foodways functioned as "not only mirrors of their society, marking and reflecting social change, but also as catalysts of these changes."[122]

The inclusion of "mainstream" recipes reflected the interest of Mennonite women in eating modern, and suggests they were using recipes and cookbooks that were not Mennonite. In her memoir, Anne Konrad reflects on learning about "'English' cooking and baking" in her Home Economics class at a Mennonite high school in British Columbia. Using a government-issued cookbook that included instructions on "English roast beef dinners served to your husband's boss when he is invited to dinner," Konrad also learned to experiment with "fancy" dishes such as Jell-O salad and tomato aspic.[123] As revealed by the cookbooks they produced and also the ones they used, many Mennonite women of this era were negotiating the transition from rural traditional cooking to an urban modernity that reflected their changing roles. This shift, never completely one way, saw them preparing traditional Mennonite *zwieback* (using a cookbook or not), while also attempting a French *soufflé* or opening a can of tomato soup. Food and gender theorist Laura Shapiro described this as "a culture of struggle, negotiation, and nuance."[124] I certainly experienced this in my growing up years in the suburbs, where my mother continued to make Russian Mennonite *borscht*, and in the summer, *rollkuchen* with watermelon, but increasingly preferred to serve casseroles with canned soups and other easy-to-prepare meals.

Cookbooks as Political Statement

To the extent that Mennonite cookbooks exhibited culinary and homemaking practices that were evolving in response to a modernizing world, the very labour activity involved in their creation also had a political message. With limited access to "recognized status-bearing discourse," which in the church and conference might include sermons, reports, and meeting minutes, for women the printed and distributed cookbook was a form of "public participation."[125] It was an assertion of women's place and labour within the structure of church and community. Cookbooks can thus also be read for their political meanings, safely situated within the non-threatening context of culinary instructions.

The rationale for the *Treasury* publicizing recipes designed to feed large groups was to indirectly assert women's fundamental roles in the running of large Mennonite conference gatherings. While women did not have a voice in the discussion and decision-making of Mennonite bureaucracies until the late twentieth century, their culinary labour was essential to the functioning of meetings that brought the men together. Indeed, the first sentence of *Canadian Mennonite Cookbook* (published in 1965) states that "throughout centuries of recorded history, food has played a leading role as a force behind many great events [including] conferences, banquets, dinners or other occasions where important decisions have been made."[126] In the writing down, compiling, and publishing of recipes for serving large groups, women's institutional labour was no longer hidden from view. The women knew how fundamental their food offerings were to the functioning of the more public spaces of church and community.

Furthermore, by writing down and publishing their recipes, women were transforming the repetitive, oftentimes tedious and intensive labour of making meals into chores of dignity rather than drudgery. Their work became indelible, noticed, and worthy. The attribution of individual recipes to specific women was not unlike an artist's name on a canvas or a minister's name on a written sermon. Indeed, the fact that recipes, when appearing in published cookbooks, reached many more people than most sermons spoken by men from a pulpit suggests that their work had a public face far surpassing their church institutions.

Cookbooks put forward the value of food preparation, and also the social power associated with feeding people, whether within the familial household or within a large community venue. Anne L. Bower holds that community cookbooks highlight women's "power within the home as angel, minister, nutritionist, manager."[127] The political aspect of cooking for one's family was implied in the preface to *Canadian Mennonite Cookbook*, which stated, "So, too, can food be used by every clever homemaker to influence persons and events which can enrich the happiness of a home and its members."[128] Sounds almost subversive! However distasteful the idea of domestic manipulation might be to twenty-first-century sensibilities, the possibility that a woman's culinary labour could enhance her influence on people and events is significant for social eras when her power was circumscribed by limitations placed on women's public and institutional involvement.

By the latter decades of the twentieth century, Mennonite women were politicizing their cookbook creations even more, offering culinary texts that Ken Albala describes as "complete food ideologies."[129] A succession of what might be termed "social justice" cookbooks, also referred to as "world community cookbooks," began appearing in the mid-1970s. The first of these was Doris Janzen Longacre's immensely successful *More-with-Less Cookbook*, advocating cooking methods and ingredients that used less of the world's resources. In short, the purpose of the project was to "challenge North Americans to consume less so others could eat enough."[130] First published in 1976, the *More-with-Less Cookbook* had sold 840,000 copies in forty-seven printings twenty-five years later, and had far surpassed the expectations of its creators.[131] A fortieth anniversary edition was published in 2016.

Subtitled *Recipes and Suggestions by Mennonites on How to Eat Better and Consume Less of the World's Limited Food Resources*, the book was politically ahead of its time – and not without critics – in responding to the food crisis of the 1970s and, in particular, in suggesting that North Americans eat less meat and thus reduce the amount of grain grown for meat production. With recipes drawn from many global cultures focused on the eating of grains and legumes, the cookbook was eagerly taken up by a generation of Mennonites and other North American social activists. I was not alone as a young adult who, inspired by the "more-with-less" agenda, prepared endless dishes of inexpensive lentils and rice throughout my university years. One convert to vegetarianism described Longacre's project as a "food revolution," intended "to change the world."[132] Others have correlated *More-with-Less* with what are perceived as overall Mennonite values of simple living.

In his analysis of the *More-with-Less Cookbook*, Matthew Bailey-Dick argues that it molded a Mennonite identity based on principles of discipleship (serving and helping others) and simple living, and thus was extremely important as a shaper of ideology and values within the Mennonite community but also well beyond.[133] Similarly, another analyst of the cookbook, who was involved in its creation, commented, "If you consider the theological teaching and witness of this cookbook, its impact far outweighs that of most Mennonite writings in theology and ethics."[134] Other writers have pointed to the theological foundations of simple eating embedded in Longacre's treatise of social transformation. Its pervasive themes of "simplicity, fellowship, scriptural allusions and practical culinary instruction" resulted in a cookbook like none other produced by Mennonites to that point.[135] Susie Guenther Loewen, who grew up with the *More-with-Less Cookbook*, also highlights the theological nature of the book's premise, referring to Longacre directly as "a female Mennonite theologian hiding in plain sight."[136] Yet, the seeming need to elevate Longacre and her book to the disciplinary category of theology suggests that culinary writing alone does not have status as a serious genre of thought.

Another analysis, by Melanie Springer Mock, proposes that *More-with-Less*, in addition to reflecting "Mennonite tradition, theology, and change," is also a "coveted symbol" of her relationship with her mother.[137] In that sense, Longacre's cookbook is similar to the Jewish *A Treasure for My Daughter*, analyzed by Andrea Eidinger, but it marks the intergenerational passing of culinary change rather than preservation of tradition. While the collection included a few traditional Mennonite recipes, *More-with-Less* stretched the culinary experiences of Mennonites (and thousands of others) by its inclusion of recipes from many global cultures, by its emphasis on whole grains and legumes rather than "meat and potatoes," and by its lesser emphasis on rich desserts. As Springer Mock argues, the book spoke to the urbanization and assimilation that occurred for most Mennonites by the mid-1970s, and also helped to "facilitate" change, especially for women who were "straddling" traditional and modern roles in their lives.[138] The transformation that occurred when Mennonite women shifted from use of Showalter's *Mennonite Community Cookbook* to Longacre's *More-with-Less* was "revolutionary" in terms of the impact it had on lifestyle changes within families.[139] The revolution was not only one of environmental sustainability, but was also a feminist one. The transformation, and political statement, continued in 2021 when Jo Snyder authored *The Vegan Mennonite Kitchen: Old Recipes for a Changing World*, which includes recipes from Showalter's famous cookbook but using plant-based ingredients. Snyder's project honours her grandmothers and the "comfort food" of her "Mennonite roots" while addressing an environmental crisis that includes "unnecessary cruelty, suffering, pollution and the psychological human toll of factory farming."[140]

The *More-with-Less Cookbook* was followed in 1991 by *Extending the Table: A World Community Cookbook*, a compilation that declared itself to be "in the spirit of *More-with-Less*" but focused on global education through foodways by sharing stories and recipes from ordinary people and places around the world. One analysis suggests the book was inspired by "a multiplicity of lifestyle and food experiences" brought to North America by Mennonite missionaries and Mennonite Central Committee workers in the global south.[141] Indicating that the book was not just another collection of international cuisine, author Joetta Handrich Schlabach stated her belief that "the experience of preparing new foods and meeting people through stories can broaden our understanding of other people and their problems."[142] In this case, the labour of cookbook production reflected and also elicited a late twentieth-century interest in transnational relationships, international connections, and global understanding. Globalization became a catchword for Mennonites, I think, only after *Extending the Table* appeared.

Continuing the tradition of cookbook as socio-political statement is a 2005 collection by two Mennonite women titled *Simply in Season*, organized around the theme of cooking with foods that are in season in a given locale – "recipes that celebrate fresh, local foods."[143] Once again in tune with the times, *Simply in Season* offered practical and simple approaches to eating local, seasonal, and fairly traded foodstuffs; the authors organized the recipes around foods that were locally available (depending on the region) during the four seasons of the year. Here again, it is largely women's labour – from producing the dishes, to articulating the recipes, to compiling them in a collection, to using them in daily meal preparation – that shaped an identity for Mennonites responding to a changing social and cultural environment. While Mennonites have so often followed the ideological bandwagon on a wide range of social issues, in the case of cookbooks, they were leading it.

From Cookbook to Food Blog

Many people argue that the printed published cookbook is a historic relic, as most of us turn frequently to the internet for cooking ideas and instructions. Perhaps in between the *Mennonite Treasury* and allrecipes.com is the food blog, a genre that has exploded in popularity in the twenty-first century. Many food blogs go well beyond a recipe mandate to offer a kind of culinary life-writing, with stories, reflections, and recollections from the blogger's personal food history. One essayist describes them as a "new form of memoir" that allows for "the study of contemporary domestic culture."[144] There are plenty of Mennonite-themed food and cooking blogs to be found. Some clearly fit the memoir or culinary autobiography, such as Kerry Fast's *With a Whisk, a Colander and a Rolling Pin*, which is replete with stories from her personal past and present, enlivened with food observations and recipes.[145] A unique blog I introduced earlier is *MennoNeechie Kitchen*, authored by Lance Cote, an Indigenous man raised in a Mennonite home who enjoys cooking and sharing the traditional foods prepared by his foster mother.[146]

Most food blogs declaring themselves as Mennonite in some respect speak to a desire to honour female ancestors, to retain or recover Mennonite roots, or revive recipes in danger of disappearance. In this, they are not unlike printed cookbooks. For example, Katie blogs on *The Shoofly Project* (the reference is to Pennsylvania German shoofly pie) and says this in her introduction: "How I love that my family's story is a Mennonite one. Our food is our most tangible cultural artifact, our palatable heirlooms."[147] A Kansas woman blogging about a *Year of Mennonite Cooking* (in the tradition of the film *Julie and Julia*) chose to explore the recipes of her heritage when her grandmother's copy of Showalter's *Mennonite Community Cookbook* began to fall apart; she describes the project as a "journey through the land of cream, lard, noodles and corn to revisit some recipes from my past."[148] Also inspired by the *Julie and Julia* phenomenon, Valerie Showalter blogged a year, and more, of cooking through the *More-with-Less Cookbook*, described as a "conscientious Mennonite culinary journey."[149] The *Mennonite Girls Can Cook* cookbook, described earlier, began as blog, with recipes posted daily for ten years beginning in 2008. The project was launched as a "whim" to share "Mennonite heritage recipes."[150] In addition to food-focused blogs, there are numerous blogs by self-identified Mennonites with a food or cooking section – further reinforcing the association of Mennonites with foodways.[151]

Upon her death at the age of ninety, it was said that Mary Emma Showalter, author of *Mennonite Community Cookbook*, had "made a great contribution to Mennonite community, nutrition, and public identity."[152] This is a modest statement that reveals a great deal about the impact of Mennonite culinary writing on community and society. The extent to which Showalter saw this as her life's work is demonstrated by her memorial stone; beneath her name and dates appear the words "Author of The Mennonite Community Cookbook." If understood in terms of their wider goals and impact, cookbooks have served as a female voice in the otherwise male-dominated discourse on Mennonite beliefs and identity. This is true whether one refers to *The Mennonite Treasury of Recipes* – a simple compilation that celebrated traditional notions of Mennonite ethnicity while reflecting a mid-twentieth century emphasis on domesticity – to the polished *More-with-Less Cookbook* that situated North American Mennonites on the cutting edge of political calls for attention to inequities in global resources. Both were and continue to be immensely successful within their respective realms. Cookbooks shaped Mennonite cultural self-understanding and also generated external perceptions and knowledge about Mennonite historical development, ethnic identity, and beliefs and values.

Cookbooks, of course, generally reflect kitchen cupboards that are full – not to mention refrigerators, freezers, and cellars – and cuisines that are rich and abundant. This was not the case for many Mennonite households in widely varying times and places. Some Mennonite cookbooks may in fact have been produced as a subconscious gesture to replace memories of famine with experiences of feasting. The "painful memories" obliquely referenced in *Mennonite Girls Can Cook* may have been about hunger and starvation, the theme of the next chapter.

Prips

Recipe by Sue Barkman

Prips is a coffee substitute made from roasted grain that was often used during times of food insecurity and when coffee was expensive or unavailable. This recipe is taken from the *Mennonite Heritage Village Cook Book*, edited and compiled by Sue Barkman.

Step 1
Wash, drain and place in large kettle: 1 gallon barley
Cover this with skimmed milk and bring to a boil. When it has reached the boiling point, turn it off and let it set for 4–5 hours.

Step 2
Spread the milk-soaked barley on the table or drain board and let it dry overnight or for at least 12 hours.

Step 3
Spread the semi-dried barley on a cookie sheet or biscuit pan, taking care not to let it be any thicker than 1 inch. Bake in a hot oven (about 375 degrees) until it turns a dark brown, but is not burnt. This should be stirred often to evenly brown the mixture. At the end of the cooking time, spread 1 tablespoon molasses over the mixture and stir it to mix evenly.

Step 4
Follow the same steps as stated above only use 1 gallon wheat.

Step 5
After both grains have been processed, mix them together and grind. Make a beverage as you would coffee.

4

Food Trauma

Memories of Hunger and Scarcity

In the aftermath of the American war in Vietnam, millions of refugees fled Laos, Cambodia, and Vietnam. Between 1975 and the early 1980s, Canada admitted 70,000 refugees, many under a new immigration program allowing private sponsorships. Some of the newcomers were sponsored by Mennonite churches and households, who covered resettlement costs for a year. While most of the newcomers had not heard of Mennonites before coming to Canada, the hospitality and support of Mennonite families and church communities led to the emergence of Mennonite congregations led by new Canadians in various parts of the country; this occurred in the United States as well. These Mennonites, of very different ethnic, ancestral, and religious backgrounds from the majority of Mennonites in Canada, nevertheless shared experiences of hunger and food scarcity, especially with Mennonites who emigrated from the Soviet Union in the twentieth century.

Refugees from Laos, for example, fled across the Mekong River to United Nations refugee camps in Thailand, a dangerous journey because of the river's fast flow and patrols by the military with orders to shoot. They were escaping a dire economic situation and the violent communist regime that took control of Laos in 1975. They had survived over a decade of warfare, which always brings food deprivation. Even with supplies of sticky rice to start their refugee journeys, those who spent weeks walking through thick forests and over mountains often wondered where the next meal would come from.[1] Among those escaping Laos were the Hmong, an ethnic minority that eventually established Mennonite churches in Canada and the United States. Individuals and families that fled South Vietnam, also under communist rule at war's end, had a comparable experience, although their stories included dangerous travel by boat on the South China Sea, where many lives were lost due to pirate attacks and boats capsizing.[2] The experience of refugees from Southeast Asia resonates with the history of my own ancestors who survived famine in the Soviet Union in the early 1920s, and especially with that of my in-laws, who survived the Holodomor in Ukraine, fled their homes in 1943, and travelled as refugees through the European warfront during the Second World War.

Mennonites in North America and Europe are often associated with food abundance, but food scarcity, famine, and starvation are also part of their historic and contemporary realities. As Hasia R. Diner points out in her study of hunger and foodways of Irish, Italian, and Jewish immigrants in America, "No people's history is devoid of episodes of want."[3] Even if the deprivation varies dramatically in degree or length, and may be nonexistent for particular individuals or generations, or barely remembered for others, all population groups have hunger in their history. Certainly, scarcity or hunger has not been experienced by all Mennonites to the same degree. Particularly in the global south, where the majority of the world's Mennonites live in the twenty-first century, food security – or lack thereof – reflects the socio-economic and political conditions in particular regional and national settings.

Hunger has long-term effects, physically and psychologically, as memories of past deprivation influence people many years later, and sometimes across generations. While writings about food, especially in the context of twenty-first century "foodie" culture, are often about pleasure-filled experiences, the opposite response to food is equally important. Memories of hunger create a stark counterbalance to narratives replete with food richness and plenty. And even once a reliable and ample supply of food has become part of their new reality, people who have experienced hunger often partake of food in a manner that reflects past deprivation.[4] That is, the fear of scarcity, even in the midst of abundance, motivates the attitudes and behaviour of those with lived experience of hunger. Indeed, one of the reasons food is so important in some Mennonite households is exactly because histories of deprivation are a generation or less away. Those who survived famine and starvation live with what has been called "food trauma" – defined by S. Holyck Hunchuk as "the enduring physical and psychological injury resulting from food deprivation."[5] Such trauma is evident in personal memoirs and community narratives of Mennonites who survived the tumultuous era of the twentieth-century Soviet Union. It likely also exists in the psyches of Mennonites who fled Southeast Asia as refugees in the late 1970s, or Congolese or Ethiopian Mennonites struggling with limited financial resources to properly feed their children in countries beset by violent conflict in the twenty-first century.

Food scarcity changes a people's cuisine and food practices – in the moment, and in times that follow. Food theorist Massimo Montanari points out that food preservation – an art at which some Mennonites excel – developed historically in response to famine and hunger. The motivation of culinary history, he says, is "to discover how mankind, with effort and imagination, has sought to transform the pangs of hunger and the anguish of nutritional privation into potential occasions for pleasure."[6] I immediately think of my mother-in-law, Elizabeth Wall Born, who was severely malnourished as a child in early 1930s Ukraine, and whose food preservation activity in Canada was legendary. Montanari's theory suggests that hunger, whether in immediate experience, or feared, or remembered, is at the root of humanity's foodways. This chapter explores hunger and food scarcity in the Mennonite past and present. Much of what follows is drawn from twentieth-century histories of Mennonites who migrated to Canada from the former Soviet Union, but I also include examples from other times and places.

Food Scarcity across Time and Space

Hunger and food scarcity have existed for Mennonites during eras of persecution or repression, during warfare, during migration and settlement, and of course, during larger political and economic upheavals facing all of society. Interestingly, an Old Order Mennonite woman in Ontario, Bevvy Martin, refers to food insecurity among early Anabaptists in the sixteenth century. Reflecting on her own proclivity to not waste food, Martin is quoted as saying, "When the Mennonites were over in Switzerland yet they got chased around by those that didn't like their peace-loving religion and I guess they had to eat whatever they could get."[7] While there is little research on Anabaptist foodways, Bevvy's understanding links possible shortages to persecution of her religious ancestors. Furthermore, sixteenth-century Anabaptists likely experienced precarity in the food supply as did others in Europe when a growing population, prolonged cold temperatures, and cyclical droughts meant that everyone was "trying to survive in a world where food was a valuable commodity."[8]

Food scarcity occurred in contexts of resettlement and relocation. Mennonites who migrated to the Americas in the seventeenth, eighteenth, and nineteenth centuries experienced severe challenges during the early years of settlement. About 18,000 Mennonites left Ukraine in the late nineteenth century, establishing settler communities in the American Midwest and on the Canadian prairies. On arrival in Manitoba in the 1870s, "Food was by far the greatest problem. There had not been enough time to grow vegetables, and they had next to no cows, chickens or pigs and therefore no milk, meat or eggs. Day after day they ate noodles made from water, flour and some lard. Flour, beans and some small rations of meat were bought with money borrowed from the Mennonites in Ontario."[9] Another settler in the same era recalled that many people almost starved in the first year: "My father-in-law related that he was once given two potatoes," Abram Janzen said. "He took them home to his wife as though they were the finest of delicacies." These early prairie settlers of necessity took out loans from the government, with Mennonites in Ontario acting as guarantors: "This was called a 'bread debt' and amounted to $92,000."[10]

Mennonites who settled in Paraguay also depended on other Mennonites for their survival. Those who migrated there as refugees in 1948 received food aid from North America, but "the meals were very monotonous, mostly rice which could be easily stored."[11] Sarah Peters, who immigrated to Loma Plata, Paraguay in 1927, recalled that the planted grain seeds brought from Canada received lots of rain and sunshine, and thus sprouted and grew, but no crop matured.[12] When nineteen-year-old Johann J. Janzen arrived in Paraguay in 1930 (having left the Soviet Union via China), he was told by a girl from the Menno Colony (established in 1928) that they ate "beans without any fat, twenty-one times a week. The beans were cooked in water to which a little salt was added, and then the meal was ready for the whole day."[13]

My own grandparents, who emigrated from the Soviet Union to rural Manitoba in 1924, found themselves in severe poverty and in a "similar situation" to a neighbouring family that was "without a cow, meat and fuel" and hadn't had bread for "two weeks." Since there was no money for wood or coal, my grandparents drove (seemingly they did have some fuel) fifteen miles to the forest to collect brush for household heat and cooking.[14] The onset of the Depression half a decade later deepened their food hardship, as it did for others, especially those on the hard-hit prairies in Canada. Some Ontario Mennonites sent food to Saskatchewan, though some church leaders in Ontario also complained about the requests from the west.[15] A Saskatchewan community also received a financial gift from a Mennonite church in India, as a "token" of the latter's "compassion for the destitute community" in Canada.[16]

One published memoir that stands out for me because of its many stories of food shortage, as opposed to more typical Mennonite narratives that chronicle plenty, is that of Helen Janzen, an Old Colony church (one of the conservative branches) member who lived in rural communities in Saskatchewan. Helen was born in 1917, the eighth of sixteen children. She married and raised nine children with little help from her husband. Birthing and raising her children during the hardship years of the Depression and Second World War, Helen lamented the inadequate milk and eggs for her young ones; she worried about her son's lack of weight gain: "but I couldn't change his diet. We couldn't afford any other food."[17] In the winter of 1943, with her husband away at a logging job and not sending any money home, Helen feared she would run out of food altogether: "All these children to take care of, and I was pregnant all the time – it was so hard." Helen remembered this as "one of the most difficult and lonely times of my life, and my chest always felt tight and painful."[18] Even though these recollections are interspersed with anecdotes of food gifts such as flour and pork, the tone in her memoir is the overwhelming fear of food scarcity and her inability to care for her children. Things improved when she began receiving a family allowance of six dollars per month, although she also received government social assistance after someone reported the family as "very poor." While Helen did not like receiving "welfare," she was able to clothe her children and send them to school, and her husband was "happier ... because I could make better meals for the family." Although her children did not complain about suppers of soup and bread, her husband did not think this made for a "proper meal."[19]

Annie Goertz, born in 1919 in Saskatchewan, also recalls Depression-era hardships. The cows did not give milk in winter because they lacked feed and so the family had no milk for porridge or to drink. Her family and all the neighbours were on "Government Relief" for more than a year and received boxes of dried fish and canned fish called "Chicken Haddie," which she describes as "a novelty at first."[20] Goertz also remembers anticipating Christmas when she and her siblings put plates out on Christmas Eve, normally to be filled with peanuts, candy, and a tangerine in the morning. One year, her mother told them not to put out the plates because there was nothing to put on them. In the morning, there was one peppermint for each child.[21] The poignancy here is obvious.

Newly arrived in Canada from the Soviet Union, the David and Agatha Fast family experienced financial hardship in the 1930s, although food costs were kept down because much of what they ate was produced on their farm. Like others, they roasted grain to make the coffee substitute *prips*, although "regular coffee was purchased for Dad" and one daughter was allowed to drink any that her father didn't finish.[22] Gender inequities around food may have intensified when there was less to share in a household.

Prips comes up frequently as a symbol of food adaptation that occurred during times of scarcity. Susan J. Fisher describes it as a foodstuff consumed during "trying times" – years of early settlement, the Depression, or in conditions of poverty. Fisher notes that for poor families in southern Manitoba, breakfast fare was *prips* with bread, salt, and onions.[23] Helen Janzen recalls that they made *prips* because they could not afford coffee. They made it by soaking barley in milk, then roasting it in the oven; they added chicory for colour and to take the bitterness away. Then it was ground and stored in syrup pails.[24] *Prips* had somewhat of a revival in late twentieth-century households attempting to live sustainably: I remember the smell of roasting grain in the house of my newly married sister and her husband, who made many dietary choices in the spirit of "more-with-less."

Even after the Depression, during the supposedly prosperous postwar decades, Mennonite families who chose to resettle to remote areas within Canada – some to escape modernization – also experienced food scarcity. The large size of some families exacerbated this scarcity. Tena Friesen's parents and twelve siblings moved to northern Alberta in the 1950s. Their "limited supply" of groceries – they could not even purchase bread – created a cooking challenge for Tena's mother, as did the lack of "modern conveniences" in the home. The persistence of so-called traditional Russian Mennonite foods may have made that challenge easier.[25] Basic and familiar foods like *borscht* and other soups, pancakes, *rollkuchen*, and baking powder biscuits required minimal ingredients and were comforting in the midst of stresses created by displacement.

Food insecurity also occurred in contexts of famine, whether climate-induced or politically forced. For the Mennonite church in Ethiopia, called Meserete Kristos, the hardships resulting from repression by a Marxist-Leninist dictatorship were exacerbated by famine in the 1980s. Although religious persecution declined in the 1990s and churches reopened, cyclical droughts continue to cause hardship for Mennonites and others in that country.[26] Severe famine also plagued Mennonite mission workers and their converts in India in the late nineteenth and early twentieth centuries.[27] And food insecurity continues to be part of daily life for Mennonites living in regions of the world where poverty and conflict seem chronic. This is true in the Democratic Republic of Congo: although the country is resource-rich, it is riven by governmental corruption, exploitation of its resources by international corporations and governments, and ongoing violent conflict. The approximately 200,000 Mennonites in that country live with ongoing food hardship resulting from political and economic instability, as I learned during a visit there in 2012.[28]

Food Trauma and Famine in the Soviet Era

Food deprivation in Mennonite history is perhaps most widely chronicled for the Soviet period, beginning in the years following the Bolshevik revolution in 1917 through to the end of the Stalin era in the early 1950s.[29] Mennonites who lived in settlements in present-day Ukraine and Russia felt the impact of famine, food shortages, and food seizures that accompanied war, invasions, revolution, and other conflict throughout the twentieth century. Several-year famines in the early 1920s and early 1930s affected almost all Mennonite households, although Mennonites fared better than their Russian and Ukrainian neighbours. Civil war in the early post-revolutionary years brought disease and challenged food security, as did Joseph Stalin's political and economic war on his citizenry in the 1930s and after. The Second World War and refugee experience also brought scarcity and hunger for those who fled their homes. Food deprivation, leading to many deaths by starvation or malnutrition-related illness, was worst for individuals and families sent into exile within the Soviet Union from the late 1920s through the war years, and for those repatriated to sites of hard labour at war's end. Memory sources such as letters, diaries, and memoirs offer glimpses into food trauma experienced by Mennonites who emigrated from the Soviet Union in the 1920s and after the Second World War, and also for those who did not leave.

While the Russian diet is remembered as a simple but hearty diet, rich in fat and carbohydrates, those who lived through famines in the early 1920s and 1930s and wartime shortages knew severe deprivation firsthand. The contradictions between a cultural heritage that included a rich mixture of food traditions from the Netherlands, Prussia, and Ukraine and the lived experience of near-starvation became part of the historical self-identity of Mennonite immigrants to the Americas. Just as the years of prosperity and self-sufficiency are often described with reference to bountiful tables, community feasts, and the daily tasks of growing, harvesting, and preserving foodstuffs, the years of hardship are conveyed in narratives that centre on the existential details of physical sustenance. The deep emotional pain of watching family members die of starvation, and for women especially, the inability to feed one's children, remain a subtext beneath concrete descriptions of scarcity. For Mennonites whose later lives were ones of economic prosperity and abundance of many kinds, a focus on food – for some to the point of obsession – emerged exactly because of the lived experience of hunger.

The famine in Ukraine in the early 1920s followed an already tumultuous period after the First World War when Mennonite property-owners were plundered by anarchist terrorists and many families experienced rapes and murders; in some cases, entire families were massacred. Civil war between the Bolshevik army and Tsarist loyalists fought in southern Ukraine brought further turmoil, and in its wake typhus and other diseases that claimed hundreds of lives.[30] One estimate is that 500 Mennonites died during the famine of 1921–1923.[31] A decade later, millions of Ukrainians and other Soviet citizens starved to death in the Holodomor (Great Famine) – the forced famine engineered by the Stalinist state – although it is suggested that Mennonites "suffered relatively few deaths" during this time.[32] Nevertheless, the fear of starvation was real.

During both famine eras, traditional diets were modified – often to the extreme – in response to growing food shortages. Unusual measures were taken to prepare familiar foodstuffs: one memoir describes searching the fields for beets and cabbage left behind after harvest, to use in soup, but "there was no meat to make their beloved Borscht taste the way they remembered it."[33] Historian John B. Toews describes the kind of foodstuffs people resorted to: "As the famine intensified late in 1921, anything edible was included in the menu – dried pumpkins or beets, chaff, dried weeds, ground-up corncobs, the remains of processed linseed, dogs, cats, gophers, and such carcasses as were available."[34] Anna Sudermann described the fall of 1921 as the "first colossal famine. It was a time when we learned to value our bread and recognize its enormous meaning for nourishment of the population in its deepest sense."[35] Walter Jansen, a child at the time, recalled that people ate "dogs, cats, rats and crows," and mentioned rumours of cannibalism. His daily ration was "one slice of bread and a bowl of milk, oats and millet" though they were without bread for three months.[36] My great-uncle Franz was six years old during the height of the famine and recalled that his favourite snack was a slice of soggy bread with salt sprinkled on it.[37] In 1922, fourteen-year-old Gerhard Martens helped his mother butcher a sickly young horse that provided horse meat for the family for several months.[38]

In some examples of life writing, the details of food insecurity are both specific and shocking. From the journal of Herman Neufeld, a Mennonite bishop, we read,

> Famine raged everywhere. Everything that was edible was utilized; boiled leather (not a bad taste), ground corn cobs made into soup, horses, dogs and cats. There were a large number of pigeons in our loft and all were good breeders. Thus the young, when fully grown, as well as some older pigeons, became part of our diet. In addition, Abram (son) had acquired a number of rabbits. They also bred quickly and added to our food supply. The death rate from starvation, typhus and/or both

continued to increase. From February onward more and more Mennonite adults and children began to join the beggars. It was heartrendering [sic] when one day in March, my late sister's children from Alexeevka came to beg for food.[39]

In her published diary, written on the backs of evaporated milk can labels included in relief packages, Anna Baerg wrote in March 1922, "I have heard that some people have even eaten their own children." She went on to describe her own family's less desperate situation: "Although we haven't actually starved, we are hardly ever full. Today at lunch, for example, there was buttermilk and water, thickly cooked wheat with a sauce made from milk, oil, and onions, and a small piece of bread. Bread, by the way, isn't made according to the old recipe anymore – half of it consists of clay. And last time we added old, brewed *Prips* grounds to the dough. Not long ago we would have pushed the concoction away in disdain. Now we don't even ask how it tastes just as long as it's edible."[40]

The evaporated milk that Anna Baerg's family received was welcome food aid from North America, delivered by the newly formed Mennonite Central Committee. This organization, launched in 1920 with the express purpose of relieving hunger in Ukraine for Mennonites and others, would become pivotal in responding to global food insecurity in the century that followed.[41] After food aid arrived, life improved for Mennonites in the Soviet Union. For example, at a Christmas Eve celebration in the town of Halbstadt in Ukraine, people brought *zwieback* baked with "American flour," and once again enjoyed sugar with tea.[42] Food relief did not come only from Mennonites overseas. Agatha Fast recalled that, during the years of civil war in 1918–19, when Mennonite families, including her own, were fleeing their villages to escape the violence of bandits, they sometimes received food aid from their Russian neighbours: "At the time we fled into the village from Shelannaja, one of [the Russians] brought us some sauerkraut, another, a small pail of honey, and a third, a hen."[43] In this moment of need, socio-economic and ethnic hierarchies, at least those that existed from a Mennonite viewpoint, were turned upside down.

Despite the food relief and temporary optimism for the future under a new communist state, the hardships and fear of these years prompted a mass exodus from the Soviet Union and saw some 25,000 Mennonites migrate to Canada and South America from 1923 through 1929. Those who were unable or unwilling to leave in the 1920s faced more food hardship a decade later. In many respects, memory sources of famine in the 1930s and scarcity in the years that followed reflect even more desperation than is expressed in the previous decade. Once again, the items consumed as "food" for sustenance can hardly be imagined by the descendants of those who survived.

Recollections of this time include stories of eating acacia flowers, tree bark, sawdust, cornstalks, thistles, and sweeping out granaries and silos to salvage whatever kernels of corn or grain might be left behind. Elsie K. Neufeld's creative writing about her mother Susanna Siemens Klassen relates that children trapped field mice to fry, and Susanna "caught drifting acacia blossoms, and imagined them hearty food." Forks and knives became "redundant."[44] Susanne Willms Thielman's memoir describes how her brothers caught sparrows that were then cleaned and roasted or boiled. This, she said, was a welcome addition to their regular fare of "water soup," which consisted of hot water with a few grains of barley, linseed, or buckwheat.[45] She also recalls when one of their old horses could not stand anymore and her father called the veterinarian to confirm that the horse was fit for human consumption. While carving up the carcass, the butcher could not prevent himself from eating handfuls of raw horsemeat. The horsemeat kept them, as well as relatives and neighbours, alive for many weeks.[46] Otto Klassen describes how, in 1933, they put the family dog to sleep and made soap out its carcass. The soap was then traded for bread with communist officials: "Fortunately, for a short while we were saved from starvation," he recalls.[47]

Desperation drove some people to pick kernels of grain from dried cow's manure and "to eat the fetid carcasses of dogs, cats, and mice."[48] Small rodents seemed to be among the easiest new foodstuff to incorporate into the daily diet. Margaret Siemens Braun recalled eating rabbits, gophers, and mice: "We were hungry. In winter, we caught field mice ... I was pretty good at it. I was eleven years old. The mice were skinned and we could sell the pelts." Braun's mother would put the meat in ice-water overnight and the next day they would eat roasted mouse.[49] With parents compelled to work on collective farms, it was often children who became responsible for food foraging. In 1933, ten-year-old Maria Hildebrandt, together with her five-year-old brother, gathered weeds to cook in salt water to feed the very ill and starving families. Her grandparents died of starvation that year and many families were seriously ill.[50] It is possible that some households, out of desperation, went way beyond mice consumption. In her family memoir, Anne Konrad suggests that people resorted to cannibalism as well, although we learn little more from such inferences.[51]

Letters sent abroad provide an idea of how the lack of food and creative ways of devising edible foodstuffs preoccupied the thoughts and activities of families. Maria Regehr, writing to family in Saskatchewan, Canada in 1930, said, "we are eating as poorly as never before in our lives," the next year describing how she cooked with "seeds, grasses, moss, and worms. Anything that moves provides protein."[52] Mariechen Peters recounted the food hardships in a 1931 letter to her sister in Canada: "Very few remain in Gnadenheim (Molotschna) who have bread. They live on gruel, and there isn't enough of that. They don't have many potatoes. Sister Sara only had ½ pound corn flour left for the children. She and Peter were eating gruel."[53] Similarly, Maria Bargen wrote to her children in Canada in 1932: "It seems so hard to live through the experiences here. We have had no bread at all for 2 months. We have had no flour in the house and very little hope for any in the future. There are only 5 months until the harvest, and then perhaps we can get some potatoes."[54] Even when bread was occasionally available, Maria Regehr wrote that it was apportioned in small amounts and was "such wet, heavy and sour bread – not made with wheat flour but from rye or barley. The thought of wheat flour is beyond our imagination."[55]

One strategy was to forage in fields for kernels and seeds remaining after crops were harvested. After the fall harvest of 1931, people obtained any edible remains from cornstalks and sunflowers, a practice common "even in very rich settlements." However, this "gleaning of the leftover" was outlawed in 1932, thus reinforcing the famine underway.[56] Alongside the forced famine of the early 1930s, drought set in to cause even more scarcity. In the summer of 1934, one letter-writer to relatives in Canada said they had waited for rain until writing more; the previous year "there was no meat [but] at least we had cornmeal bread and beets, as well as onions and beans," but this year the "vegetables have not sprouted, and not even the watermelons."[57] What is especially interesting about these letters to Canada is that they acknowledged the food hardships created by the 1930s Depression; one Soviet Mennonite wrote to a Canadian, "Once again to ask for help from you goes against the grain since it is not much better where you are."[58]

Many letters were published in German-language Mennonite newspapers in Canada and the US during the hardship years. For example, a 1929 letter from the far east of the Soviet Union, published in the *Mennonitische Rundschau*, pleaded, "Help us hunger is painful ... Can't write well because my hand has become weak because of my hunger." The writer asked readers to "save us so that we can live."[59] Such published letters generated sympathy among North American Mennonites but also created a disparity in historical experience that would shape familial and intra-religious relationships for decades to come.

Despite challenges to the food supply in parts of North America in the 1930s, some Soviet Mennonite families benefited from aid sent from overseas. After waiting for many months, one family received several dollars in the mail and looked forward to the "Canadian feast" they would enjoy; on another occasion they received a parcel with flour, sugar, and rice "which saved us from starvation."[60] The day after Christmas 1932, Helene Dueck's mother wrote to her family in Canada: "Everyone is starving because all the grain had to be delivered and there is nothing to buy. The horses that are working in the fields are falling like flies. When they die people fight over the dead animals. The children are constantly asking for bread."[61] Occasionally they would be sent a bit of money, five dollars perhaps, to purchase staples like flour and sugar. One poignant story is that of a boy named Haenschen, in exile in Siberia with his family in 1933. In the midst of severe hunger, a few dollars arrived from a relative in America that would allow them to purchase rice. Haenschen then dreamed of eating his favourite meal, rice pudding cooked with milk. However, on the day his mother went to the store, Haenschen died at the age of twelve.[62]

During periods of deprivation, the Mennonite diet evolved to include foods that, under normal conditions, would not have been part of their culinary traditions. References above to eating dogs, cats, and mice make this obvious. One individual wrote that beets normally used to feed livestock were consumed as a delicacy.[63] Another described food aid from the Red Cross, "creamed flour made of rye and barley," that would normally be animal feed.[64] Mushrooms were a common part of the Russian and Ukrainian peasant diet, mainly as a substitute for meat and dairy on those days when religious observance prohibited such foods. Mennonites generally did not share this affinity, because they did not have a similar practice of religious fasting, or perhaps because their preference for a hearty meat-and-potatoes diet made mushrooms seem insubstantial. However, under conditions of hardship, during the early 1930s, during exile in Siberia, and also during the refugee flight, Mennonites too gathered mushrooms for survival.[65] For instance, Tina Dyck Wiebe, living in an orphanage in Siberia, recalled that dinner consisted of a bowl of soup made from mushrooms, and that she and her sister gathered mushrooms to eat because they were so hungry.[66] And recalling his boyhood years as a refugee, one man said that at a time when he should have been learning "reading, writing and arithmetic," he instead was learning how to "beg for food and find edible berries, leaves and mushrooms in their natural setting."[67] The role of children as scavengers for mushrooms and berries is noted in other memory sources.[68] The necessity of eating foods not normally part of their diet contributed to a long-term cultural transformation that saw Mennonites absorb Ukrainian and Russian ethnic traditions.

Massimo Montanari observes that people develop "complex survival strategies" when faced with food shortages; mainly, "while in a forced estrangement from usual practices, the strategies continue to adhere as closely as possible to the basic individual culture, and to the familiar."[69] Primarily this involves finding substitutions for familiar foods and ingredients that are scarce or unavailable. Wheat or rye bread, a mainstay of the Russian Mennonite diet, became particularly scarce, and women devised ways of baking even a semblance of the fluffy white or heavy rye bread that was symbolic of better times. Sorghum, a grain hitherto disdained, was added liberally because its sticky consistency allowed a small amount of wheat flour to go a long way. The use of what Mennonites considered "inferior grains"[70] diminished the class gap between them and their Ukrainian neighbours and workers. The amount of bread available to each person also corresponded to increasing scarcity. Susan Toews, in a letter to her family in Canada in 1931, observed that as conditions worsened, the morsel of bread became smaller: "The piece of bread does not become larger, but quite the opposite. If there is no more [bread], and many don't have any, what will happen?"[71]

It is possible that baking also became a political act, since flour put into baking would not be confiscated by authorities. Flour itself became a valuable commodity, subject to confiscation by government authorities or theft by random others. Policies of the 1930s Holodomor included punishment for withholding foodstuffs.[72] Even though they did not have enough food to meet delivery quotas placed on them, many were accused of withholding foodstuffs from the collective and were subject to warnings and possible imprisonment. The fears of retribution for unmet production placed additional stress on families already on the brink of starvation. In a letter to Canada in 1934, one Soviet Mennonite noted that a family member "had been in serious danger of losing his life for he was sleeping on the top of the chest in which most of the flour was stored." "We have bread that will probably last [through the winter]," he continued, "if it can be kept safe."[73]

When foodstuffs, particularly grains, were in limited supply because of quotas required by the communist state, the Mennonite practice of baking in large quantities may have even been a subversive act. This is suggested by one 1930 letter from the Soviet Union to Canada that begins with the statement, "Wish to send proof that we are still alive." In the "postcard," as it is called in the translated and edited collection, Aganetha Schartner Rahn writes to her brother about the difficult times, noting "We will also bake extra buns (zwieback) if we are allowed to keep them." Aganetha goes on to name her brother's decision to emigrate to Canada as "luck" and wonders if she too will experience that.[74] A year later, in a letter to his son titled "When you get this Letter we will be without Food," her husband said, "From us they have also taken the last of the flour, so that all we have now is the previously baked bread. I always said, they [the household] should just [keep on] baking, we would surely eat it."[75] Fearing the confiscation of flour, households would bake all their supplies of flour before that happened.

The food shortages, adaptations, and, at a base level, the eating of what was unthinkable, may have had important impacts, both immediate and long term, in terms of gender and mental health. One question that warrants further exploration is whether hunger and starvation had differential results for men and women. There is no statistical evidence regarding the deaths of Soviet Mennonites that would allow one to test a theory of gendered rates of starvation, yet in memory sources many women cited the need to care for and protect their children as their main, sometimes only, reason to live. Paul Fieldhouse, a specialist in food and nutrition, states, "It has long been recognized as a home-truth that when food is scarce women often do without, to the detriment of their health and strength, in order to ensure that their children receive adequate nourishment."[76] The memoirs of Mennonite immigrants abound with stories of mothers who gave the last morsel of bread to their children. Some analyses of the mid-nineteenth-century Irish famine found that overall, the mortality rates for adult women were lower than for adult men. Explanations for this are partly physiological – women's superior capacity to store body fat and their lesser caloric intake needs. Other explanations focus on women's functions as household managers, providers of "affection and consolation," and caregivers, roles that become more crucial and are therefore safeguarded during times of deprivation.[77] While acknowledging no quantitative data about gender-based rates of starvation, Oksana Kis offers qualitative analysis regarding Ukrainian women's greater resiliency to food deprivation during the Holodomor.[78]

While most Mennonite narratives speak to the physical consequences of famine years, a few sources address the mental health struggles that resulted from food scarcity – what today might be called food trauma. One letter from the village of Einlage in Ukraine to Mennonites in North America offered gratitude for food aid, yet alluded to the inner illness: "The indescribable bodily suffering, coupled with a hopeless outlook for the future, had brought about in most of our brethren a condition of mind which was worse than a mere lack of courage, rather verging on despair."[79] A report on the human situation in one region of Mennonite settlement in the 1920s, said, "the spirit and the will to live sinks, and the will to work disappears."[80] Inner struggles included spiritual despair, particularly hard for a community organized around religious beliefs including protection by God, and practices like prayer. Katie Funk Wiebe remarked that in the midst of famine in early 1920s Ukraine, her father "felt the weight of providing for the eight people around his table, but even as he added his prayers daily to those of the rest of the family, each day the meals became simpler and smaller. He had swept every corner of the mill for stray kernels."[81] In this case, the comforting ritual of prayer did not alleviate hunger.

Food and Flight

For Mennonites in the Soviet Union during the Second World War, a new form of food hardship, that which occurred during their refugee sojourn, along with general wartime scarcity, made food once again central in personal narratives. The so-called great trek of Mennonites from the Soviet Union, led by retreating German military forces, began in September 1943. Germany's two-year occupation of western

4.1 *Zwieback* served at a Mennonite church near Omsk, Siberia, Russia, in 2010.

Ukraine came to an end as the tides of war turned in favour of Allied forces. As the Soviet army advanced from the east, Mennonite villagers had barely a day or two warning to vacate their homes.

Not surprisingly, preparations centred on food, and what might last along a journey of unknown duration and destination. The choice of food was significant. Animals were butchered and the meat packed in lard for preservation. Fruit was dried and bagged. When leaving on the trek westward in 1943, Helene Dueck's family had three days to prepare: "Pigs, calves, sheep and chickens were butchered, cooked and covered with hot fat to preserve them a bit longer. Bread and buns were baked and roasted." While most household goods were left behind, they took along her mother's sewing machine because it "was her bread," as it provided a means to earn some money.[82] Wera Teichroeb, a child at the time, recalled that her father skinned and cleaned rabbits to take along.[83] Most importantly, *zwieback*, as the quintessential travelling food, was prepared in abundance. Numerous memory sources describe *zwieback* as the central food of migration. *Zwieback* became, literally and metaphorically, the food of survival and one with religious meaning, a topic I explore in more depth in chapter 5.

Most families began the trek with an ample supply of food but as weeks lengthened into months, supplies ran out and the refugees had to scavenge for meals. Mary Krueger, age ten at the time, remembered when her family's food supply was completely gone. One evening her mother gave each of the three children a spoonful of syrup with a little sugar on top, their last meal.[84] Children were sent ahead into villages to beg door-to-door, or into farmers' fields to search for grain or root vegetables left after the harvest. One woman recalled begging for food from strangers and going through the garbage.[85] Cows, brought along for their precious milk supply, were butchered. Only occasionally along the journey did the refugees stop long enough to cook a meal that might consist of some cooked potatoes, or a pot of soup, hastily prepared when a hole was dug in the ground, a fire lit, and some stones put in. Campfires had to be doused when air raids threatened, sometimes before the meal was prepared. More often than not, the daily fare consisted of bread and water.

The escape westward changed from a trek to a flight in the latter months of the war as the Red Army advanced on the eastern edges of German-occupied territory. Mennonite refugees, along with millions of other displaced civilians, found themselves in even more desperate circumstances, trying to obtain limited places on trains, trucks, and wagons and, in the midst of hurried and chaotic travel, trying to find enough to eat. In addition, flight occurred in the midst of a particularly hard winter: one woman recalled that her limited supply of bread froze so hard she was unable to cut it.[86] Katie Friesen describes her flight with her schoolmates and teachers. She was woken at four in the morning of 19 January 1945 with orders to evacuate; the Soviet army was very close. "Before leaving we took time to carry all the textbooks into the basement, just in case we would return. We wrote messages on the chalkboards, played one last song on the piano, bade farewell to our classrooms and then assembled in the schoolyard with tears

4.2   Family eating meal on refugee trek from Ukraine during the Second World War, c1943–44.

streaming down our cheeks." In the days that followed, the girls and their teachers travelled by wagon, bicycle, foot, and finally by train, barely stopping to eat or sleep. On more than one occasion, they had to abandon a hastily cooked pot of unpeeled potatoes. During a three-day stretch by train, they were lucky to receive one piece of bread per day; to quench their thirst, they ate handfuls of snow when the train stopped long enough for them to disembark.[87]

In her memoir, Helene Dueck also recalls stopping to cook potatoes but then having to flee before they could be eaten.[88] As she and her group of school friends fled the advancing Soviet army in late 1944, she repeatedly describes the meagre fare at the various stops along the way. They spent some time in the town of Weizenfels, Germany, where they stayed at a teaching training institute and received minimal nutrition: "Food was scarce in this school too. Breakfast consisted of coffee and two slices of bread so thin that one could almost see through them. At noon and in the evening our fare was potatoes in their skins with salt. When the teachers left the dining room the girls grabbed whatever was left for everyone was still hungry. Yes, hunger was our constant companion. It was war time and food was scarce everywhere."[89] Food became an obsession and procuring it by whatever means was paramount.

At war's end, many Mennonite refugees were in regions under Allied control, and gradually saw their food insecurity alleviated, some benefiting from overseas aid and within a few years given opportunities to emigrate. Others, caught in the Soviet zone of occupied Germany and Poland, existed in what Eve Kolinsky has called a "culture of physical survival" in which German nationals and displaced persons alike "lived close to starvation levels."[90] Military rations being far below what was needed for subsistence, two Mennonite women in the Soviet zone swept out the floor of a granary into a bag and brought it home, washed the grain, dried it, ground it, and made a kind of porridge soup from it.[91]

Some Mennonites in Prussia, which came under Soviet occupation, fled to refugee camps in Denmark, where provisions were inadequate. In her fictionalized biography, Ruth Reimer's family is said to have lived with seventy other German refugees in a former soldiers' barrack. Here they received a piece of bread for breakfast and supper and a dipper of thin soup for lunch. The bread was a dark sourdough – "so different from what was familiar to them." Because their diet had "changed drastically" in a short amount of time, some refugees developed intestinal problems.[92] Ruth's siblings would pick up "pea shells, cabbage leaves, or other peelings" that were thrown out the window of the central kitchen.[93] When construction workers came to the camp, the children would beg for, and sometimes receive, apples or turnips. This family remained in a state of constant hunger during their three years in Danish refugee camps.

During the periods of deprivation described above, access to food became paramount as an activity and a value in the lives of refugee families. Agatha Schmidt, a young refugee widow who fled the Soviet Union with her mother and two sisters, said, "When you are hungry you forever think about food, it is like an obsession."[94] When Helene Dueck and other school girls were waiting in the German city of

Treuenbrietzen in 1944, they were hungry and often talked about food to pass the time: "We dreamed about roast chicken, bread and butter and cookies. ... there was nothing to do but talk about our families and food. Though we were given something to eat twice a day, we always felt hungry. Coffee at noon and thin soup at supper was very meagre fare."[95]

I described earlier the incessant food-talk my refugee parents-in-law engaged in. It reflects a phenomenon prevalent among individuals experiencing deprivation and starvation. Abraham Maslow, in applying his hierarchy of human needs to food usage, said, "For the man who is extremely and dangerously hungry, no other interest exists, but food. He dreams food, he remembers food, he thinks food; he emotes only about food, he perceives only food, and he only wants food."[96] An interview project with Vietnamese refugees who settled in Montreal in the early 1980s offers supportive evidence: the foremost response to the question "What happened during the flight?" related to the lack of drinking water and food. It rated higher, remarkably, than concerns about suicides, deaths, rapes, and piracy.[97] Myrna Goldenberg has similarly observed the "preoccupation with hunger and obtaining food" in the memoirs of Auschwitz survivors.[98] This is starkly true for the recipe book *In Memory's Kitchen*, compiled by Jewish women murdered in a Nazi concentration camp.[99] Other examples of the poignant primacy of food-talk in situations of food deprivation can be found in Mennonite histories of hunger. For example, in a novel about the 1870s Mennonite migration from Ukraine to Canada, the female characters pass the long and hard first winter on the Manitoba prairie by gathering and talking about food: "For brief moments their voices came alive when they compared recipes."[100]

Descriptions of food and eating during conditions of shortage also serve to illustrate the breakdown of regular social relations and behaviour within the Mennonite community. The lack of regular meals, particularly on the trek and flight, reinforced a sense of normalcy breaking down, of life turning to chaos. The regularity of eating is a fundamental rite that maintains the structure of daily life even when there is disruption in other aspects of a routine. During times of famine, the entire day could become a preoccupation with scrounging for and preparing something edible for one's family, while on the refugee flight there was sometimes little opportunity to eat at all. Insecurity about the future was heightened when even the patterned ritual of meal preparation and eating was destabilized. Another important impact that food shortage had on social relations was to challenge ideas about family. Anne Murcott writes that the idea of the "proper" meal has much to do with the idea of "proper" family life.[101] So that the lack of adequate food and thus "good" meals as part of daily routine during the 1930s and throughout the war years coincided with the breakdown of family life – particularly related to the loss of male family members – and may have reinforced the idea that social and moral life was disintegrating among Soviet Mennonites.

The breakdown of eating routines and the shortage of food also had the effect of broadening the idea of family. With the loss of numerous individuals from Mennonite communities throughout the 1930s, the structure of families altered to meet the exigencies of the situation. Women, children, and the elderly were all that remained in most families and, as a result, living units composed of individuals with extended family or village relationships became common. Especially during the refugee flight, individuals rallied together to share limited resources – food, shelter, transportation – as well as the emotional support needed to confront fearful situations. Judith Tydor Baumel, in her study of the Holocaust, observes that the act of group food-sharing was one of the most powerful ways to create and reinforce communal bonds and mutual assistance.[102] For Mennonites, the sharing of meagre food portions solidified the bonds of village, family, and "grab bag" households in a way that never happened when individual households and families had plenty of their own.[103]

The sharing of food extended beyond the Mennonite group, and this too, could have a significant effect on how "outsiders" were viewed. Relations with Ukrainians, Germans, and later, Canadians, were often shaped in the context of accessing food. In her description of the benevolence that Ukrainian villagers showed toward her and her sister during the refugee trek, Susanna Toews writes of the "kind" "Russians" who were "good to us" – sharing their food and in one instance, offering such luxuries as apples. Because Susanna was malnourished, her sister scouted a Ukrainian village for eggs and "in a few hours had collected 150 eggs. Not one woman refused her request. These Russians were very good to us."[104] She contrasted this with the German military – ostensibly their liberators and protectors – who stole valuable foodstuffs from both the refugees and Ukrainian peasants along the way. The interaction also represented a socio-economic reversal, since prior to the Bolshevik Revolution, Mennonite colonists had by and large been much wealthier than their Russian and Ukrainian neighbours.

Food deprivation had particular social affects, but in the context of immigrant narratives and memoirs, it had figurative significance as well. When scarcity was particularly acute, certain foods became symbolic of survival and indeed life itself. Alongside *zwieback*, potatoes were mainstays of the Mennonite diet and became even more so when other foods were unavailable. As Norma Jost Voth has observed, "In the Mennonite home ... potato was king, always a staple part of the everyday diet as well as Sunday's traditional menu. Sometimes potatoes were served twice a day."[105] Eva Daniel, whose family fled their home in Prussia during the Second World War, recalled that "potato soup became our staple food on the move."[106] Potatoes became symbolic of both survival and starvation. As a means to survival, potatoes were often the last remaining food in a diet of deprivation. Anne Penner Klassen recalled in the spring of 1940, "It was becoming more and more difficult to get bread. After I had been standing in the bread lines for several days without getting any, I bought 110 pounds of potatoes for 54 rubles."[107] Mennonites exiled to Siberia similarly recall that the only thing allowing for physical survival was when the truck or train occasionally stopped by a potato field long enough for refugees to dig a few of the vegetables, build a fire, and cook them.[108] While the lowly potato kept people alive, it was also a fearful sign that starvation was not far away; even though potatoes were the preferred staple food of Russian Mennonites, when eaten alone and incessantly, they were a sign of poverty.

From Famine to Feast

By the end of the Second World War, over 10,000 Mennonite refugees had made it to the West where, once Allied relief supplies began to flow, they saw a beginning to the end of a long period of inadequate nourishment. For those in the western zones of the postwar occupation, and for the roughly 8,000 refugees who later immigrated to Canada, the previous two decades of deprivation were replaced by a time of relative abundance. In personal narratives, a border crossing to the West, the arrival at a refugee camp, or the trip to Canada are frequently marked with reference to the foods encountered, most of which offered a stark contrast to the immediate past. One example of this precedes the war. David and Agatha Fast were among the last of the large migration of Mennonites from Ukraine in the 1920s, travelling to Moscow in 1929 with hopes of getting permission to leave. When they finally crossed the border into Latvia, their first greeting was an invitation to eat. David recalled, "The children received so many chocolates, they didn't know what to do with them. And there was borscht, and meat and bread [though the latter] wasn't very tasty ... the kind we weren't familiar with."[109]

We do not know the nature of the bread served to the Fast family, but other sources appear to differentiate between the bread of scarcity and that of abundance. In her memoir of the flight from the Soviet Union, Susanna Toews makes frequent references to the food they received and ate at various points of the journey. When they finally crossed the border into Holland, she says, "we were served such food as we hadn't seen for a long time – milk, cheese, sausage, white bread and butter."[110] White bread, a symbol of prestige and plenty, marked a departure from hardship, when any morsel of dark, rough bread had been devoured eagerly. Similarly, Wera Teichroeb recalls that when her family worked on a farm in Allied-occupied Germany, they were fed well: "creamy milk, eating bread as big as watermelons and fluffy as cotton candy slathered with as much butter as we want."[111]

The preparation of some traditional Russian Mennonite foods in Mennonite agency-run refugee camps was a welcome treat after the deprivation of years prior. Justine Thiessen Warkentin recalled her arrival at the Mennonite Central Committee refugee camp in Berlin: "There on the table was a green bean soup and a plate full of bread. We could eat as much as we wanted. We could not imagine that something like this existed."[112] At a camp for refugees in Soviet-occupied Berlin, peppernuts – a small Germanic spice cookie – were baked during the night of Christmas Eve, much to the delight of Mennonite children awakening the next morning.[113] Elizabeth Klassen, recalling time spent at a Mennonite Central Committee refugee centre in the Netherlands, remembered that "on festive occasions our cooks arranged for the use of the baker's ovens [in a nearby village]. They would come back with piles and piles of *Zwieback* to everyone's delight."[114]

Along with fluffy white bread and *zwieback*, sugar was symbolic of prosperity and abundance. Sugar, expensive and often scarce, offered caloric energy, but its sweetness was also a metaphor for better times. Agnes Pauls recalled that when a Canadian medical officer in a refugee camp asked her sickly young son, "And what do you want in Canada?" the boy replied, "I want to eat myself full of chocolate."[115] The sweetness of oranges eaten on the journey across the Atlantic Ocean is highlighted in many of the narratives of those who immigrated to Canada, though rough seas often meant that food could hardly be kept down. Edna Schroeder Thiessen described the Jell-O and fruit desserts she received on her transatlantic journey in 1949, saying, "It was like being at a wedding every day!"[116]

Food memories of arrival in Canada include such things as white bread spread thickly with butter, tall glasses of milk, and sausage. One sixteen-year-old girl was enthralled with the plentiful food available during the train trip from Halifax, Nova Scotia, to Alberta: "We had never tasted such white soft bread or drank such cold rich milk before," she said.[117] Helene Dueck ate her first chocolate bar on board the ship *Tabintha* that took her to Canada in 1948.[118] When she arrived, she was given ten dollars to buy food to eat on the train journey to Alberta. She was overwhelmed by what she could purchase: "I had never seen so much white bread and such gorgeous fruit. I stood in front of the shop as if rooted to the ground. Immediately I bought 4 large loaves of white bread and a big bag of oranges ... When the train stopped at other stations and we noticed that the shops were just as full of goods, we knew that there would be no shortage of food in Canada."[119]

Mennonites who immigrated to Canada (very few resettled in the United States in the postwar era) left decades of hardship behind, yet their years of food insecurity and indeed starvation continued to be embodied in ongoing physical ailments and in memory. Individuals who experienced food deprivation in the context of war, famine, refugee flights, or imprisonment lived with memories of food trauma. This could manifest, as it did in the household of my parents-in-law, as an unstated but constant fear of food shortage or inadequacy. For this family, as for many others, the fear of hunger became "a culturally shared reality [and] a collective preoccupation reflected in actions, choices, and behavior."[120] The habit of elderly Jewish Holocaust survivors at a community centre in the UK to slip handkerchief-wrapped slices of bread into handbags and pockets reminds me of my mother-in-law's habit of filling her large purse with muffins or croissants at restaurant buffets. Ben Kasstan describes this as a "learned survival strategy from a time when life and death were hinged on having bread in your hand."[121]

The Guilt of Survival

My mother-in-law's food trauma may have emerged, in part, from knowledge that some of her relatives, including her father, who was arrested by Soviet secret police in 1938 and never seen again, remained in a state of food deprivation. The memories of Mennonites who found food abundance after migration were shaped by the guilt of their survival, a feeling that increased with the growing evidence of food trauma experienced by family members left behind to starve or live near starvation levels for a decade or more after the war. While approximately 12,000 Soviet and Prussian Mennonites migrated to North and South America after the war, tens of thousands of others were either unable/unwilling to leave or were repatriated from Europe to the Soviet Union. Until the mid-1950s, many of these were sent to the oppressive system of labour camps known as the gulag. While their fates were largely unknown in the decade after the war, letter exchanges, migration to Germany, and the publication of memoirs from this group of so-called "left behind ones" provide glimpses into desperate situations of food insecurity. Those left behind included Mennonites who were arrested and exiled within the Soviet Union – some temporarily, others permanently – during the late 1920s, through the decade of the 1930s, and during the war years.

The survivors' guilt, held by Mennonites who emigrated in the earlier movements of the nineteenth century or 1920s or post-Second World War, was intensified when letters were received from kinfolk left behind. In memory sources offering lived evidence of hardship, food shortages and acquisitions are central to personal narratives. For instance, in the early 1930s, Katja Isaak wrote the following to her relatives in Canada from her place of exile in Siberia: "I am writing this letter and tears are falling onto the paper. I am in a situation where there is no way out. I feel terrible. We have again been sent to another place. The food is worse too. With this food I cannot survive. Yesterday morning we got bread and now it is already the second day and have received no food. No bread, no water, no soup. I felt very sick to my stomach today."[122]

Mennonites sent into exile as alleged *kulaks* or subversives wrote that they received fish soup and bread only twice during a week-long trip on a crowded freight train, while others received no food at all.[123] Deprivation continued and often became worse in labour camps, where food rations were reduced or withheld as a form of punishment and as a means to control the prisoners.[124] Those who were less able to work, such as women, children, the elderly, and people with disabilities, received lesser amounts of food. One Mennonite in exile wrote that "food rations were such that we received too little to live on, but enough to stop us from dying."[125] Even so, starvation-related illness and death were commonplace. For some, death beckoned as a welcome release from hardship. Jasch and Maria Regehr, exiled to hard labour in Siberia in the early 1930s, wrote to relatives in Canada, "We are completely out of bread. We only eat soups but have to do very strenuous work, so that one feels like lying down and dying."[126] This family also wrote that sleep was a welcome reprieve from the strenuous labour and inadequate food because it "can dull the hunger pangs we suffer."[127] Their letters frequently mention people dying of starvation.

Suicides were not unknown among individuals feeling the desperation of loss and hunger. One man (unnamed), whose family was exiled to Siberia at the beginning of the Second World War, wrote this about his mother's state of mind that led to her almost taking her own life: "One day we too had nothing left to eat in the house. We had nothing for supper, nor was there any possibility of getting something for the next day. The torture of hunger and our hopeless, wretched conditions proved to be too much for our mother. Father had been torn away from us in the early thirties. All our property had been stolen, and we had been deported. Now here we were, soon to starve, as so many had already done."[128]

Some Mennonites sent into exile or prison fared better food-wise, but nevertheless longed for the familiarity of foods from home. Jacob D. Suderman, imprisoned in a labour camp in eastern Siberia in 1933, wrote to his relatives, "Our diet is probably good, but poor on variety. Currently we are getting salted meat and that does not make me happy. At times one has potatoes and meatballs, but one can only dream about *vareniki*."[129] In a similar vein, he wrote, "The tomatoes do not taste as good as at home, they are picked green and there can be no thought of melons and watermelons."[130] Jacob was executed in 1937.

Among those repatriated from Europe at war's end, refugee Helene Dueck's mother and sisters were sent back to the Soviet Union to do hard labour in Siberia. Helene's family worked at railroad-building, receiving 600 grams of bread per day that had to be divided among the children, the sick, and the elderly. With the little money she received, Helene's mother bought rye that she roasted and mixed with water to make a mush. "If she had a potato she would add it and they were happy. They had no vegetables, fruit or meat, so mother was nearly blind from lack of vitamins in her diet."[131] On Sundays, she would go to nearby villages to sell whatever goods they had for food. Helene's younger sister Anni, too young to work on the railroad, would ride a train (hanging on the steps because they had no tickets) into the mountains to collect wild onions which she would then sell at a market to buy staple foods like potatoes.[132] Gerhard, Helene Dueck's brother, was a prisoner of war and sent to the gulag in Siberia. Everything he did was motivated by the need for food. He was prepared to sell his dirty underwear for food, but nobody wanted it, taking pity on him instead by giving him some potatoes and onions.[133]

Helene Dyck Funk, among a group of 200 women and children in Fergana (present-day Uzbekistan), also recalled the scarcity: "Our food consisted of heavy bread and soup made of grass cooked in water, but at least it was something hot. I rose very early every morning to volunteer help loading the trucks at the bakery, gleaning any crumbs that fell. In summer on the way home we sometimes found mulberries and saved some for the next day. Many, *many* died of starvation here. On Sundays we helped shake fruit trees and sometimes were given a bit of food for this."[134] Hunger eased in the summer because weeds such as stinging nettles could be picked and made into soup or blended with whatever grain was available to make small breads. Aganeta Janzen Block, repatriated with her four children to central Siberia, did sewing "but only for food like milk, potatoes and other things – anything that was edible, but not enough to satisfy our needs ... You can't even imagine or believe how poor we were, yet not even the abdomen of the weakest of my children swelled with hunger."[135] She recalled the many women whose children died of starvation because they received no rations. Her niece and biographer Katie Funk Wiebe, who told Aganeta's story from letters received from her aunt in Moscow many years later, said, "For years hunger was as real as the hard boards on which she lay at night, the extreme cold as sharp and cutting as the knife used by the camp inmate delegated to cut bread rations into precise portions, down to the tiniest crumb."[136]

Multiple generations of Mennonites who survived (or did not) the Soviet era experienced gradations of food insecurity that ranged from temporary shortages and limitations, to long-term diet inadequacy, to death by starvation. Those at the less dire end of this spectrum of hunger lived with guilt over their own survival, while those who knew near-starvation carried the physical and mental repercussions of that hunger for the rest of their lives.

The Memory of Hunger

As many of the above examples illustrate, the role of memory is especially important when considering narratives of food scarcity. One poignant example comes from the Second World War. At the end of the war, Helene Dueck, a Mennonite refugee from Ukraine, found work on a wealthy farm in Germany. She had lost her family through the political events of Stalinization and in the refugee flight. Even while she survived and was able to migrate to Canada, her written memoir recounts the trauma of this era. One recollection exhibits how a food memory functioned as a metaphor for her emotional state. "As dirty and sweaty as I was," she said, "I had to sit at the table with the [farm-owners] and their guests. In my bowl of meagre soup there was one single dumpling. That told me that hunger would be my companion here too. The dumpling in my soup was lonely just like me, I thought."[137] The dumpling, even though it may have been better food fare than she had experienced in preceding years, not only reminded her of her food deprivation as a refugee, but symbolized her loss of home and loved ones.

Numerous memoirs like Dueck's point to the crucial need some felt to never forget those periods of hardship. Sometimes foods are associated with transformative moments in an individual's life. For example, for Mennonites whose fathers were disappeared during the Stalin purges of 1936 to 1938, the tragedy of loss was tied, in memory, to particular foods. Henry Bergen said this about his father's arrest on 10 June 1938: "As I remember it, life, before Dad was taken, was comfortable. There occasionally were white buns on the table and a pig was butchered each fall. With Dad gone things changed."[138] Henry associated the presence of his father in his life with good food. Anny Penner Klassen Goerzen related the following story about the arrest of her husband Johann in 1938. On that day she had cooked his favourite *vereniki* (spelled *Wareneki* in her account) with cottage cheese inside; later the two had visited the garden and seen the first cucumber that was growing but she had told him to let it grow longer before picking it. That night the Soviet secret police arrived and arrested her husband. "That day I couldn't eat the leftover *Wareneki*. I could not get myself to eat that first cucumber either, for it drove me to tears. After that, whenever I made *Wareneki*, I always thought of that last evening. And every year when the first cucumber was ready for picking I was reminded of that evening, and I couldn't hold back my tears."[139] In this case, food items gave Anny concrete memories of her husband, whom she had married only three years before his arrest and about whom her recollections may well have been rather dim without those tangible memory prods.

Because food is so everyday, it is an easier subject to talk about – in both oral and written forms – than violence, death, or moral ambiguity, for instance. Memories of food deprivation or abundance also function to veil complicated histories during wartime, whether personal experiences of sexual violence, morally questionable choices, ideological alignments, or complicity in violence.[140] Research on Mennonites and the Holocaust offers important and startling evidence that some Mennonites had personal affinities with National Socialism and collaborated with the Nazi regime during the Second World War.[141] This important research does not, however, probe the issue of memory to any great extent. How does guilt over such complicity become hidden in professions of unknowing or in memories of physical need at the time? During the Second World War, as the German army occupied Mennonite settlements in Ukraine, political affinities were tested. Many Mennonite families living in Soviet Ukraine when the German occupation occurred from 1941 to 1943 were required – and were willing – to provide food and lodging for German soldiers. For instance, Wera Teichroeb, in her memoir, says about the occupation, "Finally they arrive! My mother cooks and looks after eight of them and they treat us very well."[142] Starvation became political. The Mennonites hated the communists who starved them and welcomed the Germans because finally they had enough to eat. How much did their experience of having enough to eat influence their attitudes toward the German occupation? When fleeing from the Soviets on the eastern front in 1944, after arriving in the German Reich, Helene Dueck says, "Friendly Hitler boys brought us a cup of milk right away which refreshed and strengthened us. After that we were served a wonderful hot soup and then were allowed to stretch out on our straw beds that had been prepared for us."[143] Later they were received by "a friendly Socialistic Women's Group" who "served us a nourishing bean soup which we thoroughly enjoyed. With satisfied stomachs and renewed strength we went off to our future home ... A few Hitler boys showed us the way."[144] The intense physical need for sustenance may have functioned, in memory, to downplay knowledge of the actual ideology and actions of the "Hitler boys."

Food trauma was manifest in behaviours that crossed generations. Hildegard Martens, for example, correlates her father's harsh attitude and threats of punishment over her resistance to eating meat with his own experience of famine in the Soviet Union in the 1920s, including an occasion when he helped his mother butcher their weak horse for food.[145] I sometimes wonder if my own grandmother's debilitating depression was related to the years of food insecurity in the Soviet Union in the early 1920s. My memories are of a woman who spoke little and exhibited minimal emotion, but I do recall her always trying to get me to eat more and finish what was set on the table, as if food could make everything better, and perhaps even repress, or heal, her memories of deprivation and violence in her childhood and young adulthood.

Food deprivation is as much a part of Mennonite identities as food abundance, past and present. I propose that the emphasis on abundance in foodstuffs and foodways associated with Mennonites, both external and self-generated, arises in part exactly because hunger was often close at hand. Throughout their 500-year history, and in many global environments, Anabaptists and their descendants experienced hunger and starvation. Whether the result of environmental or politically motivated famine, or food limitations during early moments of settlement, or shortages resulting from war and refugee flights, or from state-imposed starvation measures, many Mennonites hold the lived experience of food insecurity in their bodies and memories. This is true for Mennonites with Russian, Ukrainian, and Soviet ancestries, who have chronicled and spoken about that deprivation in many sources. However, it continues to be a reality for Mennonites in poor countries around the world, and for some racialized Mennonites in rich countries, a topic I acknowledge as a gap in this discussion.

As people of religion, Mennonites often turned to prayer and hope in God in response to severe food deprivation. I explore the connections between food and religious faith and practice in the next chapter.

Anarsa

Recipe by Rishita Nizel Nath

Anarsa is a food for festive times made by some Mennonites in India. This recipe represents the method for making *anarsa* in Chhattisgarh state, where I travelled with guide Cynthia Peacock. Cynthia, who lives in Kolkata, is a leader in the Mennonite community in India and reached out to women for this recipe on my behalf.

Ingredients
2 cups Raw Rice
1 cup Molasses or Jaggery
6–8 full Cardamom
2 tsps full Fennel seeds

Method
1. Soak rice in water for 3 days – keep changing water twice or thrice a day.
2. On the 4th day, drain the water, spread on a thin muslin cloth and sun dry till all water is absorbed.
3. When fully dried, put the rice in a mixer, add the cardamom (peeled) and fennel and grind to a powder.
4. Keep aside.
5. Take a pan, add 2 glasses of water and in that add the molasses and bring to a boil. The consistency must be such that when you test with a spoon, it will be sticky and thick. Keep a little aside for later use if necessary.
6. Add the rice powder mixture and keep mixing till it is formed into a dough. Remove from fire and cool it till you are able to make small balls with your palms. Then press each one and flatten it and keep aside on a sheet. Taste and if it needs more sweet, add the set aside molasses to the dough before making the whole into small balls.
7. Add enough veg or cooking oil in a pan to deep fry and when hot enough, add one and if it floats, the oil is ready.
8. Fry all a few at a time depending on how large your pan is.

5

Breaking and Baking Bread Together

Food and Religious Practice

In March 2015, I joined a group of women for conversation about food and other things at their Mennonite church in Ranchi, Jharkhand State, India. I learned about the common ritual of *Mutthi Daan* (translated for me as handful offering), whereby women set aside a handful of rice each day while preparing the family meal. Those handfuls accumulated until brought to church, where the women's collective offering of rice was sold to raise funds for activities in the church. The regularity and, as one woman said, the "prayerful" way in which this was enacted put women into a sacred space within the spiritual life of the congregation. More recently, the collection of rice has been replaced by the collection of monetary donations.[1] This localized ritual connected the household to the church directly and demonstrated that food is often at the heart of religious-based charity, meeting the needs of others within and outside of the church. This particular ceremony brings together the major themes that follow – caring for those in need, food-based rituals in the church, food as essential to community, and a food item, in this case rice, as symbolic of spiritual meaning.

In the introduction, I noted that some people critique any deliberate linkages between Mennonites and food because the former category is considered a purely religious one and the second purely cultural. It is good to keep this distinction in mind, but the two categories should not by necessity always be separate. Indeed, a

Waterloo, Ontario rabbi proposes that "cuisine is a great example of religion and culture going hand in hand."[2] Historian Hasia R. Diner, who also acknowledges resistance to studying food and religion together, reminds us that "since food constitutes the core of life and religion seeks to imbue meaning to life, a deep and inextricable bond must bind what we humans eat with our understanding and engagement with the sacred."[3] Most world religions, in varying degrees, incorporate beliefs and practices that are food-related. Scholars Michel Desjardins and Ellen Desjardins speak to the intersection of food and religion in Canada specifically, noting that "commensality – the act of eating together – helps people get through long, cold winters."[4] They also observe that "sermons and biblical texts might be fodder for theologians, but food is universally significant."[5] Religion itself involves all the senses, and exists "in accord with basic, natural experiences of eating and breathing, seeing and speaking."[6] Daniel Sack corroborates this in *Whitebread Protestants*, offering that "food ... calls attention to our senses and to our bodies, and it plays a central role in church life."[7]

Anyone who is part of a faith community knows that food is involved at many moments, whether it is the community-building that happens at potluck meals, or the daily or seasonal religious rituals that are central to faith practice, or in the living out of beliefs through food charity. Food-focused religious rituals and practices are central to many of the world's faith traditions: fasting during Ramadan and eating halal for Muslims; the Seder meal and eating kosher for Jews; food gifts offered by Buddhists to fill themselves with the divine presence; beef restrictions by Hindus; non-violence in the diet of Jains; and the potlatch ceremony of some Indigenous nations, for example. Christians also associate certain foods with special religious occasions, although practices vary widely. Food-related religious rituals are less central to Protestant Christianity and even less emphasized – indeed rejected – in most evangelical or iconoclastic denominations. Yet, reflecting in his memoir on his love of traditional Mennonite foods, Ted E. Friesen says, "Food is one of the few Mennonite sacraments."[8] In the human yearning to imbue spiritual expression with everyday practices, and vice versa – to sanctify daily tasks – Mennonites connect certain moments in the Christian year and family lifecycles with their cultural foodways.

Alongside specific food practices, Mennonite religious emphases on community, simple living, and, in contemporary settings, environmental sustainability, allow one to situate the practical and functional nature of food within a framework of religious faith and practice. One woman, speaking about the *More-with-Less Cookbook*, said simply, "our interaction with food is a way to express our faith."[9] Lovina Eicher, an Amish woman and cookbook writer, states, "Whether it be a 'grocery shower' for a shut-in or a new mother, or offering food for donation to help raise money for medical bills, food plays an important part in our faith."[10] Lovina's understanding of faith represents what is described as "lived religion" – the recognition and embrace of the sacred in everyday practices and routines.[11]

Mennonite practices of food charity and justice, culinary ritual, and commensality all emerge from values and actions deriving from their religious beliefs and varied historical sojourns. In this final chapter, I explore food in Mennonite religious practice and argue that the topic of foodstuffs and foodways is not only a cultural one.

Food as Spiritual Symbol

While certain foodstuffs have tangible and ritualistic roles to play in Mennonite religious ceremony and events, other foods appear in more symbolic ways. The handful of rice in the ceremony of *Mutthi Daan* symbolizes generosity and elicits prayerfulness for those participating in the practice. Watermelon and *zwieback* were, for Russian Mennonites, foods with special cultural importance, but also emerged at moments of religious experience or expression. That watermelon-eating might even function as religious ritual is suggested by one man quoted in *Mennonite Foods and Folkways*: "Next perhaps to its unquestioning faith in baptism, the Mennonite heart hugs the watermelon above all things."[12]

We might chuckle at this, but watermelon does indeed appear in Mennonite memory at moments high in religious meaning. Reflecting on her grandfather's death in Ukraine before the Bolshevik revolution, Helene Dueck wrote that on his deathbed he said farewell to everyone, but also asked if the watermelon that the herdsman gave him had tasted good, since he had not been able to eat it.[13] His idea of what constituted a good watermelon may well have summed up his entire life story as he prepared to die, hoping no doubt that in heaven all the watermelon would be sweet and juicy. Helene was among thousands of Mennonites who fled their homes in present-day Ukraine in the midst of the Second World War. On the refugee journey she recalls resting for several weeks in a Ukrainian village near the Mennonite settlement of Sagradowka. Some of the refugee travellers went to visit the settlement and "were received with open arms. It was the season for watermelons. How we enjoyed the juicy fruit – it was a reminder of home."[14]

Even during times of food insecurity, watermelon appears in Mennonite memoirs as a sign of hope. In 1930, one letter from the Soviet Union to Canada spoke about watermelon abundance. In describing her garden productivity, Aganetha Schartner Rahn said, "We already have plentiful watermelons stored in the shed, very nice ones and also many other melons, nice ones. It is impossible to eat so many. We are feeding the melons to the cows."[15] Some first-generation immigrants to Canada recalled that watermelons in Ukraine were sweeter and remained available when many other foodstuffs were scarce. When sugar was scarce, watermelon syrup was made and smaller melons were pickled for eating in winter.[16] Susanne Willms Thielman devotes an entire section of her memoir to the making of watermelon syrup in her childhood village in Ukraine, noting it was a "basic food" in her family, given that white sugar was considered a "delicacy." Watermelon itself was an "important part of our diet," she recalled.[17]

When Sarah Peters' family immigrated to Loma Plata, Paraguay in 1927, watermelon was the first food noted in her memoir. Sarah's mother planted seeds in September and by December, "the huge watermelons looked great." Since they had no gifts for Christmas, they "rejoiced over the large watermelons which would be ripe for Christmas." On Christmas Eve day, a hot wind scorched the garden, baking the melons white, and so the women quickly made watermelon syrup.[18] Memoirist Connie T. Braun, reflecting on a 2005 tourist trip to visit her father's former village in Ukraine, described a figurative communion service – breaking bread together – that occurred when a village resident sliced a watermelon for the visitors. When Braun's father later said it was not as sweet as he remembered it from his childhood, his memory of "sweeter times" was hiding the years of turmoil and loss he experienced in that same place.[19] Watermelon is a constant memory prompt in the novel appropriately titled *Watermelon Syrup*. Based on a real-life account of a Russian Mennonite woman's life in Canada, the novel's main character recalls "the feel of watermelon juice running down" her chin as she reveals pre-migration memories clearly divided between the beauty and prosperity of her childhood and the violence, including the rape of her mother, that beset her family in 1919.[20] Watermelon is symbolic of sweetness and better times.

For individuals wrenched abruptly and involuntarily from their homes, food holds much religious meaning, not only because certain foods, like watermelon, are symbolic of the homes left behind, but also because hunger is linked so closely to physical and spiritual despair. In oral histories and written memoirs, foods stories or allegories often emerge at crisis moments in an individual's life. The quintessential Russian Mennonite foodstuff, *zwieback*, discussed in previous chapters, figures prominently in this regard.[21] Foremost, this white flour bun is a travel staple. In preparation for departure, first in the nineteenth century, and then in the 1920s and 1940s, Mennonite women baked hundreds of *zwieback* and roasted them for the journey. When roasted properly, thoroughly dried out, and cooled, they can last for several months without turning rancid. In the novel *Katarina: Mennonite Girl from Russia*, the protagonist and her mother filled four pillowcases with roasted *zwieback* for their journey to Canada in 1873 and to sustain them in the early weeks of settlement.[22] Kornelius and Elizabeth Neufeld, who left Ukraine for Canada in 1875, similarly filled "pillowcase after pillowcase" with roasted buns, on the advice of others who had already made the voyage.[23] Among the "few possessions" of Mennonite settlers to Kansas in the 1880s was "Turkey Red wheat, toasted zwieback, determination, resourcefulness, and love of the land." Describing her ancestors' food for the journey, Naomi Gaede-Penner compared *zwieback* to the "hardtack" of sailors, "something that would not spoil, something to eat in the absence of perishable food, something that would endure for the long voyage."[24]

Typical is this description by one man who recalled his family's journey to Canada in 1923: "Mother roasted buns in the oven in order to dry them out so they would not go moldy on the trip. When they were roasted, they kept for months. Many a little youngster was raised as a baby with a portion of dry bun soaked in coffee, sprinkled with sugar, wrapped in cloth as a soother."[25] In another example, Mary Konrad Epp recalled her mother's food preparations in anticipation of their trip from Siberia to Moscow and departure for Canada in 1929: "Day after day I watched Mama bake zwieback, many, many of these double-decker buns. Mama toasted them in a warm oven until they were dry and I liked them crispy that way – but why did Mama want bags full? 'To eat on the train trip,' was Mama's hurried reply."[26]

Beyond their qualities as the perfect travel food, *zwieback* are prominent in Mennonite memory sources in which emotions of loss and sadness accompany the experiences of leaving homes, saying good-bye to loved ones sent into exile, and preparing packages for those in prison, for example. The life-giving potential of this modest breadstuff is epitomized in Tina Dyck Wiebe's description of her mother's death in exile in Siberia. The family was severely malnourished and suffering from scurvy when a package of food arrived from relatives: "At last the sleigh came with a package. How much joy! But Mother was hardly able to smile as Father opened it. He soaked a roasted *Zwieback*, and tried to feed her. But she only looked at it with big eyes as she sank down in her pillow. She whispered with her lips: 'I don't need it anymore.' It was barely audible. 'No, No! You cannot die!' Father cried out in despair. 'Don't leave me alone with the children!' But Mother never opened her eyes again."[27] The faint hope that, if nothing else could save her, then maybe the taste of *zwieback* would bring her back to life, brings deep meaning to this foodstuff.

Yet *zwieback* was also about looking to the future, and roasting and packing them in sacks became a ritual of hope and movement forward. To state it simply, as long as there was *zwieback*, God existed for people who were in despair. Even beyond situations of sorrow, *zwieback* functioned symbolically to mark sacred and celebratory moments. Theologian John Rempel wrote that in his childhood household, *zwieback* were baked only for Sundays, weddings, and funerals and thus, for him, "symbolized a way of life, a way of measuring time." They signified "movement from ordinary time to sacred time."[28] Rempel suggests that *zwieback* were more than just bread, but of course bread itself, because of its biblical significance, carries religious meaning as life-giving.

Referring to its religious qualities, historian Aaron S. Gross says, "bread is always more than bread alone."[29] For Mennonites, wheat flour baking, as Ben Nobbs-Thiessen observes, "was inextricably linked to social and religious life," and when it was absent, they "pined for wheat."[30] The central Christian symbol of the communion meal, whereby Christ's body is received (for Mennonites, symbolically) in the eating of the bread, reinforces this connection between bread and life. Thus, when those in need of food receive bread, it does more than satisfy hungry stomachs or meet nutritional requirements. It carries hope for survival and a better future. Given its metaphoric meaning as life-giving and a source of salvation, bread is the foodstuff cited most often in stories of unexpected fortune. Numerous anecdotes or references to bread or *zwieback* appear in stories that are about more than just giving bread, but about giving life.

In her memoir, Marianne Zwittag Pauls says, "Bread is the basis of our sustenance," something she came to appreciate during her years as a refugee eating "nothing but potatoes and radishes."[31] Anny Goerzen relates the story of when her mother, brother, and sister-in-law were arrested by the Soviet secret police in 1939. As the prisoners were being loaded up, soldiers guarded the house and prevented the remaining family members from going outside. Anny's ten-year-old sister climbed out of the bedroom window and ran to the store to buy bread, which she threw to the prisoners on the truck.[32] Not only was this a story of a girl's bravery, but the bread was symbolic of important family ties and a gift of what was most fundamental to survival. In another story, bread given to men in prison camps in the Soviet Union was used to hide messages. Helene Dueck reflected on the courage of her mother, who set out in the cold and snow and wind to visit her husband who had been arrested the day before (in 1938). She had baked a loaf of bread and hidden a note inside that said she loved him and would never forget him. She didn't know if they would give him the bread but wanted to give him courage.[33]

Stories of food also emerge in accounts of miraculous moments when death from starvation seemed imminent. Agatha Schmidt remembers an incident from the time of severe famine in Ukraine in 1932–33:

> That our family ever lived through this time is truly a miracle. One time I remember mother baked a "korshik" [flatbread] which she divided into four equal parts. After we had each eaten our portion she said: "Children, that was the last flour. We have no food left for tomorrow." Then she took us into the living room where we all knelt down while she prayed with us. That evening a knock came at the door. Then the figure of a woman thoroughly shrouded to conceal her identity, came in, set a freshly baked loaf on the table and disappeared into the darkness once more. We had no opportunity even to thank her, and to this day we have never discovered the identity of our benefactor who took risks to help us.[34]

In a similar account, Peter Epp describes the experience of his wife who, alone with five children and expecting the sixth, fled Poland ahead of the Soviet army in the winter of 1945. In her haste to leave, she left behind her bag of provisions and had only one loaf of bread with her. He continues, "But God was always there! When her hope had all but vanished, my wife found a kettle with warm boiled potatoes on an abandoned farm."[35] Walter Loewen, a child at the time, describes an incident on their refugee journey out of Ukraine in 1943: "In time we arrived at a town with a sugar manufacturing plant. Mother walked up to the German manager and asked for some food. He insulted her, calling her a beggar woman and chased her away. Mother cried. Then we met a Russian lady who gave us a bread. This was not an ordinary bread, but a shiny, artfully braided and decorated bread, a work of art! It was obviously produced with much love and respect! With thankful hearts we admired the bread before we ate it, for this woman had given us more than just a bread! May God bless her for it."[36]

Food deprivation also intersected with Mennonite religious ideals when questions of morality were involved. In cases such as theft of food, perspectives on right and wrong became situational for Mennonite refugees fleeing their homes during and after the Second World War. Stealing food from farmers' fields or from employers' kitchens when one's family was starving, or a woman allowing sex in exchange for food for her children – all these actions went against Christian beliefs about right and wrong. These were among the kinds of activity condemned by Canadian Mennonite church leaders who called for a program of religious rehabilitation for postwar Mennonite refugees in North and South America.[37] Yet, communities that had not lived through severe deprivation could not empathize with the crisis of food insecurity experienced by many Mennonites. Margaret Siemens Braun described that insecurity in the late 1930s in Ukraine when, after her father was arrested and disappeared, her mother and siblings collectively tried to keep starvation at bay. She recalled they stole apples, pears, and watermelons from other villages: "I don't call it stealing because we were hungry. But if we got caught, we would be arrested."[38] Accusations of immorality for such actions caused a crisis of conscience for Mennonites who sought to preserve life in the midst of death that surrounded them. Braun's daughter-in-law reflected, "We wish stories to be black and white, but in between lie all the gradations of survival."[39]

Bread-related food practices hold symbolic meaning for other immigrant and religious communities. For Bhutanese Hindu refugees in the United States, the staple food *sel-roti* (a flatbread) is prepared in such a way that when people eat it together they are reassured of meeting again. The batter is intentionally overlapped in the frying oil to symbolize the overlapping of lives and thus "signal the hope of return and reunion."[40] Even while food is often viewed as having only material meaning, especially for Mennonites who separate the physical from the spiritual in sometimes rigid ways, individual foodstuffs such as bread function as symbolic companions to religious practices and emotions. Of course, bread is not only consumed for individual sustenance but is shared so that others can thrive as well.

Food Charity and Justice

Mennonites are known for their food charity and food justice, arising from religious principles of discipleship – following the teachings of Jesus Christ – and mutual aid. Hubert L. Brown described the principle of mutual aid in straightforward terms: "The Anabaptists [predecessors to Mennonites] gathered food, money, and clothes for those in need."[41] Notions of economic justice and/or caring for those in need are enshrined in numerous Mennonite statements of faith and doctrine, including in cookbooks. In the *More-with-Less Cookbook*, author Doris Janzen Longacre offers the blanket statement, "Mennonites are … a people who care about the world's hungry."[42] At a very basic level, food charity emerges from Mennonite beliefs in helping those in need. This has occurred over time through localized community initiatives and also through national and international organizations.

Localized measures included the practice of *Mutthi Daan*, described earlier. In my own community, food charity was manifest in weekly church dinners served to unhoused, marginally housed, and others who sought social contact and good food. For four years, my family, together with a changing number of volunteers, prepared a meal for 200 people at Stirling Avenue Mennonite Church in Kitchener, Ontario. Not only was this a site for food charity, but it built a community of giving within and outside of the kitchen. Participating in a "soup kitchen" – serving those with food insecurity – is often the first, and sometimes only, exposure that wealthy Mennonites have to poverty.

An international soup kitchen is cited as a pivotal initiative in the history of Mennonite food charity. As noted elsewhere, Mennonites' primary collective non-profit relief and development agency, Mennonite Central Committee (MCC), was founded in 1920 to deliver food to starving Mennonites and others in Ukraine in the aftermath of world war, civil war, and famine. I wrote this in March 2022 as Russian military forces attacked Ukraine and we witnessed history repeat itself as Ukrainian people of all ethnicities and faiths experience food shortages when their cities and towns were bombed and as they fled those places as refugees. Mennonite Central Committee was once again attempting to send food and other needed assistance to that country, while a Mennonite charity based in a former Mennonite village provided humanitarian aid to vulnerable populations.[43] Since its inception, MCC has continued to facilitate food relief to populations across the globe: some include Mennonites but most do not. The spirit of the original soup kitchen continues with the MCC meat-canning initiative, whereby annually up to 30,000 volunteers across North America cook and preserve meat at a mobile canning operation. The cans are distributed around the world in regions experiencing food insecurity. This food charity program began in 1946 in response to postwar hunger in Europe and elsewhere, and it is still in operation eight decades later. Essayist Julia Kasdorf describes the canner as not the most "sophisticated or efficient" approach to world hunger, but, she adds, for the volunteers it "satisfies a basic human need to do something concrete in the face of cruel and confusing times."[44] Indeed, Mennonite food charity has a significant positive impact on those who give as well as those who receive the relief.

A North American manifestation of food charity occurs in annual relief sales, localized events where material goods are donated and

5.1 Lucy Santiago (right), with Glorimar Mojica (left), serves Puerto Rican-style canned meat to homeless people near the Mennonite church, San Juan, Puerto Rico, 2019.

sold to raise funds for the international relief work of Mennonite Central Committee.[45] Alongside popular quilt auctions, food is a central feature. There is a certain irony in the sale as a fundraiser for global hunger and poverty, since it often means that Mennonites feed the world by feeding – sometimes overfeeding – themselves. Indeed, the *London Free Press* described the first Ontario sale in 1967 as "Man and His Stomach."[46] The first relief sale in Canada may have been in 1920 at Herbert, Saskatchewan, but they really became an annual phenomenon in Mennonite communities across North America in the late 1950s. I often attend the sale in New Hamburg, just west of Kitchener-Waterloo, Ontario.

In May 2017, the *Waterloo Region Record* reported on the annual sale in New Hamburg with the front page headline "'Stop Eating, and Bid!' Food Rivals Quilts as Draw." Apparently, the quilt auctioneer was trying to rouse the audience into higher bids when he thought they were giving too much attention to the plentiful foodstuffs at the sale. The article described one woman eating her strawberry pie with whipped cream right out of the box while watching the quilt auction. It also noted the diversity of the food at the sale: "In addition to the spring rolls, there were pupusas from Latin America, falafels from the Middle East, and a savoury fried dough called rollkuchen that was served with watermelon slices, from a booth run by an Old Colony community near Listowel."[47]

This diversity in 2017 was a far cry from the offerings at the first Ontario sale in 1967. In the year prior, organizers of the sale sent out a call for "Pennsylvania Dutch food" – the cuisine associated with the Swiss Mennonite and traditionalists in the area.[48] The result was the sale of tea balls, apple fritters, pickled fruit and vegetables, and other fare from this tradition. Shortly thereafter, the offerings expanded to include foods from Russian Mennonites, such as *rollkuchen*. Pies also became a feature; in 1973, 4,000 homemade pies were sold, including the popular fresh strawberry pies. In the same year, a *Relief Sale Cookbook* was created and sold for four dollars; on the day of the sale, 2,500 copies were sold.[49]

By the early 1980s, the list of foodstuffs had expanded considerably, so that the 1983 New Hamburg sale included the following array of items: "Pork on bun, donuts, ice cream waffles, grape juice, rosettes, apple fritters, tea balls, popcorn, pancakes and sausage, hamburgers and hot dogs, barbecued chicken legs, sandwiches, cookies, tarts, fruit bread, cakes, candy, pies, rollkuchen, borscht, apple juice, milk and chocolate, cream buns and coffee, cut pies and ice cream, summer sausage, canned goods and noodles, vereneki, fleisch piroschke, strawberry pies, and cheese."[50] The foods were a combination of Swiss/Pennsylvania German and Dutch/Russian Mennonite foods, along with other fare. However, the next year was a turning point in multicultural offerings when newcomers from Southeast Asia, former refugees sponsored for immigration by Mennonite churches, sold egg rolls.[51] The diversity increased exponentially. While some voices argue against the notion of "Mennonite food," I suggest the convergence of foods from different cultural traditions, all prepared by self-described Mennonite cooks, creates a site for community-building within the denominational fold, rather than alienation and exclusion.

As with many other Mennonite charitable activities, relief sales in the past were highly gendered, with men often heading up the main committees and making decisions, while women contributed the labour and produced the goods sold. The introduction of a heifer sale in 1982 was viewed as a way to "present a challenge for the men in Mennonite families," after organizers "noticed that women did most of the work" at the relief sale.[52] The labour of women to prepare food, quilts, and other handwork to sell was historically an essentialized part of their accepted and allowed roles in the church. It is largely portrayed as an altruistic aspect of Mennonite outreach to those in need – funds raised went mainly to international relief and development work. Yet, as Diane Tye argues, "Church women's production of food legitimated their position as unpaid domestic workers, who were often pressured to perform important, but invisible, work that church and community members – women included – did not recognize as work."[53] This was true whether they were organizing other women to bake hundreds of pies for the relief sale, supplying meals for church suppers and funerals, or catering a wedding. Relief sale labour was an extension of women's work in the home and in their churches, although in the twenty-first century, food production at the sales is increasingly shared by all genders, young and old.

Relief sales reflected a primary orientation of Mennonite churches and organizations toward food charity and international relief efforts. In more recent times, food justice has accompanied food charity as central to Mennonite social justice work. In addition to MCC, other non-governmental agencies such as Mennonite Economic Development Associates and the Canadian Foodgrains Bank became part of a larger church-based and secular movement of "hunger politics" that arose in the 1970s and after.[54] In this context, individual and collective action was, and is, directed at local and global food inequity and unsustainability – in effect, addressing the structural causes of hunger rather than only giving food to the needy. Some women were well ahead of their time when in 1976 they proposed a "more-with-less" response to the food crisis of that era, manifest in the popular *More-with-Less Cookbook*. The cookbook's call to eat less meat and more grains so that less global food energy would go toward feeding the rich at the expense of the poor, predated Michael Pollan's call to "eat food, not too much, mostly plants" by three decades.[55]

Appeals for food justice on the part of Mennonites emerged in diverse contexts. In the early 1970s, Black, Latino, and Native American Mennonite youth in the United States joined together to support the famous food justice movement of Cesar Chavez and the United Farm Workers by passing a resolution to boycott lettuce in solidarity with farm workers' rights.[56] This kind of activism had the potential to cause inter-Mennonite strife given that many wealthy white farmers in California were Mennonite. Furthermore, the kind of food justice activism that included boycotting and picketing grocery stores selling non-United Farm Workers food products went against traditional Mennonite stances against strikes and union participation.[57] Indeed, this case of food activism saw Mennonites somewhat divided by racial-ethnic identity and revealed the racism carried by white Mennonites.

While food charity and justice are significant components of Mennonites living out their faith and values, incorporating food into seasons of the Christian year and events in congregational life are a very different site where food and religion intersect.

Culinary Rituals

Unlike many other faith groups, Protestant Christians maintain few food-related rituals as requirements of their religious practice. Historically, this may have been especially true for groups like the Mennonites who objected to, and rejected, many sacramental rites in their daily or seasonal religious lives. The only clearly observed food-related doctrine is the communion meal. Also called the Lord's Supper, when Christians eat bread and drink wine in remembrance of Jesus' last supper with his disciples, communion is one regularized food ritual practised by Protestants.

Across the Mennonite spectrum, the Lord's Supper is celebrated twice or more in the church year. The foodstuffs consumed during communion elicit less gustatory enjoyment than friction over what is appropriate to drink and eat, and how and to whom it is served. The most heated disagreement, within church congregations and across Mennonite subgroups, is whether to serve wine – considered authentic to the biblical story – or grape juice – thought to be morally correct when alcohol consumption was viewed as sinful (as it still is for some Mennonites), or considered a better option for individuals who struggle with alcohol addiction.[58] While a traditionalist view limits communion participation to baptized adults, some liberal churches call for inclusion of non-church members, non-baptized adults, and allow children to be involved by giving them grapes and crackers, for example. The move toward accommodation of individual dietary restrictions also prompted the addition of non-gluten bread items in recent decades. The nature of the food served in a communion service has thus been a point of contention in debates over tradition versus innovation, and inclusion versus boundary-setting.

The vagaries and inclinations of local congregations, as well as Mennonites' iconoclasm and separatist impulses more broadly, has allowed for a certain creativity in celebrating the communion ritual. I recall that at one alternative Mennonite church I attended, the communion meal was coffee and hot cross buns. In one missionary's memoir, communion in India was celebrated with raisin juice with a few drops of cochineal (made from dried insects) and sugar, and chapatti bread.[59] In the Mennonite church in Japan, a traditional tea bowl might be used as a common cup in communion.[60] The richness in Mennonite and other Anabaptist cooking traditions also permeated the preparation of communion bread in some contexts. For example, Mary-Ann Kirkby says that Hutterites "quite possibly make the best communion bread in the world." Unlike the high church unleavened wafers, Hutterite communion bread is "decadent" and enriched with "cream, beaten egg whites, and extra sugar" that "tastes as creamy as a custard."[61] Regardless of the exact nature of communion bread, until recently in modern Mennonite churches, bread for communion was most often the responsibility of the church deacon's wife, the deacon looking after other logistics of the ceremony. This is another example of how women's food labour "makes church possible."[62]

Other than the communion meal, ritual food customs intrinsic to church doctrine are absent. Instead, Mennonites create their own unofficial rituals that satisfy the human need to position food in religious practice. Foodways are thus part of an "everyday faith" that makes eating sacred.[63] In this, they are not unlike the Jewish people, for whom the linkage between food and religious practice is central. Hasia R. Diner, in her study of foodways that accompanied Jewish immigrants to America at the turn of the twentieth century, observes that each holiday in the Jewish calendar called for its own special dishes, few of which had "textual sanction."[64] That is, many of the special foods prepared at times of religious holidays were not required consumption for devoted Jews, but became part of tradition, enriching sacred moments with food practices. Such connections "elevated ordinary time and ordinary lives to transcendence and bore witness to the intimate connection between sanctity and food."[65] To a lesser degree, this process of "enriching" significant religious moments with special foods also occurs for Mennonites. Indeed, the everydayness of connections between food and faith is apparent in subtle stories, such as Eleanor Hildebrand Chornoboy's description of an ancestor's bread-making: Helena sang her favourite hymns while she kneaded the dough and the children would play quietly nearby, "listening to their grandma's sacred music as she prepared the bread that she would break with her family."[66] Here, the kneading and baking of bread are signalled as a sacred ritual in and of itself, made more so by the overlay of hymn-singing.

Most culinary rituals practised by Mennonites are tied to special seasons in the Christian year. Christmas is one of these. Amish writer Marianne Jantzi states it simply: "To me Christmas is family and food."[67] In her memoir, Tena Friesen describes her mother's cooking activity for several weeks before Christmas. In her household, "traditional Christmas food" included a sauerkraut soup with dill, onion, parsley, and ketchup, along with *plumi moos*, and *kringel* – a twisted fancy flat bread.[68] Sarah Peters, from a conservative Mennonite family, recalled that food for "Christmas, Easter and Pentecost was special: dried fruit mousse [soup], boiled sausages or ham, fancy delicious cookies and the best tasty buns."[69] Sensory historians would no doubt make much of the Mennonite cookbook comment that "the fragrance of the kitchen was probably enough to kindle the Christmas spirit."[70]

The notion that Christmas equals family and food may be true across the globe. Indian Mennonite women have incorporated *anarsa*, a food for special occasions from their South Asian culture, into religious celebrations such as Christmas and Easter. On Christmas Day, before going to church, women – in the northeast region of India that I visited – cook a special meal consisting of meat, fried rice called *chutney pulao*, and sometimes *papadam* (thin cracker or flatbread). Two or three days before Christmas, they make *anarsa*. After church, families invite each other for lunch and continue to do so with neighbours and friends into the evening and night until everyone has finished eating. According to Suniti Masih, "In this way women express their gratefulness and love and share their Christmas joy with each other."[71] Similarly, Mennonites in the Mexican state of Chihauhau hosted a "parade of lights" in December 2019 in order that both Mennonites and Mexicans could celebrate Christmas in a context where both groups lived in fear of drug cartel violence. After the parade, the two groups gathered at the Mennonite museum for *tamales*, a Mexican food enjoyed by both cultures. As Rebecca Janzen suggests, events like this, which include shared foodways, serve to "traverse religious and ethnic borders."[72]

A common Christmas food in Russian Mennonite households is peppernuts (*pfeffernüsse*), small spice cookies with northern European origins. During the Christmas season, my mother always made peppernuts, either hard or soft, as did my grandmother. One of my former male colleagues baked them in mammoth batches and, as a seasonal workplace custom, they were eagerly anticipated by all of us – Mennonite or not. Now, I make them too and have learned there are as many different ways to make peppernuts as there are bakers and recipes. These Christmas-time peppernuts carry no explicit religious meaning, nor is their consumption required of a practising Mennonite, but they do link me to the cultural and also religious past of my grandparents. They add a celebratory component to events in the Christian calendar, thus allowing traditionally ritual-averse Mennonites to move beyond the solemn piety of religious practice to include material and sensory enjoyment. Their centrality to the season is suggested by Simone Horst, who comments, "To me, Christmas has well and truly arrived when the peppernuts are made."[73] The religious meaning implicit in peppernuts goes beyond the Christmas season. For example, among some Mennonites in Paraguay, peppernuts cut with a thimble were used as bread during the communion service, thus taking on a sacred character.[74]

Russian Mennonite peppernuts are not unlike the South Asian *anarsa*. I first learned about *anarsa* from a group of women in the Bihar Mennonite Mandli in India. Lily Kachhap, a leader within the Mennonite women's organization, described to me the time-consuming process of making *anarsa*, that begins with several days of soaking raw rice, then drying and grinding it finely to powder; it is then mixed with sugar or jaggery (unrefined cane sugar), and optional ingredients like coconut, nuts, or dried fruits are added. The mixture is shaped into flat or round shapes and then fried in oil.[75] I learned quickly that, as with peppernuts, there are many variations according to the style and preferences of the cook. In fact, the debates I witnessed about preparing *anarsa* were as animated as the discussions about the "authentic" way to make peppernuts at my Canadian Mennonite workplace.

One woman declared that every Christian home would have *anarsa* at Christmas, while another said that when Mennonite women began making it in the weeks of Advent, their non-Christian neighbours would come around hoping for a taste. Some sources say that *anarsa* is a traditional Hindu food associated with the festival of Diwali (festival of lights), which normally occurs in mid to late autumn. It was interesting to ponder the migration of this special treat from Hindu kitchens during Diwali to Mennonite-Christian kitchens just a few weeks later at Christmas. These Indian Mennonite women came to associate their *anarsa*-making with a religious season.[76] While peppernuts and *anarsa* are different in culture, taste,

5.2 *Anarsa*, a special food prepared by some Mennonites in India at Christmas, 2015.

and ingredients, they hold similar meaning for Mennonite women of different ethnicities.

The next food-related season in the Christian year is that of Lent and Easter. Lent, the forty days of preparation and fasting before Easter, begins with Shrove Tuesday when many Christians eat rich foods ahead of the period of fasting or abstinence from particular foods. While many Mennonites eat pancakes on what is sometimes called "pancake Tuesday" or "fat Tuesday," most Mennonites do not follow this with abstinence from oil or eggs or other rich foods for the Lenten season. Indeed, the satirical news site *The Daily Bonnet*, which pokes fun at all things Mennonite, regularly posts an article on "Reverse Lent," during which Mennonites, noted for their nonconformity with the world, "cease their regular practice of abstaining from anything pleasurable and instead take up a wide variety of unhealthy habits."[77] While this is a comical perspective, it is not without some historical accuracy. In fact, the Anabaptists in the sixteenth century participated in a movement of rebellion against the Roman Catholic church by breaking existing laws regarding fasting during Lent. In Zurich, Switzerland, in 1522, they publicly consumed sausage, an event commemorated as the *Wurstessen* (sausage-eating) affair, and re-enacted in 2022 by Mennonites across the world.[78]

Although Mennonites do not have a religious tradition of food abstinence during the forty days preceding Easter, those with ancestry in Ukraine do mark the resurrection of Jesus Christ with eating a sweet bread called *paska* (the root of the word meaning Passover) that symbolizes the breaking of the Lenten fast. This celebration of the resurrection is honoured both materially and symbolically as the egg and sugar-laden *paska* rises along with Jesus Christ. Sometimes it is baked in coffee tins so that it will be tall and seemingly reach the heavens. Sufficient rising is key to a successful *paska* and Ukrainian women had a particular prayer – *Bog na pomotsch* (God help me) – when putting the loaves in the oven to bake. Some Mennonites followed this practice of "asking for God's blessing and help in making this holy bread."[79]

Because *paska* is a difficult foodstuff to perfect, it is cause for admiration and pride – or shame, as the case may be. The decorations added to *paska* range from icing with candy sprinkles to elaborate sugar roses and doves. Historically, some bakers in Ukraine, Mennonites included, even put their *paska* in the windows for passersby to see. Still today, many Mennonite churches hold a breakfast after or prior to the Easter Sunday service. For Mennonites of Dutch-Russian ancestry, *paska* is the centrepiece of these potlucks. The inevitable comparison of who in the congregation makes the best *paska* for Easter breakfast may seem to desacralize a pivotal event in the Christian year, yet it indirectly honours the culinary role of women in bringing meaning to the moment. Now, of course, men have entered the *paska* competition. Matthew Froese began making *paska* during the Covid-19 pandemic. Unable to attend church and family gatherings, he said, "making *paska* helped me feel a little more like Easter was still happening. It still smelled and tasted like Easter." He offered that the "tactile and sensory" aspect of making and eating paska also rooted him in the traditions of his grandmother.[80]

While *paska* is a signature dish in the Russian Mennonite tradition, for Swiss Mennonites like Lorna Shantz Bergey doughnuts were the food most associated with Easter, and were often dunked in maple syrup that was fresh in early spring.[81] In the Indonesian Mennonite context, an Easter tradition is to be given a *telur bebek asin* (a salty duck egg), while at New Year's, people eat *kue keranjang* (a basket of cakes). Bread and rice are given out at Christmas.[82]

In my own ancestral tradition, the New Year was marked with *portzelky*, a deep-fried fritter with raisins. The fritters are like the Dutch *oliebollen*, thus connecting back in time to the earliest locale of the Russian Mennonite sojourn, while the name is derived from a Low German phrase meaning "tumbling over" which is what these balls of dough do when put into hot oil.[83] A New Year's Eve service was a tradition in some churches, followed by a communal meal where *portzelky* was served, as it was at home the next day after the morning church service.[84] One memoir describes New Year's *portzelky* in Ukraine being offered by Mennonites to neighbours who knocked on their doors, in keeping with a Slavic tradition that saw people go door to door offering New Year's wishes.[85] In this custom, a food exchange became a site at which Mennonites interacted with their Ukrainian neighbours outside of the regular encounters of labour and social class hierarchies. The way in which foodstuffs intermingled with religious ideas is suggested in a Low German poem recited when someone wanted the taste of a freshly made *portzelky*: "I saw your chimney smoking. / I knew what you were making. / The tasty New Year's Fritters. / Give me one – I'll stand still. / Give me two – I'll start walking. / Give me all three, four and five, / I'll wish you the Kingdom of Heaven."[86] Here, a food gift was reciprocated with a blessing from heaven.

Thanksgiving, observed in many religions and cultures, was historically an opportunity to celebrate the abundance of the agricultural harvest. Many Mennonite churches decorate their church sanctuary with a "horn of plenty" – carefully arranged vegetables and other foodstuffs that symbol abundance and gratitude. In North America, Thanksgiving is marked in the months October and November, but in India it is combined with the Christmas season since the harvest occurs in December. In this context, missionaries invited people to bring offerings to church services and, since it was "easier to give gifts in kind," food was the main form of offering and included rice, chickens, eggs, garden produce, sugar cane, and homemade sweets.[87]

The centrality of specialty foods in marking moments in the Christian year may have been more pronounced in the past when church life itself was at the centre of Mennonite communities. Indeed, in the early settlement years, the Swiss Volhynian Mennonites in Kansas were called "holiday people" by their English neighbours because they always seemed to be visiting and feasting.[88] "Holiday" foods also serve as a reminder of poignant events in history, such as the anecdote about refugee women baking peppernuts in Berlin. In cultural contexts where Mennonites are a minority as Christians or because of their ethnicity/nationality, they may adopt food practices of their surroundings – whether because such practices are appreciated or because Mennonites wish to "fit in." While particular foodstuffs reflect common regional or national cuisine, when they are incorporated into the seasonal life of Mennonite churches, they become ritualized. This can be localized to individual churches. Ellery Penner describes one example of localization in Indonesia: "A special food in the community is *tumpeng* (cone-shaped rice). It is eaten every year in April, in celebration of the church's birthday. Every three months there is a potluck party at church. People bring snacks such as bread, fried bananas, fried treats (known as *gorengan*), fruit, and cookies. This tradition is specific to their church; each church does things differently."[89]

While there are specific foods that Mennonites prepared to coincide with moments of the church year, I can't identify any foods that Mennonites explicitly restricted. Although there are many jokes, in reference to culinary blandness, about Mennonites resisting spices, herbs, or flavour! Indeed, writer Jan Braun jokingly describes Mennonite cooking as "endless iterations of butter, flour, potatoes, and meat."[90] In one memoir, the story is told about a couple who, upon becoming "deadly sick" after a pig butchering, believed that God was telling them not to eat pork, as was indicated in the Old Testament. They abstained for the rest of their lives, although their children eventually did eat pork.[91] One of my uncles became a vegetarian after witnessing his neighbour butchering a pig. As a child, I thought him very unusual for this practice, which was unfamiliar at the time. Indeed, meat was a central foodstuff in a Mennonite diet, as the sausage-eating affair of 1522 suggests. Norma Jost Voth writes that "Mennonites were great pork eaters"[92] and references a popular Mennonite Low German saying: "He thinks highly of short prayers and long sausages."[93] However, one nineteenth-century treatise by Peter Wiens, a Mennonite teacher in Russia who studied naturopathy, strongly criticized Mennonites for their unhealthy diet overall, but especially their love for pork, offering that God made a good decision in forbidding the Israelites to eat pork. Wiens said, "if we followed this practice we most certainly would be happier."[94]

While contemporary Mennonites might fast on occasion, mainly for health or ethical reasons, or even during the weeks of Lent, this was by and large not part of their dietary history. Indeed, religious fasting, particularly abstinence from meat on particular days of the week, was rejected by Protestants already during the Reformation era.[95] One woman, however, recalled that, in her desperation to experience religious conversion and assurance that she was "saved," decided to fast, only drinking water and homemade Postum (brand name for a roasted grain coffee substitute, much like *prips*). For her this was a form of "punishment" for her sins; her fast lasted only a week and ended when the "Holy Spirit" spoke to her in the outhouse.[96] Another woman, a Mennonite missionary in India in the early twentieth century, fasted on the day she received a letter from her twin sister in the aftermath of the Bolshevik revolution of 1917. The sister wrote about the hardships of starvation and violence saying, "Both the Reds and the Whites let us starve."[97]

While nonconformity, unworldliness, and plainness were, and are, required of many Anabaptist-Mennonite groups in varying degrees, as tangible manifestations of religious ideals, this was not applied to food. Indeed, the irony of Mennonites' reputation for food abundance (even excess) alongside repudiation of most other "sins of the flesh" was not lost on some observers. In the early twentieth century, journalist Victoria Hayward visited Mennonite homes in southern Manitoba and remarked on their rich diet: "The Mennonites are not vegetarians like the 'Douks' [Doukhobors] but eat meat of all kinds, and fish. Macaroni, homemade, is a staple dish, also noodle soup. But plemm-moase [sic], a sort of pudding-soup made of stewed fruit, prunes, raisins, etc., thickened with flour, seems to be the national dish. And their cottage-cheese dumplings served with cream and melted butter, made a dish fit for a king. There were other good things to eat, chickens, eggs, fried crabapples, etc." Hayward then commented that "the Mennonites may be a plainly dressed people, but they certainly live well as to food."[98] Hildegard Martens's 2018 memoir also points to the contradiction between her mother's emphasis on "good food" and her need to "adopt the anti-pleasure stance of the church."[99] It is possible that, since plain and uniform dress codes existed in various Mennonite subgroups, as well as among the Amish and Hutterites, women were drawn to richness, and sometimes fanciness, in their food production.

Food as a subtext in the Christian message gives women a sense that they preside over the sacred, especially in the past when their ecclesial roles were limited. Because food preparation is often within the female realm of household activity, food-related rituals can provide women with a special and sacred space and role within their religious community. Other ceremonial events, not part of the Christian year yet an intrinsic part of religious practice in which food is a central feature, include weddings and funerals. Here too, women in Mennonite contexts played a significant role. And while there are no specific food requirements for these events, custom, culture, and church are interconnected in the creation of long-held assumptions of "how things are done."

My mother-in-law considered a wedding meal without two meats and several desserts hardly proper. When we attended a wedding reception in her community – a stand-up affair with only raw vegetables, tiny sandwiches, and squares – she declared the couple not really married at all! So that when planning my own wedding, I was less worried about my in-laws' reaction when they learned I was not taking their family surname than I was about what the meal would be. In other communities, a standardized menu for weddings and funerals existed, even if there was no particular rationale for it, beyond custom. According to Karen M. Johnson-Weiner, Amish wedding meals in Lancaster County, Pennsylvania, include a casserole of chicken and stuffing, along with mashed potatoes and gravy, as well as "creamed celery, cabbage, applesauce, dinner rolls, peaches and pears, 'Indiana salad' (green Jell-O with pineapples, cream and Cool Whip), donuts, and pies."[100] *Kringel* – deep-fried bread twists or twisted buns – appear at weddings, funerals, and family gatherings of Low German-speaking Mennonites;[101] perhaps they are saved for these special times because they are so labour-intensive. Subgroups modify a menu in order to differentiate themselves and set boundaries, or to cater to preferences that evolve over time. Along with specific foods, producing a wedding meal could involve ritualistic behaviour such as when and how particular food items were prepared, and by whom. One Mennonite cookbook that reflects on the role of food in church life, observes that dating rituals included couples serving coffee and tea together at wedding meals, as a way of matchmaking perhaps, but also to mimic the bridal couple.[102]

Over time, changes in food-related technology had an impact on weddings. In conservative communities, once electricity was allowed and refrigerators and freezers entered homes, a longer wedding season became possible since large quantities of food could be kept cold and thus weddings could be planned outside of a busy harvest season.[103] The move away from agrarian living for all kinds of Mennonites meant that food for weddings was, and is, increasingly outsourced from households to commercial caterers and businesses. Even though a bridal couple's families may no longer produce and prepare much of the wedding meal in the twenty-first century, some communities maintain an event-specific menu.

Even more so than at weddings, the particular foods called for at the funerals I attended as a child seemed to hold a near ritualistic place in the overall service. Funeral foods, whatever they might be, are not in themselves sacred, yet, as Sandra M. Gilbert proposes, "even while addressing ordinary bodily needs, the secular has a kind of ritual function on such an occasion."[104] In my Russian Mennonite tradition, raisin bread was always served at funerals. Swiss Mennonites and Amish frequently refer to "funeral mustard."[105] Among Old Order Mennonites in Ontario, a particular funeral cuisine exists but has changed over time. Old Order church member Nancy Martin recalled that while pies were funeral food in her grandmother's era, in the present "bread, buns, and orange-flavoured cookies" are standard fare, along with applesauce, and cabbage slaw and pickles.[106] Among the Ontario David Martin/Independent Old Order Mennonites (who are most separatist), the funeral meal also includes creamed potatoes and dried apples with stewed prunes.[107] Yet another conservative group has a slightly different meal; according to Marion Roes, the Old Order Amish funeral meal is "usually potato salad, cold meats and bread for sandwiches, coffee and water," and dessert of some kind.[108] Yet other churches have only simple meals of bread and buns with coffee. For example, Tena Friesen recalls a "traditional funeral *Vaspa*" of buns, sugar cubes, and coffee in her Old Colony church in northern Alberta.[109]

There is no clear reason why these foods are specific to funerals, other than they make for light meals but are substantial enough to sustain travellers. While sources often point to a sameness in funeral meals, the menu varies in different contexts, suggesting that Mennonite subgroups, congregations, and even families create their own funeral meal traditions. It is common for families to request particular foods that are favourites of the deceased. At the funerals of my parents-in-law, a German cake called *bienenstich* (bee sting) was requested by the family as homage to their mother and father. Rituals of menu also exist in traditionalist communities that host home-based church services. The reason for this, proposes Johnson-Weiner, is that "a standard menu, like uniform dress and Ordnung [Rule of Order] restrictions on household furnishings, serves as a symbol of the community, helps reduce any temptation to show off, and limits the amount of time and effort meal preparation might otherwise take."[110]

In rural communities up to the mid-twentieth century, preparing food for the funeral meal was a communally shared ritual. In her memoir, Hilda J. Born observed that neighours "try to share the grief" by cleaning the yard of the deceased and by bringing ingredients for bun dough to the "afflicted home" where they were mixed and then distributed back to homes for baking.[111] The role of food as a response to the grief inherent in death and funerals is not unique to Mennonites, but the communal nature of Mennonite church life, along with the importance of food itself, reinforces this linkage. For example, Mennonite pastor Renee Sauder describes the food she received and prepared in response to deaths of family members, and also her recollection of church funerals: "When someone dies, you cook. But bereavement is not the time for exotic recipes. It's a time for the familiar, the traditional, for what is easy to prepare." Hence, funeral food, in its simplicity and familiarity, is also "comfort food." Sauder also suggests that, "food shared in the midst of sorrow allows for a moment of respite, of grace."[112] The rituals of funeral food, along with the practice of bringing food to the family of the deceased, point to the "indispensable role of ritual in reinforcing community."[113]

Community and Commensality

Gathering to share a meal after a funeral is an acknowledgment that the deceased is no longer at the table, pointing to the centrality of eating *together*. The idea, practice, and importance of eating together is part of every culture and religion. Food historian Jeffrey M. Pilcher says that "commensality, the sharing of food and drink, forges bonds of group identity." With the decline of regular shared meals in modern times, ceremonial and celebratory mealtimes, such as Thanksgiving and Christmas, he proposes, "carry even greater emotional weight."[114] Writer Connie T. Braun states this idea evocatively when she says, "Food imparts the flavor of belonging."[115] When people eat together, they obtain a sense of belonging, at least most of the time; for people

5.3   Mennonite church meal, Reedley, California, 1960s.

with eating disorders or restrictions, eating with others may induce discomfort or estrangement. Eating together in a church context elevates the religious meaning of gathering. Indeed, Daniel Sack observes that American Protestants go to church "not for the doctrine or the ethics, but for the community – a community usually built and sustained around food."[116] Eating together and thereby building community is perhaps the most important way in which food and religion come together for Mennonites.

The Mennonite practice of commensality is directly related to the high ideals they hold for notions of community. At the Mennonite post-secondary institution where I taught, community was called the "C-word" – sometimes derisively but mostly with affection – because of the strong emphasis placed on it as an activity and a value. Community is intrinsic to Mennonite religious practice because, from early manifestations as an idealized egalitarian movement, the Anabaptists aimed to read and understand the Bible together. They viewed the church as people gathered together, practising their beliefs as a collective, rather than as individuals. This value is common across Mennonite subgroups and global locations. For example, Hendy Stevan Matahelemual, who worked as a minister in both Indonesia and the United States, says, "North American and Indonesian Anabaptists have in common ... our sense of community. We build our lives around the community, and food is an important part of this."[117] He proposes that cross-cultural food exchange is central to the religious work of reconciliation across divides.

While food commensality was, and is, important in church settings, other sites of gathering were equally important for Mennonites, especially historically. Historian Frieda Esau Klippenstein comments, "In actual healthy, kin-based, rural Mennonite communities such as could be found in southern Manitoba or in Ontario, Mennonitism had more to do with functioning, intertwined family-centered communities than with churches as institutions."[118] Over time, Mennonites developed what has been termed the "social congregation," a religious community with social programs that promoted cohesion within the church and also attracted members away from increasing entertainment opportunities in secular society.[119] The increasing number of church suppers, usually prepared and served by what were called women's auxiliaries, as well as potluck meals where everyone contributed, resulted in a "boom time" for the construction of kitchen additions at churches in the later twentieth century.[120]

The value of community itself, whether focused on food consumption or not, is a core "belief" for some Mennonites. Ideas and ideals of community pervade Daniel Shank Cruz's study of queer Mennonite literature, even if the institutional Mennonite church "community" has frequently rejected queer Mennonites.[121] Karen Allen, who immigrated to Canada from South Africa, and is of English and Welsh ethnic heritage, experienced the dilemma of being an outsider in conversation about traditional Russian Mennonite foods, such as "schmaundt fat (cream gravy) and farmer's sausage." Yet, it was the "great comfort in being swept along with the communal aspect of this culture" that drew Allen to a Mennonite church community.[122] Elaine

Enns, in listing the "key church practices" of her Mennonite ancestors that she embraces, includes "table fellowship," which functioned to nurture "values of inclusion and abundance" and also was "a space for instruction as a child, and remembering as an adult."[123]

Mennonite practices of gathering at a meal could offer implicit meaning about identity, even if unintended. For example, in a study about the "Mennonite Dinner" or "Mennomeal" – a four decades-long college community ritual in Wheaton, Illinois – the authors propose that the weekly dinner became "emblematic of what being Mennonite means in a context where Mennonites are little known."[124] In the United Kingdom, theologian Andrew Davis found that, in contrast to other denominations, within Anabaptist circles, "sharing meals was seen as vital to developing discipleship" – the belief in following Jesus' example.[125] Cookbook author Jo Snyder commented that, although she had not attended church in decades, one of the beliefs she maintained from her Mennonite upbringing was a "'Big Tent' philosophy – gathering people around the table and serving up 'kindness, nourishment and a sense of belonging.'"[126] And, in an article about an Ontario Mennonite man's "ministry" of baking and sharing butter tarts, Barb Draper concludes that "connecting with others and building community work well when there is food to share."[127] While there is no Mennonite precept that correlates religious observance with commensality, subliminal linkages between Mennonites and food, along with emphasis, almost to the point of requirement, on building community, has led to the embedded notion that eating together is what Mennonites "do."

Some manifestations of commensality occur within the church institution itself. In many congregations, potluck meals are akin to religious observance. According to one source, potluck advocates consider them the equivalent of the communion meal in a modern era.[128] One observer described potlucks as "complex social interactions,"[129] at which people, often women, were tested for the popularity and acceptability of their contributions. For individuals without a Mennonite ancestral background, potlucks could be "intimidating" and "scary" because of high expectations of what

5.4 Potluck meal at Rajnandgaon Mennonite Church, India, 2015.

was suitable to bring.[130] In my own household, there have been half-serious conversations about whether to switch congregations because of the quality of the potlucks. Potluck meals are not limited to any one Mennonite tradition, nor even to Mennonites. When visiting Mennonite churches in India in 2015, I was the guest of honour at a potluck meal following the evening service; I was struck by my familiarity, not with the dishes themselves, but rather with the patterns of conversation, the variety of foods put out, and the manner in which the cooks (both men and women) talked about each other's contributions. When churches closed during the Covid-19 pandemic, I dare say adherents missed the potluck gatherings as much as, if not more than, the in-person church services. Commensality just doesn't work on a Zoom platform. Whether in the context of a potluck meal or not, the success of church congregations was directly related to the membership's practice of gathering together to build community, more often than not over food. Describing her mother's prolific baking activity for church functions, Diane Tye says, "Sharing a cup of tea and a sweet made congregations more cohesive and helped build communities."[131] The food was not an extraneous element to church life, but in fact allowed communal relationships to occur at all.

Commensality is perhaps best displayed in conservative Mennonite subgroups where there is no differentiation between the church, the community, and extended family networks. Among separatist groups such as the Old Order or Old Colony Mennonites, church and community overlap and might be considered indistinguishable. In these settings, eating together is part of the everyday rhythms of life, yet also part of unique customs and traditions. I recall attending a service at an Old Order Mennonite meetinghouse, after which I was invited to a member's home for the noon meal. This was part of a custom whereby households in the district where a Sunday service was held were prepared for guests who were not formally invited yet expected to arrive. I was fascinated by the way the hostess prepared the table for the meal; she had a cupboard with numerous boards to enlarge the table for up to twenty people, and rolls of plastic table covers cut to lengths appropriate to the many table setting options. She was ready for a group of five or twenty, or more! This practice suggested to me that hospitality and commensality were as much part of Sunday as a sacred day as was the meetinghouse (church) service itself.[132]

Food was central to, and indeed fuelled, community-based practices such as barn-raisings and pig butcherings. Pig butchering was a communal activity, sometimes described as a ritual, that is discussed at length in numerous memoirs and community histories.[133] Norma Jost Voth says that Mennonites developed their love for pork and the custom of community butcherings in sixteenth-century Prussia; indeed, the Vistula Delta where Mennonites lived was called the "lard pot" or "grease" pot.[134] Detailed accounts of butchering "bees" appearing in many family and local histories, as well as cookbooks, address the important aspect of community gathering, apart from the stores of food that result. Historian Catherine Wilson has analyzed rural work bees as "not only an economic and social exchange but also a process through which shared values and a collective identity were created and communicated."[135] In her memoir, Marlene Plett said the butchering bee was "an example of how to build up rather than tear down a community."[136]

In a typical butchering bee, several households joined together for the day, with men, women, and children all given gender and age-specific roles. Children were often exempt from school for the day. In her memoir, Helen Reimer Loewen describes in detail the tasks at a pig butchering, saying "it was almost a celebration."[137] Tena Friesen's 500-page autobiography has an entire chapter devoted to the pig-butchering bee, describing it as a "Mennonite tradition" and a "very important and exciting day" on the mid-twentieth-century Canadian prairies.[138] Similarly, Eleanor Hildebrand Chornoboy's folkloric compilation has a section on "Butchering Bees" that offers a detailed account of the highly ritualized event – the cleaning of the utensils, preparing of food for participants, the slaughter of the pig, and cutting of the carcass from the bone. The end result was that "a pig running around on all four trotters was turned into bacon, ham, *Jreewe* (crackings), farmer sausage, liver sausage, ribs, and pork roasts."[139]

Butchering was a highly communal activity, one memoir noting that "typical Mennonite co-operation is shown at this time."[140] According to one account of hog butchering in the Mennonite community on Pelee Island, Ontario, up to five families came together on what was described as "an exciting day for the family." Early in the morning, the 500-pound hog was killed, bled, then hung from a tree to remove organs and begin carving. Later the carcass was laid on a long wooden table and the men carved the meat to produce sausage, ham, lard, headcheese, pickled meat, and spare ribs. After the noon meal, sausage was ground and put into the clean intestines, while other parts of the animal were boiled in the giant cauldron in order to render as much lard as possible. Everyone – male and female, old

5.5   Pig Butchering, Ukraine, c1910.

and young – had a task and role to play.[141] While very communal in nature, butchering bee tasks were clearly delineated by gender. Called "frolics" among the Amish, butchering a pig or cow saw men doing the killing, dressing, and smoking, while women processed the meat into jars or as sausage, or prepared small cuts for smoking or freezing.[142]

The community aspect of the event was enhanced by eating as well as producing pork products together. Breakfast was ready when the workers arrived and might include "coffee with fresh cream; homemade raspberry, strawberry, rhubarb, and Saskatoon jams, made from the summer's harvest, and freshly baked buns."[143] The noon meal itself meant significant labour for women and might consist of "roast chicken or roast duck, potatoes, pickles and a dessert of *Obstmoos* [fruit soup], pies, or thick rice with cinnamon and sugar." The break in late afternoon typically offered "coffee, *Zwieback* and peppernut cookies."[144] At the end of the day, the shared meal included outputs from the day – liver sausage, fresh ribs, and cracklings, the little meat bits that float to the top when lard is rendered in the cauldron.[145] This is an example of a butchering bee in a Russian Mennonite community, but comparable gatherings occurred historically in Swiss Mennonite settings and today in places like rural India or the Democratic Republic of Congo. At a large church gathering I attended in the latter country, a cow, goat, or ox was slaughtered each day and prepared right on the site of the meetings.

Commensality was not without political meaning, in past and present. It could serve to diminish conflictual relationships within a community or counter church practices that explicitly divided people within the group. Reflecting on the meaning of communal eating within Hutterite colonies, Mary-Ann Kirkby quotes a member who said, "'It's darn hard to have three meals a day with someone you have a grudge against.'"[146] Theologian Irma Fast Dueck gave an account of the communion tradition as remembered from her childhood years in southern Manitoba. In preparation for the communion meal on Sunday, her mother would bring a jar of *borscht* to other church members, as a way of "making things right" with people in the fellowship before taking communion with them. As the remembered tradition went, if the jar was returned empty, the giver would know that "all was well" in the relationship; however, if the jar was returned still full of soup, there was more work to be done.[147] The incorporation of food-related customs into relationship-building is widespread across the Mennonite spectrum. In the Mennonite church in Japan, the inclusion of the traditional Japanese tea ceremony helps to realize "mutuality and reciprocity" while prioritizing the group over the individual.[148]

However, commensality was challenged when Mennonites opted for strict church discipline practices that included placing excommunicated individuals under the ban or shunning them for violating church rules. Extreme forms of shunning meant no social or business interaction with individuals who had broken church rules. Thus, even while couples remained married (divorce being a sin and disallowed), social contact with the banned party was not allowed. Wilhelmine Reimer's husband, Jakob, was put under the ban in late nineteenth-century Manitoba and she was instructed to avoid and shun him, but she could "prepare his food and place it where he can receive it."[149]

Eating together and showing hospitality through food could also function as a political statement of inclusion. Writer Kerry Fast interviewed individuals participating in the 2016 Pride event in the historically Mennonite town of Steinbach, Manitoba. The offering of a traditional Russian Mennonite menu – *borscht*, bread, *rollkuchen*, and watermelon – was one way for a Steinbach family to demonstrate a "complex, politicized hospitality; it was also a way for them to demonstrate that 'Mennonite' and being welcoming of LGBTQ people were not incompatible." Acknowledging that Mennonite beliefs and theology were often used to justify a position of condemnation and exclusion, foodways, "as a stand-in for Mennonite culture, could be the first step in communicating the capacity of Mennonite faith and church life to be inclusive," according to the host.[150]

The pleasure of eating together, the preparation of holiday foods during the religious season, and the calling to bring relief to those with food insecurity serve, I argue, to unite Mennonites, at least symbolically, even more than their common religious beliefs. At a food sale, Mennonites from diverse backgrounds and with diverse languages, histories, cultural customs, and worship practices find common ground. While their congregational life remains separate, their food life has come together. It is in the intentional planning for and preparation of traditional cultural foods at specific times of the year that Mennonites are immersed in the everyday spirituality of Advent and Lent, within an overall religious framework that is otherwise minimalist in sensory expression and experience. Eating together, essential to authentic community, is as much a part of religious practice as prayer and hymn-singing, although it is often considered tangential to doctrine and theology.

Conclusion

In the end, I return to the question posed in the introduction: what does it mean to "eat like a Mennonite"? Ultimately, the answer to that question accords with the multiple identities of the eater – their ancestral history, their gender, their global location, their socio-economic class, their family traditions, and their own personal dietary likes and dislikes. Asking the question how to eat like a Mennonite is an inconvenient one. Some will laugh. Some will be indignant. Some will contest the idea at all. Nevertheless, in light of the popular perceptions about Mennonites, in their own eyes and in those of "outsiders," it seems a necessary question to consider.

It is necessary because, despite the advance of social-historical scholarship on Mennonites and related groups, there is more work to be done on the importance of domestic space, cultural change, and everyday religious practice in the past and present lives of individuals who identify with these groups. The field of food studies itself would benefit from greater attention to religion and ethnicity, not as quaint culinary categories but as dynamic and evolving forces in how and what people eat. I hope this specific study contributes to such inquiries. Studies of ethno-religious groups often take the duality of ethnicity and religion as a given whereby these categories exist in conflict or complementarity with each other. This field too must incorporate human behaviour that goes beyond fixed cultural characteristics and patriarchal institutions, and instead acknowledges the overlapping existence of ethnic and religious identities.

The category of "Mennonite food" must be deconstructed and reimagined, even though it should not be discarded altogether, in my opinion. Mennonites of Russian and Swiss ancestry did not create or own any foodstuffs, or very few, but appropriated aspects of their cuisine from surrounding cultures. There is no singular culinary category of "Mennonite food," even while the label is applied widely, by the general public and by Mennonites themselves. Yet, Mennonite food has become a category of analysis based on food adoptions, adaptations, and attitudes, in different times and places, that evolve according to preferences and styles within subgroups and households, and that are preserved or forgotten and possibly reclaimed across generations.

What constitutes "Mennonite food" first of all results from the climate, the soil, the plants, the animals, and the humans that Anabaptist-Mennonite groups encountered as they migrated across the globe, for many reasons, to new environments. When Mennonites brought one foodstuff from a past cultural environment to a new settlement context, that unfamiliar foodstuff became known as Mennonite food. An example would be eating *portzelky* (Dutch) or *vereniki* (Ukrainian) in Paraguay. Or eating Dutch apple pie in Ontario, Canada. Or eating *queso menonita* in Mexico. At the same time, they adopted, adapted, and absorbed foodstuffs and foodways from these new environments into their own diets. Sometimes, hitherto unfamiliar foods and methods of preparation became new and central features of Mennonite cuisine. Alternately, existing foodways changed and adapted as new ingredients were introduced to familiar recipes. Varying degrees of separation and group cohesion on the part of Mennonites encouraged the development of these specialized food identities. These food adaptations were, of course, shaped by embedded prejudice on the part of Mennonites toward the cultures they encountered and sometimes displaced or dominated. Thus, inequalities and differential status were also applied to foodways, although new cuisines were easier for Mennonites to incorporate than most other cultural traits.

Furthermore, the notion of "Mennonite food," long defined by historic Swiss and Russian categories, is of necessity challenged by the incorporation of other ethnicities under the Anabaptist-Mennonite umbrella. The idea that Congolese *foufou* or northern Indian *anarsa* or Laotian-Canadian spring rolls could be Mennonite continues to prompt fresh answers to the question. In these contexts, food practices are more closely related to seasonal religious ritual, or food charity, than they are to cultural uniqueness. What the pluralism of Mennonite ethnic and cultural identity indicates is that Mennonite foodways are significant not only because of their continuity over time, but exactly because they have evolved and adapted when interacting with other cultures or when they emerge from new national contexts altogether. Acknowledging the centrality of both food and spiritual traditions in the lives of virtually everyone may prompt an embrace of the idea that religion and culture are constantly interacting.

Along with adoptions and adaptations of specific foodstuffs and foodways, the idea of Mennonite eating practices must be analyzed with regard to attitudes. The dramatic contrast between abundance and starvation that is lived experience for some Mennonites shapes their emotional and behavioural relationship with food. A yearning for abundance, sometimes to the point of obsession, may exist exactly because food deprivation is within recent memory or is even lived reality. Eating habits and outlooks are closely related to how food, and those who prepare it, are remembered, whether those memories arise from nostalgia or trauma. More work is needed to explore and elevate the disjuncture between stereotypical Mennonite food abundance and the attitudes of individuals with eating disorders or food dislikes and restrictions.

The notion of Mennonite food is also a bodily response, indeed a reaction, on the part of Mennonites themselves to the need for religious ritual and practice that is otherwise limited in their church lives. Food obsession fills the emptiness created by the plainness and simplicity that seemed to go with humility, at least historically. Pride in food was not condemned, unlike pride in physical appearance, clothing and adornment, artistry of many kinds, houses and vehicles, or wealth. While simplicity in attitude and materiality – the more-with-less ideal – is a commendable Mennonite trait, embraced especially by post-pandemic and environmental calls for less consumption, such a demeanour can leave a void. The human desire for beauty, personal and communal artistry, and religious practice that is not only words and deeds but is "felt" and "sensed," has led to the inclusion of foodways with spiritual meaning into household and church life. Vocal music, especially hymn-singing, also functions this way, but that is a topic for a different study.

Curiosity about Mennonite food may actually be on the rise, as more and more Mennonites themselves, especially non-traditionalists, are less engaged with religious or institutional manifestations of that identity, but want to retain or develop connections with their cultural and ancestral roots. Furthermore, the food practices and food businesses of conservative Mennonites are increasingly attractive in a post-Covid-19 environment where many people are seeking food security, sustainability, and self-sufficiency in a localized context. The idea that food produced by such Mennonites is healthy, wholesome, and unprocessed contributes to a notion that an identity-based cuisine exists. As well, the strong desire for personal connections and communal belonging within society as a whole, also enhanced by the experience of pandemic isolation, highlights the value of commensality – eating together in community – a long-held central practice for Mennonites. The persistence and popularity of cookbook literature that is in some manner identified as Mennonite reinforces all of these trends.

This book is about Mennonites, but it is also about food. I hope that it compels readers – Mennonite and not – to think intentionally about the food we eat, why some foods are special to us, why some foods are disagreeable to us, why we eat certain foods at certain times, and what are the cultural origins of foods we think are "ours." When we eat, all our multi-layered identities come together and create individual responses shaped by physical realities, ancestral histories, gendered selves, and socio-economic situations. We indeed are what we eat.

Notes

Introduction

1 Staebler, *Sauerkraut and Enterprise*, 27–8.
2 Barkman, *Mennonite Heritage Village*, 11.
3 Braun, *A Village Saga*, 121.
4 Friesen, *Pushing Through Invisible Barriers*, xiii.
5 *The Daily Bonnet* website, accessed 15 July 2019, https://dailybonnet.com/. In 2023 *The Daily Bonnet* changed its name to *The Unger Review*, https://www.ungerreview.com/.
6 Plett, *I Am a Mennonite*.
7 The Buggywhip IPA is produced by Abe Erb Brewing Company, named after a Mennonite settler in Waterloo, Ontario; see https://abeerb.com/. The reference to the Amish ale is from Weaver, *As American as Shoofly Pie*, 172. This book will not offer an analysis of Mennonites and alcohol; see the special issue of *Preservings*, 43 (2021).
8 Johnson-Weiner, *The Lives of Amish Women*, 114. The Amish, most numerous in the United States, are closely related to Mennonites in origins, beliefs, and practices.
9 Weaver, *As American as Shoofly Pie*, 174.
10 Burtt, "Growing Organic," 14.
11 Williams, "Eat Like a Mennonite."
12 Although my book title does not relate directly to Julia Kasdorf's essay "Writing Like a Mennonite," I want to acknowledge the similarity in titles. Eating, like writing, is an activity that allows Mennonites to express memories that are often silenced. See Kasdorf, *The Body and the Book*, 167–89.
13 Redekop, *Making Believe*, 73.

14 St George, "North West Mounted Police Report," 88.
15 Voth, *Mennonite Foods and Folkways*, 1: 295–6.
16 See, for example, Wiebe, "On the Mennonite-Métis Borderland," 111–26.
17 Neufeldt, "Settler Colonial Conscripts," 1–19.
18 For information about Mennonites worldwide, see Mennonite World Conference website: https://mwc-cmm.org/. The five-volume *Global Mennonite History Project*, with a volume for each continent, provides detailed overviews of these migration and mission histories.
19 Scholarship on diverse aspects of food proliferated in almost all fields of study from the 1980s onward. In the Canadian historical context, see the introduction and essays in Iacovetta, Korinek, and Epp, *Edible Histories, Cultural Politics*.
20 Coppolino, "Telling Afro-Caribbean Stories."
21 Plakias, *Thinking Through Food*, 34.
22 Fischler, "Food, Self and Identity," 279.
23 Diner, *Hungering for America*, 10.
24 Bertram, "Icelandic Cake Fight," 28.
25 Lorenzkowski, *Sounds of Ethnicity*, 35.
26 Petö, "Food-Talk," 152–64.
27 Gabaccia, *We Are What We Eat*.
28 Martin, "What Is the Spirit Saying," 6.
29 Goossen, "The Pacifist Roots of an American Nazi."
30 Epp, "I Am from the Mennonites," 34.
31 Warren Belasco, quoted in Diner, foreword, *Feasting and Fasting*, 11.
32 Brandt, "In Praise of Hybridity," 130.
33 Hinojosa, "From Goshen to Delano," 201–12.
34 Hinojosa, *Latino Mennonites*, x.
35 Montanari, *Food Is Culture*, 140.
36 Quoted in Klassen-Wiebe, "Minority Mennonites," 25. *Schmaunt fat* (correct spelling) is a rich pork-based gravy made with cream that is common in Russian Mennonite cooking.
37 Desjardins and Desjardins, "The Role of Food," 78.
38 Dueck, *Negotiating Sexual Identities*, 26.
39 Cruz, *Queering Mennonite Literature*, 8.
40 Dueck, *Menno Moto*.
41 Janzen, *Mennonite in a Little Black Dress*, 106.
42 Hossack, video of lecture in Mennonite/s Writing Series at Conrad Grebel University College, Waterloo, Ontario, 7 March 2012.
43 Harder, *Mostly Mennonite*, 239–40. *Zwieback*, a two-layered white bread bun, and *rollkuchen*, deep-fried fritters, are both traditional Russian Mennonite foods.

44 Rempel, *Letters of a Mennonite Couple*, 237.
45 Weier, "Where Am I Now?"
46 Frayne, "Saving Grace," 4, 8.
47 Yoder and Huff, "The Best Education Happens around the Table," 137.
48 Hinojosa, *Latino Mennonites*, 86.
49 Ibid., ix.
50 Francis, "Food in the Contemporary UK Anabaptist Movement," 11–31.
51 Klassen, "Worscht Bits," 12.
52 Redekop, *Making Believe*, 10.
53 For recent scholarship on Mennonites and identity, see especially the essays in Zacharias, *After Identity*.
54 Klassen, "What's Bre(a)d in the Bone," 242.
55 Exploring the relationship between food and memory also connects to the growing field of sensory and embodied history. See, for instance, Smith, *Sensing the Past*. See also Thomson, "Psychologists Explain Why Food Memories Can Feel So Powerful."
56 See my chapter, "The Semiotics of Zwieback."
57 Jones-Gailani, *Transnational Identity*, 84.
58 Hamilton, "This Year, Baking Ukrainian Easter Bread Feels Different."
59 I explore these themes in "'The Dumpling in My Soup Was Lonely Just Like Me.'"
60 Michelle, "More-with-Much-Less."
61 For numerous references to foodoir literature, see Gilbert, *The Culinary Imagination*.
62 Chornoboy, *Katarina*.
63 Zacharias, "Learning Sauerkraut."
64 See for example, Kasdorf, "When Our Women Go Crazy"; Waltner-Toews, *The Complete Tante Tina*.
65 *MennoNeechie Kitchen*, https://mennoneechiekitchen.com/.
66 "About Anna," *Mennopolitan*, www.mennonpolitan.com.
67 Borrowing from Mehta, "Toronto's Multicultured Tongues," 158. See also Fleishman, "Gender, the Personal, and the Voice of Scholarship"; Iacovetta, "Post-Modern Ethnography."
68 Iacovetta, "Post-Modern Ethnography," 283.
69 On Mennonites and agriculture, see especially Loewen, *Mennonite Farmers*.
70 For various articles about Mennonites as "A People of Diversity," see the special issue of *Journal of Mennonite Studies* 37 (2019), including my article "Cookbook as Metaphor for A People of Diversity."
71 "A Call to Cook," *Historians Cooking the Past*. I contributed a blog post titled "Where There's Zwieback, There's Hope," 9 April 2020.

Chapter One

1. Interview with Maria Martens by the author, 4 May 2012, Aylmer, Ontario.
2. Menu, Family Kitchen.
3. Ibid.
4. Del Rios Family Restaurant.
5. Menu, Pizza Haven.
6. For detail about these migrations, see, for example, Loewen, *Village among Nations*.
7. Plakias, *Thinking Through Food*, 50.
8. Many food studies scholars analyze notions of food hybridity. See, for example, Mehta, "Toronto's Multicultured Tongues"; Gabaccia, *We Are What We Eat*.
9. Brandt, "In Praise of Hybridity," 131.
10. Vallely, "The Jain Plate," 13.
11. Kaufman, *Melting Pot of Mennonite Cookery*.
12. Voth, *Mennonite Foods and Folkways*, 1:177. In volume 2 of *Mennonite Foods and Folkways*, Voth notes that some Mennonites also preferred *borscht* with beets (166).
13. Zacharias, "Learning Sauerkraut," 109.
14. Urry, "Mennonites, Migrations and Cookbooks," 4.
15. Klassen, *Mennonites in Early Modern Poland & Prussia*, 70–1. See also Thiesen, "Mennonite Nectar."
16. Weaver, "Food Acculturation," 421. See his longer study *As American as Shoofly Pie*.
17. Hostetler, *Amish Society*, 162.
18. *Pennsylvania-German Foodways*, 1.
19. Weaver, *As American as Shoofly Pie*, 25. Weaver adopts the common practice of replacing the term "German" with "Dutch."
20. Fehderau, *A Mennonite Estate Family*, 74. The humorous and satiric Mennonite news website *The Daily Bonnet* has published numerous pieces on the practice of spitting sunflower seeds, called *knackzoat* in the Low German dialect.
21. Fuchs, *Beauty and Sustenance*, 12.
22. Swartz, *Stories Our Mothers Told*, 45.
23. Ibid., 159.
24. See Kostash, *The Doomed Bridegroom*.
25. Interview quoted in Carl-Klassen and Klassen, "Rebels, Exiles, and Bridge Builders," 179.
26. Graber, "Immigrant Cooking in Mexico."

27 Interview by the author with Maria Martens, 4 May 2012, Aylmer, Ontario.
28 Graber, "Immigrant Cooking in Mexico."
29 Loewen, *Horse-and-Buggy Genius*, 152.
30 "A Mix of Mennonite, Mexican Cuisine."
31 Kneafsey and Cox, "Food, Gender and Irishness," 11.
32 Sneath, "Imagining a Mennonite Community."
33 A sampling of scholarship on this question in the Canadian context includes Driedger, "Native Rebellion and Mennonite Invasion"; Good, "Lost Inheritance"; Epp, "'There was no one here when we came'"; Wiebe, "On the Mennonite-Métis Borderland"; Neufeldt, "Settler Colonial Conscripts."
34 Mintz, "The History of Food in Canada."
35 Enns, "Facing History with Courage," 13.
36 Ibid. This story is also told in Enns and Myers, *Healing Haunted Histories*, 239–40.
37 Krause, "Emilia Wieler and Almighty Voice," 15–17.
38 Brass and Iwama, "Two Worlds, One Body," 38.
39 Neufeld, "The Amish and Their 'New' Neighbours."
40 Campbell, "Kookoom Mariah," 11.
41 Maria Campbell told this story in a keynote address at Indigenous-Mennonite Encounters in Time and Place, a conference held at Conrad Grebel University College, Waterloo, Ontario, 14 May 2022.
42 Fisher, "Seeds from the Steppe," 128.
43 Hiebert, "Indians, Métis and Mennonites," 52.
44 Interview with Joe Braun, referenced in Fisher, "Seeds from the Steppe," 130.
45 See, for example, "A History of Wilmot Township," in Bergey and Sherk, *Lorna (Shantz) Bergey*, 243.
46 Sawatzky, *Side by Side*, 8–10.
47 Ibid., 10.
48 Ibid., 14.
49 Hein and Enns, *Ufa*, 64–5.
50 Ibid., 83.
51 Ibid.
52 Fast, *In Den Steppen Sibiriens*, referenced in Suderman, *The Sudermans from Alexanderthal*, 126.
53 Nobbs-Thiessen, "Reshaping the Chaco," 606–8.
54 Klassen, *I Remember*, 180.
55 Rudolph, "dispossession," 30.
56 Story told in Wiebe, "From Bloodvein to Cross Lake," 18.
57 Cote, *MennoNeechie Kitchen*.
58 Cote, "Homemade Egg Noodles (Kielke)," in *MennoNeechie Kitchen*.

59 Enns, "Facing History with Courage," 42.
60 Gabaccia, *We Are What We Eat*, 8. This point is also made by Diner, *Hungering for America*, 9.
61 Konrad, *Down Clearbrook Road*, 100.
62 Ibid., 102–3.
63 Kauffman, *Immigrant Daughter*, 99.
64 Petö, "Food-Talk," 157.
65 Harder, *The Vauxhall Mennonite Church*, 13.
66 See chapter 5 in Bertram, *The Viking Immigrants*; Mehta, "Toronto's Multicultured Tongues," 156–69.
67 Voth, *Mennonite Foods and Folkways*, 2: 151.
68 This is described in Konrad, *Down Clearbrook Road*, 121.
69 Quoted in Hinojosa, *Latino Mennonites*, 102.
70 Hinojosa, *Latino Mennonites*, 115–16.
71 Kauffman, *Immigrant Daughter*, 174.
72 Montanari, *Food Is Culture*, 133.
73 Stucky, *The Centennial Treasury of Recipes*, 10.
74 Voth, *Mennonite Foods and Folkways*, 1: 25.
75 Kostash, *The Doomed Bridegroom*, 133–9.
76 Voth, *Mennonite Foods and Folkways*, 2: 187.
77 Graber, "Immigrant Cooking in Mexico." According to one source, by the turn of the twentieth century, there were twenty-four privately owned cheese factories in Mennonite colonies in Mexico: Friesen, *Pushing Through Invisible Barriers*, 409.
78 Nobbs-Thiessen, "Cheese Is Culture and Soy Is Commodity," 324.
79 Nobbs-Thiessen, "Reshaping the Chaco," 592.
80 Voth, *Mennonite Foods and Folkways*, 2: 188.
81 Koop and Dyck, "The Band Plays On," 47.
82 Teichroeb, "A Child Remembers War and New Beginnings," 9.
83 Ibid., 15.
84 Ibid., 18.
85 Nobbs-Thiessen, "Reshaping the Chaco," 579.
86 Ibid., 587. Material is from the Mennonite newspaper *Mennoblatt* in the 1930s.
87 Braun, *At This Table*, 95.
88 Klassen, *I Remember*, 128–9.
89 Doerwald, "Mate," 14.
90 Dueck, *Menno Moto*, 263.
91 Bergman, "The Mennonite Obsession with Yerba Mate."
92 Nobbs-Thiessen, "Reshaping the Chaco," 587.
93 Ibid., 590.

94 Braun, *At This Table*, 95.
95 Boerner, *Jakob Unger*, 203.
96 This topic is further explored in Epp, "Returning Home."
97 Friedlander and Hecht, "The Powers of Place," 35.
98 Braun, *Silentium*, 128. See also Holtzman, "Food and Memory."
99 Khan, "Juthaa in Trinidad," 262.
100 Smucker, "Faith versus Culture," 241.
101 Information gleaned from conversations at Lao Evangelical Mennonite Church, Kitchener, Ontario, 25 May 2012.
102 "International Food a Crowd-Pleaser," B1.
103 Martin, "'Mennonite' Not Eaten Here."
104 Loewen, Loewen, and Shepherd, "Food without Borders," 109.
105 Montanari, *Food Is Culture*, 133.
106 Pilcher, *Food in World History*, 71.
107 *Portzelky*, of Dutch origin, are a popular New Year's food in Russian Mennonite households.
108 Ellery Penner, who had conversations about food with Mennonites in Indonesia while on a year-long voluntary service assignment there in 2012, shared this perspective with me.
109 Chen and Hartono, "Transforming Conflicts through Food."
110 "Indonesian Food."
111 Unrau, *A Time to Bind and a Time to Loose*, 28.
112 Swartz, *Stories Our Mothers Told*, 126.
113 Ibid.
114 Ibid.
115 Ibid., 134.
116 Schroth, *Curry, Corduroy and the Call*, 22.
117 Bertsche, *Congo*, 29.
118 *Foreign Missions Africa*, 43–4.
119 Peters, *Walk with Me*, 45.
120 Loewen, Loewen, and Shepherd, "Food without Borders," 102–5.
121 Entz and Penner, *Missionary Meals around the World*, 3.
122 Pepper, *Called and Faithful*, 30–2.
123 Peters, *Walk with Me*, 32.
124 Toews, *Glances into Congoland*, 36.
125 Loewen, Loewen, and Shepherd, "Food without Borders," 107.
126 Swartz, *Stories Our Mothers Told*, 122–3.
127 Goertz, *Miss Annie*, 94.
128 Bertsche, *Congo*, 27–8.
129 Wiebe, *Sepia Prints*, 25.

130 Loewen, Loewen, and Shepherd, "Food without Borders," 103.
131 Labun, *Margaret Suderman*, preface.
132 Quoted in Unrau, *A Time to Bind and a Time to Loose*, 56.
133 Toews, *Spices of India*, i.
134 Wiebe, *Sepia Prints*, 76.
135 Quoted in Unrau, *A Time to Bind and a Time to Loose*, 33.
136 Schroth, *Curry, Corduroy and the Call*, 162.
137 Unrau, *A Time to Bind and a Time to Loose*, 32.
138 Quoted in Unrau, *A Time to Bind and a Time to Loose*, 32.

Chapter Two

1 Hostetler, *Mennonite Life*, 14–15.
2 Staebler, *More Food That Really Schmecks*, 12, 15. This volume was preceded by Staebler's *Food That Really Schmecks*.
3 Staebler, *Sauerkraut and Enterprise*, 25–36.
4 Androsoff, "A Larger Frame," 298–316.
5 Eicher and Williams, *The Amish Cook at Home*, xi.
6 Funk, *Mennonite Valley Girl*, 9.
7 Unrau, "Mennonite Pioneer Days," 21.
8 Hind, "The Mennonites of Manitoba," 97, 99.
9 Hayward, "Mine Host–The Mennonite," 195.
10 Loewen, *Horse-and-Buggy Genius*, 151.
11 Margaret Reimer, in a presentation at the conference "Still/Moving: Stories of Low German-Speaking Mennonite Women," King's University College, Western University, London, Ontario, 26 August 2016.
12 Wiebe, *The Storekeeper's Daughter*, 163.
13 Friesen, *Memoirs*, 9.
14 Loewen, Loewen, and Shepherd, "Food without Borders," 110.
15 Funk, *Mennonite Valley Girl*, 20.
16 Voth, *Mennonite Foods and Folkways*, 2: 6.
17 Friesen, *Pushing Through Invisible Barriers*, 133.
18 Inness, "Introduction," in *Kitchen Culture in America*, 4.
19 Neuhaus, *Manly Meals and Mom's Home Cooking*, 94, 190, chapter 9; Paul Freedman, "How Steak Became Manly"; Contois, *Diners, Dudes, and Diets*, 1.
20 Sharpless, *Cooking in Other Women's Kitchens*, 1.
21 Procida, "No Longer Half-Baked," 198. A similar point is made by Avakian and Haber in "Feminist Food Studies," 1–26.
22 Belasco, "Introduction," in Belasco and Scranton, *Food Nations*, 8.
23 Le Dantec-Lowry, "Reading Women's Lives," 118.
24 Avakian, *Through the Kitchen Window*, 6.

25 Randall, "What My Tongue Knows," 122.
26 Tye, *Baking as Biography*, 5.
27 Ibid., 25–6. A pivotal study was DeVault, *Feeding the Family*.
28 Cancian, "'Tutti a Tavola!,'" 209.
29 Gabaccia, *We Are What We Eat*, 180.
30 Braun, *Silentium*, 126.
31 Kirkby, *Secrets of a Hutterite Kitchen*, 134. Hutterites are a communal religious group with Anabaptist origins and bearing some similarities to Mennonites.
32 There are many studies detailing this outcome of the pandemic. See, for example, the United Nations report, "Whose Time to Care."
33 Poem by William Siddall, referenced in Epp, "Yeowomen of Yarrow," 122.
34 Klassen, "What's Bre(a)d in the Bone," 241.
35 Jones-Gailani, *Transnational Identity*, 94.
36 Cassidy and El-Tom, *Moving Meals and Migrating Mothers*, 9.
37 Groening, "Grandmother Remembers."
38 Friesen, *Pushing Through Invisible Barriers*, 273.
39 Fast, *A Day of Pilgrimage*, 80.
40 Penner, "Memories of *Schaaldouak*."
41 Stucky, *The Centennial Treasury of Recipes*, 5.
42 Betty Jane Hegerat, quoted on back cover of Hossack, *Mennonites Don't Dance*.
43 "Interview with Rhoda Janzen," 49.
44 Gilbert, *The Culinary Imagination*, 144.
45 See Redekop, *Making Believe*.
46 Stucky, *The Centennial Treasury of Recipes*, 5.
47 Martens, "The Artist as Homemaker," 13.
48 Born, *Maria's Century: A Family Saga*, 123.
49 Martens, *Reimer Legacy*, 22.
50 Schroeder, "Zwieback from Saint Johanna," 27.
51 Wiebe, *Displaced*, 115.
52 Braun, *Silentium*, 124.
53 Miller, "Pies at the Potluck," 9.
54 Hildebrand, *Reflections of a Prairie Community*, 11.
55 Voth, *Mennonite Foods and Folkways*, 2: 197.
56 Stucky, *The Centennial Treasury of Recipes*, 160.
57 Enns, *Preacher's Kids on the Homestead*, 69.
58 Plett, *The Road from Edenthal*, 117.
59 Bergey and Sherk, *Bergey: Her Literary Legacy*, 189.
60 Voth, *Mennonite Foods and Folkways*, 2: 146.
61 Braun, *A Village Saga*, 67.
62 Plett, *The Road from Edenthal*, 160.
63 Driedger, "Grandma's Soup Expressed Love and Care."

64 Friesen, "Tribute to Linie Krahn Friesen."
65 Fast, *A Day of Pilgrimage*, 40.
66 Kauffman, *Immigrant Daughter*, 5.
67 Konrad, *And in Their Silent Beauty Speak*, 241–2.
68 Friesen, *Pushing Through Invisible Barriers*, 133–4.
69 Wiebe, *Displaced*, 105.
70 Staebler, *Sauerkraut and Enterprise*, 29.
71 Wiebe, *Displaced*, 50.
72 Jantzi, *Simple Pleasures*, 186.
73 Fuchs, *Beauty and Sustenance*, 6.
74 Braun, *A Village Saga*, 51–2.
75 Sawatzky, foreword, in Fuchs, *Beauty and Sustenance*, 1.
76 Fuchs, *Beauty and Sustenance*, 10.
77 Klassen, "Russian Mennonite Food History."
78 Wiebe, *Displaced*, 98.
79 Jones-Gailani, *Transnational Identity*, 94.
80 Enns and Myers, *Healing Haunted Histories*, 85.
81 Giesbrecht, "The Everydayness of a Dairy Farm," 187.
82 Konrad, *And in Their Silent Beauty Speak*, 241.
83 Sawatzky, *Side by Side*, 76.
84 Konrad, *Down Clearbrook Road*, 240.
85 Braun, *Silentium*, 134.
86 Evans, "Telling Stories," ii.
87 Wiebe, *Fonn Onjafäa*, 1.
88 Wiebe, *Memories of Our Parents*, 204, 209.
89 Eidse, *Light the World*, 15.
90 Enns and Myers, *Healing Haunted Histories*, 95.
91 Kasdorf, "When Our Women Go Crazy."
92 Wiebe, *A Strong Frailty*, 118–19.
93 Tye, *Baking as Biography*, 82.
94 Freedman, "How Steak Became Manly."
95 Neufeld, *Mary Neufeld and the Repphun Story*, 200.
96 Loewen, Loewen, and Shepherd, "Food without Borders," 101.
97 Kauffman, *Immigrant Daughter*, 99.
98 Janzen, *My First Ninety Years*, 55.
99 Sawatzky, *Side by Side*, 75.
100 Dueck, *Journey to Freedom*, 14–15.
101 Neufeld, *A Family Torn Apart*, 47.
102 Klassen, *Going by the Moon and the Stars*, 91.
103 Dueck, *Journey to Freedom*, 127.
104 Driedger, "From Country to City," 6.

105 Kauffman, *Immigrant Daughter*, 210.
106 Dueck, *This Hidden Thing*, 27.
107 Ibid., 79.
108 Epp, "The Mennonite Girls' Homes of Winnipeg," 109.
109 Klippenstein, "'Doing What We Could,'" 152.
110 Kasdorf, "Working Away," 228.
111 Ibid., 231.
112 Riekman, "Helen Kliewer Bergman," 12.
113 Quoted in Thiessen, *The City Mission in Winnipeg*, 68.
114 Klippenstein, "The Modern Mennonite Housewife," 5–6.
115 Gilbert, *The Culinary Imagination*, 18.
116 Tye, *Baking as Biography*, 17.
117 Loewen, Loewen, and Shepherd, "Food without Borders," 104.
118 Inness, *Secret Ingredients*, 10.
119 Hussain, "Bateta Champ."
120 Barolini, "Appetite Lost, Appetite Found," 234.
121 Wade-Gayles, "'Laying On Hands' through Cooking," 97.
122 Adorno, *Las mujeres flores*, 17.
123 Konrad, *Down Clearbrook Road*, 240.
124 Borger, "Mennonite Domestic Workers," 32.
125 Wiebe, *Displaced*, 2.
126 Bergey and Sherk, *Bergey: Her Literary Legacy*, 188.
127 Peters, *The Plain People*, 47.
128 Voth, *Mennonite Foods and Folkways*, 2:18.
129 Braun, *A Village Saga*, 77.
130 Fast, *A Day of Pilgrimage*, 43.
131 Pető, "Food-Talk," 160.
132 Ibid.
133 Chornoboy, *Faspa*, 37.
134 Wiebe, *The Storekeeper's Daughter*, 144.
135 Masih, "Mennonite Indian Women," 5–6. Suniti Masih is a retired nurse who is part of the Dhamtari Mennonite Church in northern India.
136 Interview with Maria Martens, by the author, 4 May 2012, Aylmer, Ontario.
137 Roth, *Willing Service*, 128.
138 Bergey and Sherk, *Bergey: Her Literary Legacy*, 63–5.
139 Ibid., 231.
140 See Loewen, *Horse-and-Buggy-Genius*, 34–5. Also the Kitchen Kuttings website: http://www.kitchenkuttings.com/
141 Johnson-Weiner, *The Lives of Amish Women*, especially chapter 6 on "Homemakers and Breadwinners."
142 Buddle, "Gender and Business," 401–7.

143 Pilcher, *Food in World History*, 4.
144 Szabo, "Men Nurturing through Food," 18–31. This dichotomy is also described by Neuhaus in *Manly Meals and Mom's Home Cooking*, 94.
145 Quoted in Roth, *Mennonite Men Can Cook Too*, 287.
146 Roth, *Mennonite Men Can Cook Too*, 295.
147 See, for example, Neuhaus, *Manly Meals and Mom's Home Cooking*, chapter 9; Dummitt, "Finding a Place for Father," 209–23.
148 Neufeld, "Thank you!" 7.
149 Loewen, "Memories," 5.
150 Montanari, *Food Is Culture*, 116–17.
151 Trollinger, *Selling the Amish*, 65–6.

Chapter Three

1 Lee-Poy and Brown, *Food for the Journey*. I am grateful to Lee-Poy and Brown for allowing me to reference their cookbook in this way. Some of the material in this chapter is drawn from my chapter, "More than 'Just' Recipes."
2 Matsomoto, "Apple Pie and Makizushi," 258.
3 Harris-Aber, "Claiming a Piece of Tradition," 148.
4 Jones-Gailani, *Transnational Identity*, 83.
5 Murray, *The Naked Anabaptist*, 27. Theologian Malinda E. Berry has also made this observation: see Berry, "The Gifts of an Extended Theological Table," 306n3.
6 Yoder, *The Politics of Jesus*; Longacre, *More-with-Less Cookbook*.
7 Driedger, "The *More-With-Less Cookbook* Changed Everything."
8 Bailey-Dick, "The Kitchenhood of all Believers," 155.
9 Inness, *Secret Ingredients*, 2.
10 Neuhaus, *Manly Meals and Mom's Home Cooking*, 2.
11 Theophano, *Eat My Words*, 6.
12 Driver, *Culinary Landmarks*, xvii. See also Cooke, "Canada's Food History through Cookbooks."
13 Gold, *Danish Cookbooks*, 176.
14 Theophano, *Eat My Words*, 9.
15 Ibid., 122.
16 Jansen, "'Family Liked 1956,'" 55.
17 Ireland, "The Compiled Cookbook."
18 Albala, "Cookbooks as Historical Documents," 230.
19 Pauls, *Canadian Mennonite Cookbook*, iii.
20 Albala, "Cookbooks as Historical Documents," 232.

21 Tye, *Baking as Biography*, 35.
22 Eidinger, "Gefilte Fish and Roast Duck."
23 For more about cookbooks as immigrant documents, see my article "Eating across Borders."
24 Theophano, *Eat My Words*, 8.
25 Bardenstein, "Transmissions Interrupted," 357.
26 Albala, "Cookbooks as Historical Documents," 229.
27 Berry, "The Gifts of an Extended Theological Table," 284.
28 Bower, "Bound Together," 2.
29 Gabaccia, *We Are What We Eat*, 182.
30 Voth, *Mennonite Foods and Folkways*, 2: 273.
31 Braun, *A Village Saga*, 117.
32 Abraham P. and Margarethe (Kroeger) Regier fonds, Hist.Mss.1.275, Mennonite Archives of Ontario, Waterloo, Ontario. Translation help from Dr Aileen Friesen.
33 Vasvári, "En-gendering Memory."
34 Kirkby, *Secrets of a Hutterite Kitchen*, 193.
35 Staebler, *Sauerkraut and Enterprise*, 28.
36 For instance, Good Books, a Mennonite and Amish specialty publisher in Pennsylvania, produced a series of recipe collections for slow cookers that appeared numerous times on the *New York Times* bestseller list and sold thousands of copies.
37 Stucky, *The Centennial Treasury of Recipes*, 5.
38 Davis, "The Woman behind 'Mennonite Community Cookbook.'"
39 Showalter, *Mennonite Community Cookbook*, x.
40 Davis, "The Woman behind 'Mennonite Community Cookbook.'"
41 Neuhaus, "The Way to a Man's Heart," 532. While Neuhaus's article is about the United States, the same could be said about Canada.
42 Mumaw, "A Tribute to Mary Emma Showalter Eby," 10.
43 Showalter, *Mennonite Community Cookbook*, x.
44 Davis, "The Woman behind 'Mennonite Community Cookbook.'"
45 Showalter, "Community Cookbook Author Retires from Teaching," 4.
46 Ibid.
47 Email communication, 9 June 2008, from Levi Miller, director, Herald Press.
48 Email communication, 9 June 2008, from Levi Miller, director, Herald Press. Quoting email from Levi Miller to Philip C. Kanagy.
49 Jan Braun, foreword, in Snyder, *The Vegan Mennonite Kitchen*, 12.
50 Weber, *Friendly Favourites*.
51 Weiskopf-Ball, "Cooking Up Change."

240 Notes to pages 124–31

52 Email communication from Lauren Block of Derksen Printers on 22 July 2020 indicated that 14,000 copies had been sold since 2008, at which point the number was approximately 350,000.
53 *The Mennonite Treasury*, 1.
54 Ferguson, "Intensifying Taste, Intensifying Identity," 696.
55 Ibid.
56 *25 Jaehriges Jubilaeum*, 13.
57 Ibid., 27. Translation by Helen L. Epp.
58 Ibid.
59 Penner, "The Mennonite Treasury of Recipes," 53–4.
60 Ibid.
61 Ibid.
62 Ibid.
63 Ibid.
64 Obituary of Anna Derksen Rosenfeld, 7.
65 Durksen, "Just around the House," 8.
66 *History of Manitoba Mennonite Women in Mission*, 51. The commercial success of the *Treasury* was followed a decade later by the publication of *Canadian Mennonite Cookbook*. First appearing as a compilation of recipes by the Altona (Manitoba) Women's Institute, the cookbook had gone through twelve editions by 1980 and sold 90,000 copies.
67 Tye, *Baking as Biography*, 121.
68 Braun, *Silentium*, 124–5.
69 Redekop, *Making Believe*, 27.
70 "Interview with Miriam Toews," 2.
71 Theophano, *Eat My Words*, 12.
72 Newman, "The Rich History and Profitability of Church Cookbooks."
73 "Helping Others."
74 Gabaccia, *We Are What We Eat*, 181.
75 Penner, "The Mennonite Treasury of Recipes," 54.
76 *Canadian Mennonite Cookbook*.
77 In 2003, the book was titled simply *Mennonite Cookbook* and published by Whitecap Books in Vancouver, BC.
78 Voth, *Mennonite Foods and Folkways*, 1:33.
79 *The Mennonite Treasury of Recipes*, 22–3.
80 Loewen, "The Poetics of Peoplehood," 339.
81 Harris-Aber, "Claiming a Piece of Tradition," 143.
82 Voth, *Mennonite Foods and Folkways*. A similar volume focusing on the Pennsylvania German cultural tradition is Good and Pellman, *Cooking & Memories*.

83 Harder, *Mennonite Ethnic Cooking*, i.
84 Turner, *From Oma's Kitchen*.
85 Roth, *Mennonite Men Can Cook Too*.
86 "Mennonite Girls Can Cook Becomes a Live Comedy."
87 Schellenberg et al., *Mennonite Girls Can Cook*, 12.
88 Ibid.
89 Ibid.
90 Kelting, "The Entanglement of Nostalgia and Utopia," 362.
91 Schellenberg, *Mennonite Girls Can Cook*, 12.
92 *Mennonites Girls Can Cook* (blog), accessed 4 March 2019.
93 Helmuth, *Hope's Table*, 9.
94 See Trollinger, *Selling the Amish*, 56–6.
95 Staebler's cookbooks were published by major Canadian publisher McClelland and Stewart.
96 Good Books, a long-time publisher of Mennonite and Amish themed books, was acquired by Skyhorse Publishing in 2014.
97 Steiner, "Horst, Isaac Reist."
98 All of these cookbooks were self-published. *Potato Potential: All Eyes Turn to Potatoes* (1985); *Just Loafin': 50 Recipes for Various Breads from Mennonite Kitchens* (1991); *High, Healthy and Happy 3-H Mennonite Cookbooks: A Collection of Swiss-Canadian Mennonite Recipes* (1985). These are examples of about a dozen cookbooks that Horst compiled.
99 Horst, *Conestogo Mennonite Cookbook*, 37.
100 Some useful studies on race and cookbook literature include Makhijani, "A Place at the Table"; Kelting, "The Entanglement of Nostalgia and Utopia"; Ferguson, "Intensifying Taste, Intensifying Identity"; Tunc, "Louise Spieker Rankin's Global Souths."
101 *Be Present at Our Table*.
102 Penner and Peters, *The Cookbook Project*, 6.
103 Harris-Aber, "Claiming a Piece of Tradition," 150.
104 Emilia and Renpenning, *Recetario Menonita de Chihauhau*.
105 *Mama's Kochbuch*.
106 *Farmer's Kochbuch*.
107 *Kommt Essen*.
108 Funk, *Met Helen en de Kjääkj*.
109 Schellenberg, "Cooking Up a Low German Blessing."
110 Ibid.
111 Sneath, "Imagining a Mennonite Community," 213.
112 Bower, "Bound Together."
113 Neuhaus, "The Way to a Man's Heart."

114 For example, see Neuhaus, *Manly Meals and Mom's Home Cooking*, 137–8.
115 *The Mennonite Treasury of Recipes* (1982 edition), 63.
116 *The Mennonite Treasury of Recipes*, 223–4.
117 *Mennonite Community Cookbook*, 450–9.
118 Hamm, *New Bergthal Heritage and Cookbook*.
119 Iacovetta and Korinek, "Jello-O Salads," 438.
120 Theophano, *Eat My Words*, 78.
121 Harder, *Mennonite Ethnic Cooking*, 82.
122 Gold, *Danish Cookbooks*, 25.
123 Konrad, *Down Clearbrook Road*, 103–4.
124 Shapiro, *Something from the Oven*, 142.
125 Bower, "Bound Together," 5–6.
126 *Canadian Mennonite Cookbook*, iii.
127 Bower, "Cooking Up Stories," 47.
128 *Canadian Mennonite Cookbook* (1973 edition), preface.
129 Albala, "Cookbooks as Historical Documents," 231.
130 "About More-with-Less."
131 Other sources suggest sales of about 700,000 in the first twenty-five years.
132 Moses, "Recipes for a Revolution."
133 Bailey-Dick, "Kitchenhood of All Believers," 153–63. An analysis of some contemporary Mennonite cookbooks that focuses on the intersection of eating habits, social justice, and aesthetics is Trollinger, "Mennonite Cookbooks and the Pleasure of Habit."
134 Gayle Gerber Koontz, quoted in "About More-with-Less."
135 Friesen, "Primary Source Analysis of the *More-with-Less Cookbook*." A more theologically focused analysis is Berry, "The Gifts of an Extended Theological Table."
136 Loewen, "Cooking Up Discipleship."
137 Mock, "Mothering, More with Less," 257.
138 Ibid., 259.
139 Ibid., 267.
140 Epp, "Serving Up Nourishment."
141 Loewen, Loewen, and Shepherd, "Food without Borders," 100.
142 Schlabach, *Extending the Table*.
143 Lind and Hockman-Wert, *Simply in Season*.
144 Salvio, "Dishing It Out," 32.
145 Fast, *With a Whisk, a Colander and a Rolling Pin*, accessed 4 February 2022.
146 Cote, *MennoNeechie Kitchen*, accessed 4 February 2022.
147 *The Shoofly Project*.

148 *A Year of Mennonite Cooking.*
149 *More-With-Less: Thinking about Our Food.*
150 "Mennonite Girls Can Cook – Ten Years," *Mennonite Girls Can Cook.*
151 See, for example, *Finding Harmony; Mennopolitan; Rhubarb & Roses.*
152 Email communication, 9 June 2008, from Levi Miller, director, Herald Press. Quoting email from Levil Miller to Philip C. Kanagy.

Chapter Four

1 Information gleaned from conversation with members of Grace Lao Mennonite Church, Kitchener, Ontario, 25 May 2012.
2 For detail on the history of refugees from Southeast Asia in Canada, see Molloy et al., *Running on Empty.*
3 Diner, *Hungering for America*, 227.
4 Ibid., 220.
5 Hunchuk, "Feeding the Dead," 140.
6 Montanari, *Food Is Culture*, 17.
7 Quoted in Staebler, *Sauerkraut and Enterprise*, 34.
8 Bach, *The Kitchen, Food, and Cooking*, 20.
9 Schroeder, "Bergthal's Pilgrimage," 15.
10 Janzen, "A Pioneer's Life in Manitoba," 20.
11 Jansen and Jansen, *Our Stories*, 93.
12 Peters, *Walk with Me*, 6.
13 Janzen, "Paraguayan Journal," 11.
14 Sawatzky, *Side by Side*, 51.
15 Anonymous response to questionnaire distributed by the author at Seniors Retreat, Hidden Acres Camp, New Hamburg, ON, October 2017.
16 Schmidt, "The Theodore Nickel Family," 12.
17 Janzen, *My First Ninety Years*, 33.
18 Ibid., 47.
19 Ibid., 51–2.
20 Goertz, *Miss Annie*, 19.
21 Ibid., 35–6.
22 Fast, *A Day of Pilgrimage*, 36.
23 Fisher, "Seeds from the Steppe," 236.
24 Janzen, *My First Ninety Years*, 55.
25 Friesen, *Pushing Through Invisible Barriers*, 164, 184.
26 Baykeda, "First Person," 14–15.
27 See Asheervadam et al., *Churches Engage Asian Traditions*, chapter 4.

28 Notes from interview by author with Mennonite women in Kinshasa, Democratic Republic of Congo, 14 July 2012. The population number is baptized church members and thus does not include children.
29 Some material in this chapter is taken from my chapter "The Semiotics of Zwieback," 413–31.
30 For accounts of this period in Mennonite history, see, for example, Dyck et al., *Nestor Makhno and the Eichenfeld Massacre*; Neufeld and Reimer, *A Russian Dance of Death*; Toews, *The Mennonite Story in Ukraine*; Friesen, *Mennonites in the Russian Empire*, chapters 10–12.
31 Peter Letkemann, as referenced in Toews, *The Mennonite Story in Ukraine*, 54.
32 Letkemann, "Mennonite Victims of 'The Great Terror,'" 38.
33 Swartz, *Stories Our Mothers Told*, 253.
34 Toews, *Czars, Soviets and Mennonites*, 112.
35 Toews, *Sketches from Siberia*, 26.
36 Jansen and Jansen, *Our Stories*, 17. References to cannibalism can also be found in Jantz, *Flight*, 656, 661.
37 Sawatzky, *Side by Side*, 15.
38 Martens, *They Came from Wiesenfeld*, 76.
39 Quoted in Neufeld, *Mary Neufeld and the Repphun Story*, 68.
40 Peters, *Diary of Anna Baerg*, 89.
41 Important recent histories of Mennonite Central Committee include Epp-Tiessen, *Mennonite Central Committee in Canada*; Weaver, *Service and the Ministry of Reconciliation*. See also Kreider and Goossen, *Hungry, Thirsty, a Stranger*.
42 Swartz, *Stories Our Mothers Told*, 253.
43 Fast, *A Day of Pilgrimage*, A21.
44 Neufeld, "Ort und Vertreibung," 172.
45 Thielman, *Susanne Remembers*, 47.
46 Thielman, in Willms, *At the Gates of Moscow*, 9.
47 Klassen, *I Remember*, 14.
48 For a brief description of some of the foods eaten, see, for instance, Neufeldt, "Through the Fires of Hell," 28–9.
49 Braun, *At This Table*, 33.
50 "The Life and Times of Marie Hildebrandt Huebert," 2–4.
51 Konrad, *And in Their Silent Beauty Speak*, 408.
52 Siemens, *Remember Us*, 45, 65.
53 Peters, "Dearly Beloved," 59.
54 Maria Martens Bargen to her children, 2 February 1932. In Bargen, *From Russia with Tears*, 352.
55 Quoted in Siemens, *Remember Us*, 98.

56 Rahn, *Among the Ashes*, 195–6.
57 "Now the 4th Month without Rain," letter written 3 June 1934, in Rahn, *Among the Ashes*, 228–9.
58 Ibid.
59 Peter G. Schellenberg, letter dated 20 February 1929, in Jantz, *Flight*, 13.
60 Suderman, *The Sudermans from Alexanderthal*, 10.
61 Dueck, *Journey to Freedom*, 16.
62 Dueck, "Rice Pudding," 61–6.
63 Neufeldt, "Through the Fires of Hell," 28.
64 Jacob Dyck, letter dated 6 February 1929, in Jantz, *Flight*, 10.
65 Voth, *Mennonite Foods and Folkways*, 1: 29.
66 Wiebe, "Memories Written by My Life," 83–4.
67 Strempler, "Uprooted," 22–3.
68 Rahn, *Among the Ashes*, 233.
69 Montanari, *Food Is Culture*, 105.
70 Ibid.
71 Toews, *Letters from Susan*, 96.
72 Mace, "Soviet Man-Made Famine in Ukraine," 78–90. He suggests that five to seven million people in Ukraine were victims of the famine. Hunchuk, "Feeding the Dead," 149, says two to twelve million perished.
73 "After a Lengthy Wait, Finally a Letter," letter written 27 February 1934, in Rahn, *Among the Ashes*, 212–13.
74 "Dear Jacob," letter written 2 June 1930, in Rahn, *Among the Ashes*, 94.
75 "When you get this Letter we will be without Food," letter written 5 March 1931, in Rahn, *Among the Ashes*, 161.
76 Fieldhouse, *Food and Nutrition*, 116.
77 Some of these arguments are summarized in Kelleher, "Woman as Famine Victim."
78 For an analysis of gender in the Holodomor, see Kis, "Defying Death."
79 Hiebert and Miller, *Feeding the Hungry*, 395.
80 Jacob A. Penner, quoted in Letkemann, *A Book of Remembrance*, 191.
81 Wiebe, *The Storekeeper's Daughter*, 157.
82 Dueck, *Journey to Freedom*, 39.
83 Teichroeb, "A Child Remembers War," 4.
84 Krueger, "An Unforgettable Childhood Experience," 7.
85 Braun, *At This Table*, 54.
86 Wiens, *Schicksalsjahr 1945*, 22.
87 Friesen, *Into the Unknown*, chapter 5.
88 Dueck, *Journey to Freedom*, 83.
89 Ibid., 89.

90 Kolinsky, *Women in Contemporary Germany*, 26–8.
91 Interview #28. During the years 1992 to 1994, I conducted recorded interviews with Mennonites who immigrated to Canada and Paraguay after the Second World War. For the purpose of anonymity, I assigned numbers to the interviews. These interviews were digitized and are held in the Mennonite Archives of Ontario, Waterloo, Ontario.
92 Slabach, *A Place for Ruth*, 59, 61.
93 Ibid., 84.
94 Schmidt, *Gnadenfeld*, 81.
95 Dueck, *Journey to Freedom*, 87.
96 Quoted in Fieldhouse, *Food and Nutrition*, 21.
97 Lam, *From Being Uprooted to Surviving*, 86.
98 See Goldenberg, "Food Talk."
99 DeSilva, *In Memory's Kitchen*. Mina Pachter compiled the recipes. In drawing parallels between groups that engage in food-talk during situations of severe food deprivation, I am not attempting to compare their overall experiences of suffering. Clearly, the genocidal treatment of Jews in the Holocaust was significantly beyond what Mennonites experienced in the Stalin era in the Soviet Union.
100 Chornoboy, *Katarina*, 248.
101 Murcott, *The Sociology of Food and Eating*, 102.
102 Baumel, *Double Jeopardy*, 79.
103 I refer to a grab bag household as comprising individuals who may have extended familial relationships but are not a traditional nuclear family. See my chapter "The 'Grab Bag' Mennonite Family."
104 Toews, *Trek to Freedom*, 30–1.
105 Voth, *Mennonite Foods and Folkways*, 1: 29.
106 Lemke and Daniel, *Slipping the Noose*, 28.
107 Goerzen, *Anny*, 187.
108 Schmidt, *Gnadenfeld*, 72.
109 Fast, *A Day of Pilgrimage*, A12.
110 Toews, *Trek to Freedom*, 40.
111 Teichroeb, "A Child Remembers War," 5–6.
112 Quoted in Loewen, *Road to Freedom*, 147.
113 Voth, *Mennonite Foods and Folkways*, 2: 33–4.
114 Klassen, "My Experiences," iii.
115 Quoted in Loewen, *Road to Freedom*, 72.
116 Thiessen and Showalter, *A Life Displaced*, 153.
117 Kirkpatrick, "The Story of Mrs. Suse Rempel," 44.
118 Dueck, *Journey to Freedom*, 150.

119 Ibid., 151.
120 Montanari, *Food Is Culture*, 115.
121 Kasstan, "The Taste of Trauma," 355.
122 Letter of Katja Isaak, translation excerpt in Willms, *At the Gates of Moscow*, 216.
123 Neufeldt, "Reforging Mennonite *Spetspereselentsy*," 280.
124 Applebaum, *Gulag*, 208–15.
125 Quoted in Neufeldt, "Reforging Mennonite *Spetspereselentsy*," 291.
126 Siemens, *Remember Us*, 128.
127 Ibid., 146.
128 Epp, "A Mother's Faith," 119.
129 Toews, *Sketches from Siberia*, 108.
130 Ibid., 94.
131 Dueck, *Journey to Freedom*, 59–60.
132 Ibid., 60.
133 Ibid., 64.
134 Dyck, *A Pilgrim People*, 161.
135 Wiebe, *A Strong Frailty*, 59.
136 Ibid., 118.
137 Dueck, *Journey to Freedom*, 105. This anecdote frames my article, "'The Dumpling in My Soup Was Lonely Just Like Me.'"
138 Bergen, *Four Years Less a Day*, 39.
139 Goerzen, *Anny*, 153.
140 I explore some of these wartime issues as they relate to memory, though not with detailed attention to food, in "The Memory of Violence."
141 See, in particular, Jantzen and Thiesen, *European Mennonites and the Holocaust*.
142 Teichroeb, "A Child Remembers War," 4.
143 Dueck, *Journey to Freedom*, 85.
144 Ibid., 88.
145 Martens, *On My Own*, 36.

Chapter Five

1 Information from conversation on 2 March 2015 at Ranchi Mennonite Church, India.
2 Quoted in Mangalaseril, "Faith and Food Intertwined," B1.
3 Foreword, in Gross, Myers, and Rosenblum, *Feasting and Fasting*, xii.
4 Desjardins and Desjardins, "The Role of Food," 72.
5 Ibid., 76.

6 S. Brent Plate, quoted in Batten and Olsen, *Dress in Mediterranean Antiquity*, 22.
7 Sack, *Whitebread Protestants*, 2.
8 Friesen, *Memoirs*, 9.
9 Mock, "Mothering, More with Less," 262.
10 Eicher, *The Amish Cook at Home*, 136.
11 See, for example, McGuire, *Lived Religion*.
12 Voth, *Mennonite Foods and Folkways*, 1: 293.
13 Dueck, *Journey to Freedom*, 7.
14 Ibid., 47.
15 "Dear Son Jacob," letter written 15 September 1930, in Rahn, *Among the Ashes*, 113.
16 Bergen and Price, "Watermelon Syrup," 10.
17 Thielman, *Susanne Remembers*, 76–8.
18 Peters, *Walk with Me*, 5.
19 Braun, *Silentium*, 127.
20 Jacobsen, *Watermelon Syrup*, 1.
21 Some of the material in this section on *zwieback* is drawn from my chapter "The Semiotics of Zwieback."
22 Chornoboy, *Katarina*, 114.
23 Froese, *Call to Remembrance*, 14.
24 Gaede-Penner, *From Kansas Wheat Fields*, 25.
25 Ebert, *Wir Sind Frei!*, 29.
26 Konrad, *And in Their Silent Beauty Speak*, 176.
27 Wiebe, "Memories Written By my Life," 82–3.
28 Rempel, "Ritual as My Third Language," 7.
29 Gross, introduction, in Gross, Myers, and Rosenblum, *Feasting and Fasting*, 4.
30 Nobbs-Thiessen, "Reshaping the Chaco," 588–9.
31 Pauls, *Memories*, 15.
32 Goerzen, *Anny*, 166.
33 Dueck, *Journey to Freedom*, 21.
34 Schmidt, *Gnadenfeld*, 47.
35 Epp, "Memories of Difficult Years," 24–5.
36 Schmidt, *Gnadenfeld*, 75.
37 For further discussion of this issue, see chapter 2 of my book *Women without Men*.
38 Braun, *At This Table*, 33.
39 Ibid., 41.
40 Abram, "The Cooking Lesson," 187.
41 Brown, *Black and Mennonite*, 85.

42 Longacre, *More-with-Less*, 6.
43 The Mennonite Centre in Molochansk, Ukraine, is located in a building that was a Mennonite girls' school in the town the Mennonites called Halbstadt. See http://www.mennonitecentre.ca/.
44 Kasdorf, *The Body and the Book*, xiv–xv.
45 See Kreider and Goossen, *Hungry, Thirsty, a Stranger*, chapter 29.
46 Quoted in Knowles, *Piecemakers*, 63.
47 D'Amato, "'Stop Eating, and Bid!'" A1–2.
48 Knowles, *Piecemakers*, 17.
49 Ibid., 21.
50 Ibid., 25–6.
51 Ibid., 26.
52 Ward Shantz, quoted in Knowles, *Piecemakers*, 24.
53 Tye, *Baking as Biography*, 151.
54 See Sack, *Whitebread Protestants*, chapter 4.
55 Reference from Pollan, *The Omnivore's Dilemma*.
56 Hinojosa, *Latino Mennonites*, 114–15.
57 Ibid., 131. On Mennonites and unions in Canada, see Thiessen, *Not Talking Union*.
58 These debates are not unique to Mennonites. For a discussion of the diversity and debates regarding communion practices in Protestantism, see Sack, *Whitebread Protestants*, chapter 1.
59 Wiebe, *Sepia Prints*, 91.
60 Beyler, "Tea Ceremony," 6.
61 Kirkby, *Secrets of a Hutterite Kitchen*, 91.
62 Johnson-Weiner, *The Lives of Amish Women*, 109.
63 I am paraphrasing Loewen, *Mennonite Farmers*, 12.
64 Diner, *Hungering for America*, 155.
65 Ibid., 157.
66 Chornoboy, *Faspa*, 140.
67 Jantzi, *Simple Pleasures*, 54.
68 Friesen, *Pushing Through Invisible Barriers*, 99.
69 Peters, *Walk with Me*, 10.
70 Stucky, *The Centennial Treasury of Recipes*, 158.
71 Masih, "Mennonite Indian Women," 3.
72 Janzen, "Mexican Mennonites Combat Fears of Violence."
73 Horst, "Peppernuts, Theme and Variations."
74 Stories in Voth, *Mennonite Foods and Folkways*, 2:367.
75 From conversation with Lily Kachhap and other Mennonite women in India, 28 February 2015.

76 This comparison of peppernuts and *anarsa* is drawn from my published article, "Peppernuts and Anarsa."
77 Unger, "'Reverse Lent' Begins Today."
78 Rindlisbacher and Yoder, "500 Years after a Sausage Rebellion."
79 Voth, *Mennonite Foods and Folkways*, 2: 100–1. For a contemporary example of this, see Bailey-Dick, "Bog na pomotsch!"
80 Quoted in Klassen-Wiebe, "Hands-On learning."
81 Bergey and Sherk, *Bergey: Her Literary Legacy*, 68.
82 Written notes by Ellery Penner, a former student who had conversations about food with Mennonites in Indonesia while on a year-long service assignment there in 2012.
83 Voth, *Mennonite Foods and Folkways*, 2: 134.
84 Konrad, *Down Clearbrook Road*, 179.
85 Gaede-Penner, *From Kansas Wheat Fields*, 50. See also Voth, *Mennonite Foods and Folkways*, 2: 107.
86 Konrad, *Down Clearbrook Road*, 177.
87 Quoted in Unrau, *A Time to Bind and a Time to Loose*, 45.
88 Stucky, *The Centennial Treasury of Recipes*, 158.
89 Written notes by Ellery Penner.
90 Foreword, in Snyder, *The Vegan Mennonite Kitchen*, 10.
91 Goertz, *Miss Annie*, 16.
92 Voth, *Mennonite Foods and Folkways*, 2: 204.
93 Ibid., 1: 243.
94 Wiens, "*Live According to Nature*," 8.
95 Bach, *The Kitchen, Food, and Cooking*, 104–5.
96 Goertz, *Miss Annie*, 31.
97 Swartz, *Stories Our Mothers Told*, 130–1.
98 Hayward, "Mine Host," 196.
99 Martens, *On My Own*, 50.
100 Johnson-Weiner, *The Lives of Amish Women*, 77–8.
101 Lily Hiebert Rempel, quoted at "Still/Moving: Stories of Low German-Speaking Mennonite Women," King's University College, London, Ontario, 26 August 2016.
102 Penner and Peters, *The Cookbook Project*, 10.
103 Johnson-Weiner, *The Lives of Amish Women*, 71.
104 Gilbert, *The Culinary Imagination*, 36.
105 Questionnaires from Hidden Acres Seniors Retreat, New Hamburg, Ontario, October 2017.
106 Roes, *Mennonite Funeral and Burial Traditions*, 15.
107 Ibid., 35.

108 Ibid., 68.
109 Friesen, *Pushing Through Invisible Barriers*, 191.
110 Johnson-Weiner, *The Lives of Amish Women*, 106.
111 Born, *Third Daughter*, 25.
112 Sauder, "Food in the Midst of Sorrow."
113 Rempel, "Ritual as My Third Language," 7.
114 Pilcher, *Food in World History*, 2.
115 Braun, *Silentium*, 134.
116 Sack, *Whitebread Protestants*, 2.
117 Matahelemual, "Spice Up Your Life," 38.
118 Klippenstein, "Gender and Mennonites," 144.
119 Brooks Holifield's phrase is used in Sack, *Whitebread Protestants*, 64.
120 Sack, *Whitebread Protestants*, 82.
121 Cruz, *Queering Mennonite Literature*.
122 Allen, "Mennonite: Culture or Denomination?" 35.
123 Enns and Myers, *Healing Haunted Histories*, 119.
124 Yoder and Huff, "The Best Education Happens around the Table," 145.
125 Francis, "Food in the Contemporary UK Anabaptist Movement," 13.
126 Snyder, quoted in Epp, "Serving Up Nourishment."
127 Draper, "A Big Heart Filled with Butter Tarts."
128 Rempel, "Ritual as My Third Language," 10.
129 Miller, "Pies at the Potluck," 9.
130 Ibid.
131 Tye, *Baking as Biography*, 154.
132 This practice is described in Gingrich, *A Quilt of Impressions*, 57–9. See also Peters, *The Plain People*, 34.
133 Examples of this include Braun, *A Village Saga*, 112–13; Neudorf, "Pig Butchering"; Snyder, *Pennsylvania German Customs and Cookery*, 16–17.
134 Voth, *Mennonite Foods and Folkways*, 2: 202.
135 Wilson, "Reciprocal Work Bees."
136 Plett, *The Road from Edenthal*, 117.
137 Loewen, *Memories*, 4.
138 Friesen, *Pushing Through Invisible Barriers*, 119.
139 Chornoboy, *Faspa*, 45.
140 Born, *Third Daughter*, 24.
141 Fast and Neufeld, "Hog Butchering/*Schwien schlachte*."
142 Johnson-Weiner, *The Lives of Amish Women*, 109–11.
143 Chornoboy, *Faspa*, 43–4.
144 Fast and Neufeld, "Hog Butchering/*Schwien schlachte*, 7–8.
145 See, *Side by Side*, 51–2, for another long description of a butchering bee.

146 Gideon Kleinsassar, quoted in Kirkby, *Secrets of a Hutterite Kitchen*, 62.
147 Story told in a sermon at Rockway Mennonite Church, Kitchener, Ontario, on 6 April 2014, with further elaboration in an email to the author from Irma Fast Dueck, 23 March 2022.
148 Beyler, "Tea Ceremony," 9.
149 Martens, *Reimer Legacy*, 15.
150 Fast, "Steinbach Pride."

Bibliography

25 Jaehriges Jubilaeum der Steinbach Mennoniten Gemeinde 1968. Steinbach, MB: Steinbach Mennonite Church, 1968.

"About Anna." *Mennopolitan* (blog). http://www.mennopolitan.com/. Accessed 24 July 2019.

"About More-with-Less." *World Community Cookbooks*, Mennonite Central Committee. https://www.worldcommunitycookbook.org. Accessed 3 July 2008.

Abram, Dorothy. "The Cooking Lesson: Identity and Spirituality in the Lives of Hindu Refugees in America." In *What's Cooking, Mom? Narratives about Food and Family*, edited by Tanya M. Cassidy and Florence Pasche Guignard, 185–93. Bradford, ON: Demeter Press, 2015.

Adorno, Eunice. *Las Mujeres Flores*. Mexico: La Frabrica, 2011.

Albala, Ken. "Cookbooks as Historical Documents." In *The Oxford Handbook of Food History*, edited by Jeffrey M. Pilcher, 227–40. New York, NY: Oxford University Press, 2012.

Allen, Karen. "Mennonite: Culture or Denomination?" *Canadian Mennonite* 16, no. 3 (6 February 2012): 35.

Androsoff, Ashleigh. "A Larger Frame: 'Redressing' the Image of Doukhobor Canadian Women in the Twentieth Century." In Epp and Iacovetta, *Sisters or Strangers*, 298–316.

Applebaum, Anne. *Gulag: A History*. New York, NY: Doubleday, 2003.

Asheervadam, I.P, and Adhi Dharma, Alle Hoekema, KyongJung Kim, Luke S. Martin, Regina Lyn Mondez, Chiou-Lang Pan, Nguyen Thanh Tam, Nguyen Thi Tam, Takanobu Tōjō, Nguyen Quang Trung, Masakazu Yamande, and Earl Zimmerman. *Churches Engage Asian Traditions: Global Mennonites History Series, Asia*. Intercourse, PA and Kitchener, ON: Good Books and Pandora Press, 2011.

Bibliography

Avakian, Arlene Voski, ed. *Through the Kitchen Window: Women Explore the Intimate Meanings of Food and Cooking*. Oxford, UK: Berg, 2005.

Avakian, Arlene Voski, and Barbara Haber. "Feminist Food Studies: A Brief History." In *From Betty Crocker to Feminist Food Studies: Critical Perspectives on Women and Food*, edited by Arlene Voski Avakian and Barbara Haber, 1–26. Amherst & Boston: University of Massachusetts Press, 2005.

Bach, Volker. *The Kitchen, Food, and Cooking in Reformation Germany*. Lanham, MD: Rowman & Littlefield, 2016.

Bailey-Dick, Matthew. "Bog na pomotsch!" *Anabaptist Learning Workshop* (blog). 16 December 2016. https://uwaterloo.ca/anabaptist-learning-workshop/blog/post/bog-na-pomotsch.

– "The Kitchenhood of All Believers: A Journey into the Discourse of Mennonite Cookbooks." *Mennonite Quarterly Review* 79, no. 2 (April 2005): 153–78.

Bardenstein, Carol. "Transmissions Interrupted: Reconfiguring Food, Memory, and Gender in the Cookbook: Memoirs of Middle Eastern Exiles." *Signs: Journal of Women in Culture and Society* 28, no. 1 (2002): 353–87.

Bargen, Peter F., ed., and Anne Bargen, trans. *From Russia with Tears: Letters from Home and Exile, 1930–1938*. Calgary, AB: printed by the authors, 1991.

Barkman, Sue, editor and compiler. *Mennonite Heritage Village Cook Book*. Steinbach, MB: Derksen Printers, 1981.

Barolini, Helen. "Appetite Lost, Appetite Found." In Avakian, *Through the Kitchen Window*, 228–35.

Batten, Alicia J., and Kelly Olson, eds. *Dress in Mediterranean Antiquity: Greeks, Romans, Jews, Christians*. London, UK: Bloomsbury, 2021.

Baumel, Judith Tydor. *Double Jeopardy: Gender and the Holocaust*. London, UK: Vallentine Mitchell, 1998.

Baykeda, Zemedkun. "First Person." As told to Rachel Miller Moreland. *A Common Place* 10, no. 2 (March/April 2004): 14–15.

Belasco, Warren, and Philip Scranton, eds. *Food Nations: Selling Taste in Consumer Societies*. New York and London: Routledge, 2002.

Be Present at Our Table: 150th Anniversary Cookbook, Erb Street Mennonite Church, 1851–2001. Waterloo, ON: Erb Street Mennonite Church, 2001.

Bergen, Henry. *Four Years Less a Day: A WWII Refugee Story*. Victoria, BC: Trafford Publishing, 2006.

Bergen, Irene, and Louise Bergen Price. "Watermelon Syrup." *Mennonite Historical Society of BC Newsletter* 9, no. 3 (Summer 2003): 10.

Bergey, Lorna Shantz, and Vernon W. Sherk. *Lorna (Shantz) Bergey: Her Literary Legacy*. Canadian-German Folklore Series 21. Waterloo, ON: Pennsylvania German Folklore Society of Ontario, 2011.

"Bericht des 'Eben-Ezer' Nähvereins." In *25 Jaehriges Jubilaeum*, 27, translated by Helen L. Epp.

Bergman, Andrew J. "The Mennonite Obsession with Yerba Mate." *MateOverMatter*, 5 November 2017. https://mateovermatter.com/first-time-experiences/the-mennonite-obsession-with-yerba-mate/.

Berry, Malinda Elizabeth. "The Gifts of an Extended Theological Table: MCC's World Community Cookbooks as Organic Theology." In *A Table of Sharing: Mennonite Central Committee and the Expanding Networks of Mennonite Identity*, edited by Alain Epp Weaver, 284–309. Telford, PA: Cascadia, 2011.

Bertram, Laurie K. "Icelandic Cake Fight: History of an Immigrant Recipe." *Gastronomica: The Journal for Food Studies* 19, no. 4 (Winter 2019): 28–41.

– "New Icelandic Ethnoscapes: Material, Visual, and Oral Terrains of Cultural Expression in Icelandic-Canadian History, 1875–present." PhD dissertation, University of Toronto, 2010.

– *The Viking Immigrants: Icelandic North Americans*. Toronto, ON: University of Toronto Press, 2020.

Bertsche, James. *Congo: Wayside Glimpses*. Chicago, IL: The Congo Inland Mission, 1952.

Beyler, Mary. "Tea Ceremony as My Training for Ministry in Japan." *Mission Insight*, no. 12. Elkhart, IN: Mennonite Board of Missions (2000): 1–13.

Boerner, Agnes Unger, ed. and trans. *Jakob Unger: Memories*. N.p.: Agnes Unger Boerner, 2013.

Borger, Sandra. "Mennonite Domestic Workers: Intersections of Gender, Ethnicity and Religion." MA thesis, Simon Fraser University, 2010.

Born, Hilda J. *Maria's Century: A Family Saga*. Abbotsford, BC: printed by the author, 1997.

– *Third Daughter: Living in a Global Village*. Abbotsford, BC: printed by the author, 2006.

Bower, Anne. "Bound Together: Recipes, Lives, Stories, and Readings." In *Recipes for Reading: Community Cookbooks, Stories, Histories*, edited by Anne L. Bower, 1–14. Amherst: University of Massachusetts Press, 1997.

– "Cooking Up Stories: Narrative Elements in Community Cookbooks." In *Recipes for Reading Community Cookbooks, Stories, Histories*, edited by Anne L. Bower, 29–50. Amherst: University of Massachusetts Press, 1997.

Brandt, Di. "In Praise of Hybridity: Reflections from Southwestern Manitoba." In *After Identity: Mennonite Writing in North America*, edited by Robert Zacharias, 125–42. Winnipeg: University of Manitoba Press, 2015.

Brass, Janis, and Marilyn Iwama. "Two Worlds, One Body: A Conversation about Aboriginal-Mennonite Relations through Marriage." *Journal of Mennonite Studies* 19 (2001): 32–46.

Braun, Connie T. *Silentium: And Other Reflections on Memory, Sorrow, Place, and the Sacred*. Eugene, OR: Resource Publications, 2017.

Braun, Margaret, with Connie T. Braun. *At This Table: The Story of Margaret*. Vancouver, BC: Connie T. Braun, 2020.

Braun, Maria Klassen. *A Village Saga*. Manitoba: Susan Empringham, 2012.

Brown, Hubert L. *Black and Mennonite: A Search for Identity*. Eugene, OR: Wipf and Stock, 2001.

Buddle, Melanie. "Gender and Business: Recent Literature on Women and Entrepreneurship." *Histoire Sociale/Social History* 51, no. 104 (November 2018): 401–7.

Burtt, Bob. "Growing Organic: Mennonite Farmers Are Well Suited for Organic Farming." *Alternatives Journal* 34, no. 3 (2008): 14.

"A Call to Cook." *Historians Cooking the Past in the Time of COVID-19*. https://sites.google.com/view/cookingthepast/home. Accessed 5 May 2020.

Campbell, Maria. "Kookoom Mariah and the Mennonite Mrs." *Journal of Mennonite Studies* 19 (2001): 9–12.

Canadian Mennonite Cookbook: With Recipes in Metric and Imperial Measures. Toronto, ON: McLeod Publishing, 1978.

Cancian, Sonia. "'Tutti a Tavola!' Feeding the Family in Two Generations of Italian Immigrant Households in Montreal." In Iacovetta, Korinek, and Epp, *Edible Histories, Cultural Politics*, 209–21.

Carl-Klassen, Abigail, and Jonathan Klassen. "Rebels, Exiles, and Bridge Builders: Cross-Cultural Encounters in the Campos Menonitas of Chihauhau." *Journal of Mennonite Studies* 38 (2020): 173–92.

Cassidy, Tanya M., and Abdullahi Osman El-Tom, eds. *Moving Meals and Migrating Mothers: Culinary Cultures, Diasporic Dishes and Familial Foodways*. Bradford, ON: Demeter Press, 2021.

Chen, Agnes, and Paulus Hartono. "Transforming Conflicts through Food: A Surakarta Case Study." *Anabaptist Witness* 2, no. 2 (November 2015): 57–62.

Chornoboy, Eleanor Hildebrand. *Faspa: A Snack of Mennonite Stories*. Winnipeg, MB: Interior Publishing, 2003.

- *Katarina: Mennonite Girl from Russia*. Winnipeg, MB: printed by the author, 2017.
Chornoboy, Eleanor Hildebrand, Adolf Ens, and Jacob E. Peters, eds. *The Outsiders' Gaze: Life and Labour on the Mennonite West Reserve, 1874–1922*. Winnipeg, MB: Manitoba Mennonite Historical Society, 2015.
Contois, Emily J.H. *Diners, Dudes, and Diets: How Gender and Power Collide in Food Media and Culture*. Chapel Hill: University of North Carolina Press, 2020.
Cooke, Nathalie. "Canada's Food History through Cookbooks." In *Critical Perspectives in Food Studies*, edited by Mustafa Koç, Jennifer Sumner, and Anthony Winson, 33–48. Don Mills, ON: Oxford University Press, 2012.
– ed. *What's to Eat? Entrées in Canadian Food History*. Montreal & Kingston: McGill-Queen's University Press, 2009.
Coppolino, Andrew. "Telling Afro-Caribbean Stories through Food." *Waterloo Region Record*, 25 February 2020. https://www.therecord.com/living-story/9861962-telling-afro-caribbean-stories-through-food/.
Cortright, David. *Gandhi and Beyond: Nonviolence for an Age of Terrorism*. Boulder, CO: Paradigm Publishers, 2006.
Cote, Lance. *MennoNeechie Kitchen* (blog). Mennoneechiekitchen.com.
Counihan, Carole, and Penny Van Esterik, eds. *Food and Culture: A Reader*. New York, NY: Routledge, 1997.
Cruz, Daniel Shank. *Queering Mennonite Literature: Archives, Activism, and the Search for Community*. University Park: Pennsylvania State University Press, 2019.
The Daily Bonnet. https://dailybonnet.com/.
D'Amato, Luisa. "'Stop Eating, and Bid!' Food Rivals Quilts as Draw." *Waterloo Region Record*, 29 May 2017.
Davis, Melodie. "The Woman behind *Mennonite Community Cookbook*." *Mennonite* 18, no. 2 (February 2015): 12–17.
Del Rios Family Restaurant. http://delriosfamilyrestaurant.com/. Accessed 15 August 2019.
DeSilva, Cara, ed. *In Memory's Kitchen: A Legacy from the Women of Terezin*. Translated by Bianca Steiner Brown. Northvale, NJ: J. Aronson, 1996.
Desjardins, Michel, and Ellen Desjardins. "The Role of Food in Canadian Expressions of Christianity." In Iacovetta, Korinek, and Epp, *Edible Histories, Cultural Politics*, 70–82.
DeVault, Marjorie L. *Feeding the Family: The Social Organization of Caring as Gendered Work*. Chicago, IL: University of Chicago Press, 1991.
Diner, Hasia R. *Hungering for America: Italian, Irish, & Jewish Foodways in the Age of Migration*. Cambridge, MA: Harvard University Press, 2001.

Doerwald, Gunnar. "Mate." In *The Cookbook Project: Celebrating 75 Years of Meals and Memories*, compiled by Ellery Penner and Rachael Peters, 14–16. Niagara-on-the-Lake, ON: Niagara United Mennonite Church, 2013.

Dossa, Parin. *Afghanistan Remembers: Gendered Narrations of Violence and Culinary Practices*. Toronto, ON: University of Toronto Press, 2014.

Draper, Barb. "A Big Heart Filled with Butter Tarts." *Canadian Mennonite* 24, no. 7 (30 March 2020): 25.

Driedger, June Mears. "*The More-With-Less Cookbook* Changed Everything." *The Other Journal* no. 31 (Spring 2020). https://theotherjournal.com/2020/03/more-with-less-cookbook-changed-everything/.

Driedger, Leo. "Native Rebellion and Mennonite Invasion: An Examination of Two Canadian River Valleys." *Mennonite Quarterly Review* 46, no. 3 (July 1972): 290–300.

Driedger, Mary Lou. "From Country to City: Five Women Recall the Fear and Rewards of Leaving Home for the First Time." In *Embracing the World: Two Decades of Canadian Mennonite Writing: A Selection of Writings from the* Mennonite Mirror, 5–7. Winnipeg, MB: Mennonite Mirror, 1990.

– "Grandma's Soup Expressed Love and Care." *Canadian Mennonite* 25, no. 15 (14 July 2021). https://canadianmennonite.org/stories/grandma%E2%80%99s-soup-expressed-love-and-care.

Driver, Elizabeth. *Culinary Landmarks: A Bibliography of Canadian Cookbooks, 1828–1949*. Toronto, ON: University of Toronto Press, 2008.

Dueck, Abraham. "Rice Pudding–Cooked with Milk." In Dyck, *The Silence Echoes*, 61–6.

Dueck, Alicia J. *Negotiating Sexual Identities: Lesbian, Gay, and Queer Perspectives on Being Mennonite*. Berlin, Germany: LIT Verlag, 2012.

Dueck, Cameron. *Menno Moto: A Journey across the Americas in Search of My Mennonite Identity*. Windsor, ON: Biblioasis, 2020.

Dueck, Dora. *This Hidden Thing*. Winnipeg, MB: CMU Press, 2010.

Dueck, Helene. *Journey to Freedom: A Survivor's Story of the Great Trek*. Translated and edited by Agatha E. Klassen. Abbotsford, BC: printed by the author, 2003.

Dummitt, Chris. "Finding a Place for Father: Selling the Barbecue in Postwar Canada." *Journal of the Canadian Historical Association* 9, no. 1 (1998): 209–23.

Durksen, Hedy. "Just around the House: Recipe Books." *Canadian Mennonite* 10, no. 6 (9 February 1962): 8.

Dyck, Barry. "Family, Food and Spirituality." *Heritage Posting* no. 87 (June 2017): 4.

Dyck, Cornelius J., and Wilma L. Dyck, eds. *A Pilgrim People: The Dyck, Isaac, Quiring and Wiebe Story*. Saskatoon, SK: Renata and Allan Klassen, 1987.

Dyck, Harvey L., trans. and ed. *A Mennonite in Russia: The Diaries of Jacob D. Epp, 1851–1880*. Toronto, ON: University of Toronto Press, 1991.

Dyck, Harvey L., John R. Staples, and John B. Toews, eds. *Nestor Makhno and the Eichenfeld Massacre: A Civil War Tragedy in a Ukrainian Mennonite Village*. Kitchener, ON: Pandora Press, 2004.

Dyck, Sarah, trans. and ed., *The Silence Echoes: Memoirs of Trauma and Tears*. Kitchener, ON: Pandora Press, 1997.

Ebert, Myrtle V. *Wir Sind Frei! We Are Free! A Mennonite Experience: From the Ukraine to Canada*. Scarborough, ON: Lochleven, 1995.

Eicher, Lovina, with Kevin Williams. *The Amish Cook at Home: Simple Pleasures of Food, Family, and Faith*. Kansas City, MO: Andrew McMeel Publishing, LLC, 2008.

Eidinger, Andrea. "Gefilte Fish and Roast Duck with Orange Slices: A Treasure for My Daughter and the Creation of a Jewish Cultural Orthodoxy in Postwar Montreal." In Iacovetta, Korinek, and Epp, *Edible Histories, Cultural Politics*, 189–208.

Eidse, Faith. *Light the World: The Ben and Helen Eidse Story*. Victoria, BC: Friesen Press, 2012.

Emilia, Katherine Esther, and Semadeni Renpenning. *Recetario Menonita de Chihauhau*. Mexico: Conaculta, 2000.

Enns, Elaine. "Facing History with Courage: Towards Restorative Solidarity." Dmin dissertation, St Andrew's College, Saskatoon, 2015.

Enns, Elaine, and Ched Myers. *Healing Haunted Histories: A Settler Discipleship of Decolonization*. Eugene, OR: Cascade Books, 2021.

Enns, Luella Marie. *Preacher's Kids on the Homestead*. Belleville, ON: Guardian Books, 2005.

Entz, Mrs Curtis, and Dolores Penner. *Missionary Meals around the World*. Ste Anne, MB: Gospel Publishers, 1986.

Epp, Aaron. "Serving Up Nourishment with a Sense of Belonging." *Canadian Mennonite* 25, no. 8 (12 April 2021): 20.

Epp, Elise. "I Am from the Mennonites." *Canadian Mennonite* 16, no. 3 (6 February 2012): 34–5.

Epp, Marlene. "Cookbook as Metaphor for a People of Diversity: Canadian Mennonites after 1970." *Journal of Mennonite Studies* 37 (2019): 11–27.

– "'The Dumpling in My Soup Was Lonely Just Like Me': Food in the Memories of Mennonite Women Refugees." *Women's History Review* 25, no. 3 (June 2016): 365–81.

- "Eating across Borders: Reading Immigrant Cookbooks." *Histoire Sociale/Social History* 48, no. 96 (May 2015): 45–65.
- "The 'Grab Bag' Mennonite Family in Post-War Canada." In *On the Case: Explorations in Social History*, edited by Franca Iacovetta and Wendy Mitchinson, 338–57. Toronto, ON: University of Toronto Press, 1998.
- "The Memory of Violence: Soviet and East European Mennonite Refugees and Rape in the Second World War." *Journal of Women's History* 9, no. 1 (Spring 1997): 58–87.
- "The Mennonite Girls' Homes of Winnipeg: A Home away from Home." *Journal of Mennonite Studies* 6 (1988): 100–14.
- "More than 'Just' Recipes: Mennonite Cookbooks in Mid-Twentieth-Century North America." In Iacovetta, Korinek, and Epp, *Edible Histories, Cultural Politics*, 173–88.
- "Peppernuts and Anarsa: Food, Religion, and Ritual." *Anabaptist Witness* 2, no. 2 (November 2015): 87–90.
- "Returning Home: Memory and Place in Mennonite Ethno-Tourism in Russia and Ukraine." Paper presented at the Canadian Historical Association, University of New Brunswick, May 2011.
- "The Semiotics of Zwieback: Feast and Famine in the Narratives of Mennonite Refugee Women." In Epp and Iacovetta, *Sisters or Strangers*, 413–31.
- "Where There's Zwieback, There's Hope." *Historians Cooking the Past in the Time of COVID-19*. 9 April 2020. https://sites.google.com/view/cooking-the-past/where-theres-zwieback-theres-hope.
- *Women without Men: Mennonite Refugees of the Second World War*. Toronto, ON: University of Toronto Press, 2000.
- "Yeowomen of Yarrow: Raising Families and Creating Community in a Land of Promise." In *First Nations and First Settlers in the Fraser Valley (1890–1960)*, edited by Harvey Neufeldt, Ruth Derksen Siemens, and Robert Martens, 121–34. Kitchener, ON: Pandora Press, 2004.

Epp, Marlene, and Franca Iacovetta, eds. *Sisters or Strangers? Immigrant, Ethnic, and Racialized Women in Canadian History*. 2nd ed. Toronto, ON: University of Toronto Press, 2016.

Epp, Peter. "Memories of Difficult Years." *Der Bote* 70, no. 38 (13 October 1993): 24–5.

Epp, Peter, as told to. "A Mother's Faith." In Dyck, *The Silence Echoes*, 119–20.

Epp, Roger. "'There Was No One Here When We Came': Overcoming the Settler Problem." *Conrad Grebel Review* 30, no. 2 (Spring 2012): 115–35.

Epp-Tiessen, Esther. *Mennonite Central Committee in Canada: A History*. Winnipeg, MB: CMU Press, 2013.

Evans, Jennifer. "Telling Stories of Food, Community and Meaningful Lives in Post-1945 North Bay, Ontario." PhD dissertation, University of Toronto, 2015.

Farmer's Kochbuch. Chihauhau, Mexico: Women's Society of the Evangelical Missions Church, 2010.

Fast, Anne, and Elfrieda Neufeld. "Hog Butchering/*Schwien schlachte*: A Grand Occasion!" *Historian: Essex-Kent Mennonite Historical Association* 23, no. 3 (October 2012): 7–8.

Fast, Gerhard. *In Den Steppen Sibiriens.* Rosthern, SK: 1957.

Fast, Kerry. "Steinbach Pride: Becoming an Embodied Queer Mennonite Space." *Steinbach Pride* (blog). 8 November 2019. https://steinbachpride.blogspot.com/.

– *With a Whisk, a Colander and a Rolling Pin* (blog). http://kerrywhisks.blogspot.com/.

Fast, Victor. *A Day of Pilgrimage: A Document Commemorating the 75th Anniversary of the Arrival of the David and Agatha Fast Family in Canada.* London, ON: printed by the author, 2005.

Fehderau, Nicholas J. *A Mennonite Estate Family in Southern Ukraine.* Kitchener, ON: Pandora Press, 2013.

Fentress, James, and Chris Wickham. *Social Memory.* Cambridge, MA: Blackwell, 1992.

Ferguson, Kennan. "Intensifying Taste, Intensifying Identity: Collectivity through Community Cookbooks." *Signs: Journal of Women in Culture and Society* 37, no. 3 (2012): 695–717.

Fieldhouse, Paul. *Food and Nutrition: Customs and Culture*, 2nd ed. London, UK: Chapman and Hall, 1995.

Finding Harmony (blog). https://findingharmonyblog.com/.

Fischler, Claude. "Food, Self and Identity." *Social Science Information* 27, no. 2 (1988): 275–92.

Fisher, Susan Jane. "Seeds from the Steppe: Mennonites, Horticulture, and the Construction of Landscapes on Manitoba's West Reserve, 1870–1950." PhD dissertation, University of Manitoba, 2017.

– "(Trans)planting Manitoba's West Reserve: Mennonites, Myth, and Narratives of Place." *Journal of Mennonite Studies* 35 (2017): 127–48.

Fleishman, Suzanne. "Gender, the Personal, and the Voice of Scholarship: A Viewpoint." *Signs: Journal of Women in Culture and Society*, 23, no. 4 (Summer 1998): 975–1016.

Florian, Meghan. "Feast or Fast?" *Mennonite World Review* 93, no. 2 (19 January 2015): 7.

Foreign Missions Africa. Hillsboro, KS: Board of Foreign Missions, Mennonite Brethren Church of North America, 1947.

Francis, Andrew. "Food in the Contemporary UK Anabaptist Movement." *Anabaptist Witness* 2, no. 2 (November 2015): 11–31.

Frayne, Helen. "Saving Grace." Unpublished manuscript, n.d. Used with permission.

Freedman, Paul. "How Steak Became Manly and Salads Became Feminine." *The Conversation*. 24 October 2019. https://theconversation.com/how-steak-became-manly-and-salads-became-feminine-124147.

Friedlander, Roger, and Richard D. Hecht. "The Powers of Place." In *Religion, Violence, Memory, and Place*, edited by Oren Baruch Stier and J. Shawn Landres, 17–36. Bloomington & Indianapolis: Indiana University Press, 2006.

Friesen, Erika. "Tribute to Linie Krahn Friesen Given at Her Funeral." Unpublished manuscript, 2019. Used with permission.

Friesen, Isaiah. "Primary Source Analysis of the *More-with-Less Cookbook*." *Anabaptist Historians* (blog). 26 April 2018. https://anabaptisthistorians.org/2018/04/.

Friesen, Katie. *Into the Unknown*. Steinbach, MB: printed by the author, 1986.

Friesen, Leonard G. *Mennonites in the Russian Empire and the Soviet Union: Through Much Tribulation*. Toronto, ON: University of Toronto Press, 2022.

Friesen, Ted. *Memoirs: A Personal Autobiography of Ted Friesen*. Altona, MB: printed by the author, 2003.

Friesen, Tena. *Pushing Through Invisible Barriers: A Canadian Mennonite Story*. Tumbler Ridge, BC: Peace photoGraphics Inc., 2011.

Froese, Margaret. *Call to Remembrance: Abraham C. Neufeldt and Elizabeth Heinrichs, a Family History*. Alberta: printed by the author, 2001.

Fuchs, Tracy Ruta. *Beauty and Sustenance: A History of Mennonite Gardens and Orchards in Russia and Manitoba*. Steinbach, MB: Mennonite Heritage Village, 2007.

Funk, Carla. *Mennonite Valley Girl: A Wayward Coming of Age*. Vancouver, BC: Greystone Books, 2021.

Funk, Helen. *Met Helen en de Kjäakj*, vol. 1. Winnipeg, MB: Family Life Network, 2007.

Gabaccia, Donna R. *We Are What We Eat: Ethnic Food and the Making of Americans*. Cambridge, MA: Harvard University Press, 1998.

Gaede-Penner, Naomi. *From Kansas Wheat Fields to Alaska Tundra: A Mennonite Family Finds Home*. Mustang, OK: Tate Publishing, 2011.

Giesbrecht, Edward R. "The Everydayness of a Dairy Farm." In *Village of Unsettled Yearnings. Yarrow, British Columbia: Mennonite Promise*, edited by Leonard N. Neufeldt, 184–91. Victoria, BC: TouchWood Editions, 2002.

Gilbert, Sandra M. *The Culinary Imagination: From Myth to Modernity.* New York, NY, and London, UK: W.W. Norton and Co., 2014.

Gingrich, Del. *A Quilt of Impressions: Mennonite Children at School and at Home.* St Jacobs, ON: St Jacobs Visitor Centre, 2003.

Gingrich, Donna. *A Taste of Nostalgia: Recipes for Everyday.* Drayton, ON: printed by the author, 2015.

Goertz, Annie. *Miss Annie: God Sent a 3 Cent Stamp and More....* Abbotsford, BC: printed by the author, 2000.

Goerzen, Anny Penner Klassen. *Anny: Sheltered in the Arms of God: A True Story of Survival in Russia.* Fort St James, BC: printed by the author, 1988.

Gold, Carol. *Danish Cookbooks: Domesticity and National Identity, 1616–1901.* Seattle: University of Washington Press, 2006.

Goldenberg, Myrna. "Food Talk: Gendered Responses to Hunger in the Concentration Camps." In *Experience and Expression: Women, the Nazis, and the Holocaust,* edited by Elizabeth Baer and Myrna Goldenberg, 161–79. Detroit, IL: Wayne State University Press, 2003.

Good, E. Reginald. "Lost Inheritance: Alienation of Six Nations' Lands in Upper Canada, 1784–1805." *Journal of Mennonite Studies* 19 (2001): 92–102.

Good, Phyllis Pellman, and Kenneth Pellman. *Cooking & Memories: Favorite Recipes from 20 Mennonite and Amish Cooks.* Lancaster, PA: Good Books, 1983.

Goossen, Ben. "The Pacifist Roots of an American Nazi." *Boston Review.* 2 May 2019. http://bostonreview.net/philosophy-religion/ben-goossen-pacifist-roots-american-nazi.

Graber, Karen Hursh. "Immigrant Cooking in Mexico: The Mennonite Kitchens of Chihauhau." *MexConnet.* 1 January 2007. https://www.mexconnect.com/articles/2404-immigrant-cooking-in-mexico-the-mennonite-kitchens-of-chihuahua/.

Groening, Margaret Heinrichs. "Grandmother Remembers." Unpublished manuscript, n.d. Used with permission.

Gross, Aaron S., Jody Myers, and Jordan D. Rosenblum, eds. *Feasting and Fasting: The History and Ethics of Jewish Food.* New York, NY: New York University Press, 2019.

Hamilton, Sharon. "This Year, Baking Ukrainian Easter Bread Feels Different." *Globe and Mail,* 13 April 2022. https://www.theglobeandmail.com/life/first-person/article-ukrainian-easter-bread/.

Hamm, Ray. *New Bergthal Heritage and Cookbook, 1980.* Winnipeg, MB: Gateway Publishing, 1980.

Harder, Anne. *Mennonite Ethnic Cooking.* Alberta: printed by the author, 2006.

- *The Vauxhall Mennonite Church*. Calgary, AB: Mennonite Historical Society of Alberta, 2001.
Harder, Ernie. *Mostly Mennonite: Stories of Jacob and Mary Harder*. Vancouver, BC: printed by the author, 2009.
Harris-Aber, Amy. "Claiming a Piece of Tradition: Community Discourse in Russian Mennonite Community Cookbooks." *Journal of Amish and Plain Anabaptist Studies* 8, no. 2 (2020): 139–58.
Hayward, Victoria. "Mine Host–The Mennonite." In Chornoboy, Ens, and Peters, *The Outsiders' Gaze*, 191–7.
Hein, Gerhard, and Mary Enns. *Ufa: The Mennonite Settlements (Colonies), 1894–1938*. Canada: 1977.
Helmuth, Hope. *Hope's Table: Everyday Recipes from a Mennonite Kitchen*. Harrisonburg, VA: Herald Press, 2019.
"Helping Others." *Mennonite Girls Can Cook* (blog). http://www.mennonitegirlscancook.ca/p/mission-music-ukraine.html. Accessed 31 March 2021.
Hiebert, P.C., and Orie O. Miller. *Feeding the Hungry: Russia Famine, 1919–1925*. Scottdale, PA: Mennonite Central Committee, 1929.
Hiebert, Susan. "Indians, Métis and Mennonites." In *Mennonite Memories*, edited by Lawrence Klippenstein and Julius G. Toews, 50–4. Winnipeg, MB: Centennial Publications, 1977.
Hildebrand, Marjorie. *Reflections of a Prairie Community: A Collection of Stories and Memories of Burwalde S.D. #529*. Winkler, MB: Friends of the former Burwalde School District #529, 2004.
Hind, E. Cora. "The Mennonites of Manitoba." In Chornoboy, Ens, and Peters, *The Outsiders' Gaze*, 91–108.
Hinojosa, Felipe. "From Goshen to Delano: Towards a Relational Approach in Mennonite Studies." *Mennonite Quarterly Review* 91, no. 2 (April 2017): 201–12.
- *Latino Mennonites: Civil Rights, Faith, and Evangelical Culture*. Baltimore, MD: Johns Hopkins University Press, 2014.
History of Manitoba Mennonite Women in Mission, 1942–1977. Winnipeg, MB: Manitoba Mennonite Women in Mission, 1977.
Holtzman, Jon. D. "Food and Memory." *Annual Review of Anthropology* 35, no. 1 (2006): 361–78.
Horst, Isaac R. *Conestogo Mennonite Cookbook*. Mount Forest, ON: printed by the author, 1981.
Horst, Simone. "Peppernuts, Theme and Variations." *Anabaptist Historians* (blog). 23 December 2020. https://anabaptisthistorians.org/2020/12/23/peppernuts-theme-and-variations/.

Hossack, Darcie Friesen. *Mennonites Don't Dance*. Saskatoon, SK: Thistledown Press, 2010.
– Video of lecture in Mennonite/s Writing Series at Conrad Grebel University College. Waterloo, Ontario, 7 March 2012.
Hostetler, John A. *Amish Society*. Baltimore, MD: Johns Hopkins University Press, 1993.
– *Mennonite Life*. Scottdale, PA: Herald Press, 1954.
Hunchuk, S. Holyck. "Feeding the Dead: The Ukrainian Food Colossi of the Canadian Prairies." In Iacovetta, Korinek, and Epp, *Edible Histories, Cultural Politics*, 140–55.
Hussain, Arwa. "Bateta Champ." *Historians Cooking the Past* (blog). 25 May 2020. https://sites.google.com/view/cookingthepast/bateta-champ.
Iacovetta, Franca. "Famine or Feast? Gender, Food and Fascism in Transnational Contexts." In *Italian Foodways Worldwide: The Dispersal of Italian Cuisine(s)*, edited by Roberta Iannacito-Provenzano and Gabriele Scardellato, 87–114. Toronto, ON: The Mariano A. Elia Chair in Italian-Canadian Studies, 2019.
– *Gatekeepers: Reshaping Immigrant Lives in Cold War Canada*. Toronto, ON: Between the Lines, 2006.
– "Post-modern Ethnography, Historical Materialism, and Decentring the (Male) Authorial Voice: A Feminist Conversation." *Histoire Sociale/Social History* 32, no. 64 (November 1999): 275–93.
Iacovetta, Franca, and Valerie J. Korinek. "Jello-O Salads, One-Stop Shopping, and Maria the Homemaker: The Gender Politics of Food." In Epp and Iacovetta, *Sisters or Strangers*, 432–54.
Iacovetta, Franca, Valerie J. Korinek, and Marlene Epp, eds. *Edible Histories, Cultural Politics: Towards a Canadian Food History*. Toronto, ON: University of Toronto Press, 2012.
"Indonesian Food." *Mennonite World Conference*. 5 January 2021. https://mwc-cmm.org/resources/indonesian-food.
Inness, Sherrie A. "Introduction: Of Meatloaf and Jell-O ..." In *Cooking Lessons: The Politics of Gender and Food*, edited by Sherrie A. Inness, xi–xvii. Lanham, MD: Rowman & Littlefield Publishers, 2001.
– "Introduction: Thinking Food/Thinking Gender." In *Kitchen Culture in America: Popular Representations of Food, Gender, and Race*, edited by Sherrie A. Inness, 1–12. Philadelphia: University of Pennsylvania Press, 2001.
– *Secret Ingredients: Race, Gender, and Class at the Dinner Table*. New York, NY: Palgrave Macmillan, 2006.
"International Food a Crowd-Pleaser at Mennonite Sale." *Waterloo Region Record*, 23 May 2018.

"Interview with Miriam Toews." *New York Times Book Review*, 3 October 2021. https://link.gale.com/apps/doc/A677668858/LitRC?u=uniwater&sid=bookmark-LitRC&xid=7458a23e.

"Interview with Rhoda Janzen." *Rhubarb* no. 32 (Spring 2013): 49–52.

Ireland, Lynne. "The Compiled Cookbook as Foodways Autobiography." *Western Folklore* 40, no. 1 (January 1981): 107–114.

Jacobsen, Annie, with Jane Finlay-Young and Di Brandt. *Watermelon Syrup: A Novel*. Waterloo, ON: Wilfrid Laurier University Press, 2007.

Jansen, Sharon L. "'Family Liked 1956': My Mother's Recipes." In *Through the Kitchen Window: Women Explore the Intimate Meanings of Food and Cooking*, edited by Arlene Voski Avakian, 55–64. Oxford, UK: Berg, 2005.

Jansen, Walter, and Linda Jansen. *Our Stories*. Translated by Walfried Jansen. East St Paul, MB: Walfried Jansen, 2010.

Jantz, Harold, ed. and trans. *Flight: Mennonites Facing the Soviet Empire in 1929/30, from the Pages of the Mennonitische Rundschau*. Winnipeg, MB: Eden Echoes Publishing, 2018.

Jantzen, Mark, and John D. Thiesen, eds. *European Mennonites and the Holocaust*. Toronto, ON: University of Toronto Press, 2020.

Jantzi, Marianne. *Simple Pleasures: Stories from My Life as an Amish Mother*. Harrisonburg, VA and Kitchener, ON: Herald Press, 2016.

Janzen, Abram. "A Pioneer's Life in Manitoba." *Mennonite Mirror* 3, no. 4 (January/February 1974): 19–21.

Janzen, Helen. *My First Ninety Years*. Saskatoon, SK: Anita Flegg, 2009.

Janzen, Helene. "Dear Uncle and Aunt." In Dyck, *The Silence Echoes*, 224–30.

Janzen, Johann J. "Paraguayan Journal." Translated by Hilda Janzen Goertzen. *Roots and Branches: Newsletter of the Mennonite Historical Society of BC* 15, no. 3 (September 2009): 10–11.

Janzen, Rebecca. "Mexican Mennonites Combat Fears of Violence with a New Christmas Tradition." *The Conversation*, 11 December 2019. https://theconversation.com/mexican-mennonites-combat-fears-of-violence-with-a-new-christmas-tradition-127982.

Janzen, Rhoda. *Mennonite in a Little Black Dress: A Memoir of Going Home*. New York, NY: Henry Holt and Co., 2009.

Johnson-Weiner, Karen M. *The Lives of Amish Women*. Baltimore, MD: Johns Hopkins University Press, 2020.

Jones-Gailani, Nadia. *Transnational Identity and Memory Making in the Lives of Iraqi Women in Diaspora*. Toronto, ON: University of Toronto Press, 2020.

Kasdorf, Julia. *The Body and the Book: Writing from a Mennonite Life*. Baltimore, MD: Johns Hopkins University Press, 2001.

- "When Our Women Go Crazy." In *Sleeping Preacher*, 7. Pittsburg, PA: University of Pittsburg Press, 1992.
- "Working Away: Mennonite Place, Women's Space, and Plain Maids of the 1930s." *Mennonite Quarterly Review* 88, no. 2 (April 2014): 219–32.

Kasstan, Ben. "The Taste of Trauma: Reflections of Ageing Shoah Survivors on Food and How They (Re)inscribe It with Meaning." *Religion and Food, Scripta Instituti Donneriani Aboensis* 26 (2015): 349–55.

Kauffman, Tina Klassen. *Immigrant Daughter: A Monument to Poverty*. Bloomington, IN: AuthorHouse, 2012.

Kaufman, Edna Ramseyer. *Melting Pot of Mennonite Cookery, 1874–1974*. North Newton, KS: Bethel College Women's Association, 1975.

Kelleher, Margaret. "Woman as Famine Victim: The Figure of Woman in Irish Famine Narratives." In *Gender and Catastrophe*, edited by Ronit Lentin, 241–54. London, UK: Zed Books, 1997.

Kelting, Lily. "The Entanglement of Nostalgia and Utopia in Contemporary Southern Food Cookbooks." *Food, Culture & Society* 19, no. 2 (June 2016): 361–87.

Kennan, Ferguson. "Intensifying Taste, Intensifying Identity: Collectivity through Community Cookbooks." *Signs: Journal of Women in Culture and Society* 37, no. 3 (2012): 695–717.

Keshgegian, Flora A. "Finding a Place Past Night: Armenian Genocidal Memory in Diaspora." In *Religion, Violence, Memory, and Place*, edited by Oren Baruch Stier and J. Shawn Landres, 100–17. Bloomington: Indiana University Press, 2006.

Khan, Aisha. "Juthaa in Trinidad: Food, Pollution, and Hierarchy in a Caribbean Diaspora Community." *American Ethnologist* 21, no. 2 (May 1994): 245–69.

Kirkby, Mary-Ann. *Secrets of a Hutterite Kitchen*. Toronto, ON: Penguin, 2014.

Kirkpatrick, Debbie. "The Story of Mrs. Suse Rempel and Her Family." Unpublished research paper, Mennonite Heritage Archives, Winnipeg, MB, 1979.

Kis, Oksana. "Defying Death: Women's Experience of the Holodomor, 1932–1933." *Aspasia* 7 (2013): 42–67.

Klassen, Elizabeth. "My Experiences and My Flight from Russia." Unpublished manuscript, Centre for Mennonite Brethren Studies, Winnipeg, MB, 1946.

Klassen, Helen, ed. and trans. *Love & Remembrance*, Vol. 1, *Origins to 1927: From the Journals of Dietrich & Katharina (Matthies) Rempel*. Abbotsford, BC: Judson Lake House Publishers, 2012.

Klassen, Jenna. "Russian Mennonite Food History." *MySteinbach* (blog). 30 June 2018. https://www.mysteinbach.ca/blogs/8998/russian-mennonite-food-history/

Klassen, Otto. *I Remember: The Story of Otto Klassen*. Winnipeg, MB: Klassen Publishing, 2013.

Klassen, Pamela E. *Going by the Moon and the Stars: Stories of Two Russian Mennonite Women*. Waterloo, ON: Wilfrid Laurier University Press, 1994.

– "What's Bre(a)d in the Bone: The Bodily Heritage of Mennonite Women." *Mennonite Quarterly Review* 68, no. 2 (April 1994): 229–47.

Klassen, Peter J. *Mennonites in Early Modern Poland and Prussia*. Baltimore, MD: Johns Hopkins University Press, 2009.

Klassen, Victor. "Worscht Bits." *Rhubarb* no. 26 (Summer 2010): 12.

Klassen-Wiebe, Nicolien. "Hands-On learning." *Canadian Mennonite* 26, no. 2 (24 January 2022): 20–1.

– "Minority Mennonites Organize a Support Group." *Canadian Mennonite* 24, no. 22 (26 October 2020): 25.

Klippenstein, Frieda Esau. "'Doing What We Could': Mennonite Domestic Servants in Winnipeg, 1920 to 1950s." *Journal of Mennonite Studies* 7 (1989): 145–66.

– "Gender and Mennonites: A Response to Mennonites in Canada, 1939–1970, A People Transformed." *Journal of Mennonite Studies* 15 (1997): 142–9.

Klippenstein, LaVerna. "The Modern Mennonite Housewife." *Mennonite Mirror* 1, no. 9 (May 1972): 5–6.

Kneafsey, Moya, and Rosie Cox. "Food, Gender and Irishness – How Irish Women in Coventry Make Home." *Irish Geography* 35, no. 1 (January 2002): 6–15.

Knowles, Paul, ed. *Piecemakers: The Story of the Ontario Mennonite Relief Sale and Quilt Auction*. New Hamburg, ON: English Garden Publishers, 2004.

Kolinsky, Eve. *Women in Contemporary Germany: Life, Work and Politics*. Providence, RI: Berg, 1993.

Kommt Essen: Mit den Mennonitischen Frauen von Durango, Mexiko (Come and Eat with the Mennonite Ladies from Durango Mexico). Durango, Mexico: Mennonitische Frauen von Durango, Mexiko, 2011.

Konrad, Anne. *And in Their Silent Beauty Speak: A Mennonite Family in Russia and Canada, 1790–1990*. Toronto, ON: printed by the author, 2004.

– *Down Clearbrook Road: A Girl in a BC Mennonite Village, 1946–1951*. Victoria, BC: Friesen Press, 2019.

Koop, Heidi, compiler, and Dyck, Helga, editor. "The Band Plays On: Mennonite Pioneers of North Kildonan Reflect." Unpublished manuscript, Mennonite Heritage Archives, Winnipeg, MB, 1998.

Kostash, Myrna. *The Doomed Bridegroom: A Memoir*. Edmonton, AB: NeWest Press, 1998.

Krause, Carl A. "Emilia Wieler and Almighty Voice." *Saskatchewan Mennonite Historian* 13, no. 2 (July 2007): 15–17.

Kreider, Robert, and Rachel Waltner Goossen. *Hungry, Thirsty, a Stranger: The MCC Experience*. Scottdale, PA: Herald Press, 1988.

Krueger, Mary. "An Unforgettable Childhood Experience." *EMMC Recorder* 26, no. 2 (February 1989): 7–8.

Labun, Allan. *Margaret Suderman: Missionary Nurse*. Winnipeg, MB: printed by the author, 2008.

Lam, Lawrence. *From Being Uprooted to Surviving: Resettlement of Vietnamese-Chinese 'Boat People' in Montreal, 1980–1990*. Toronto, ON: York Lanes Press, 1996.

Le Dantec-Lowry, Hélène. "Reading Women's Lives in Cookbooks and Other Culinary Writings: A Critical Essay." *Revue française d'études américaines*, no. 116 (2008): 99–122.

Lee-Poy, Michael, and Thomas Brown. *Food for the Journey: Recipes and Quotations from Our Community*. Kitchener-Waterloo, ON: printed by the authors, 2007.

Lemke, Helmut, and Eva Daniel. *Slipping the Noose: Two Escape Stories*. Bloomington, IN: AuthorHouse, 2018.

Letkemann, Peter. *A Book of Remembrance: Mennonites in Arkadak and Zentral, 1908–1941*. Winnipeg, MB: Old Oak Publishing, 2016.

– "Mennonite Victims of 'The Great Terror,' 1936–1938." *Journal of Mennonite Studies* 16 (1998): 33–58.

"The Life and Times of Marie Hildebrandt Huebert (1923–1911)." Courtesy of Ruth Derksen, *Historian of Essex-Kent Mennonite Historical Association* 33, no. 2 (July 2011): 2–4.

Lind, Mary Beth, and Cathleen Hockman-Wert. *Simply in Season*. Scottdale, PA and Waterloo, ON: Herald Press, 2005.

Loewen, Harry, ed. *Road to Freedom: Mennonites Escape the Land of Suffering*. Kitchener, ON: Pandora Press, 2000.

Loewen, Helen Reimer. "Memories." Unpublished manuscript, British Columbia Mennonite Historical Association, Abbotsford, BC, 1996.

Loewen, Royden. *Horse-and-Buggy-Genius: Listening to Mennonites Contest the Modern World*. Winnipeg: University of Manitoba Press, 2016.

– *Mennonite Farmers: A Global History of Place and Sustainability*. Baltimore, MD: Johns Hopkins University Press, 2021.
– "The Poetics of Peoplehood: Ethnicity and Religion among Canada's Mennonites." In *Christianity and Ethnicity in Canada*, edited by Paul Bramadat and David Seljak, 330–64. Toronto, ON: University of Toronto Press, 2008.
– *Village among Nations: "Canadian" Mennonites in a Transnational World, 1916–2006*. Toronto, ON: University of Toronto Press, 2013.
Loewen, Susie Guenther. "Cooking Up Discipleship." *Canadian Mennonite* 19, no. 19 (28 September 2015): 4–6.
Loewen, William, Gladys Loewen, and Sharon Shepherd Loewen. "Food without Borders: Adaptive Expressions of Mothering." In *Moving Meals and Migrating Mothers: Culinary Cultures, Diasporic Dishes and Familial Foodways*, edited by Tanya M. Cassidy and Abdullahi Osman El-Tom, 95–114. Bradford, ON: Demeter Press, 2021.
Longacre, Doris Janzen. *More-with-Less Cookbook: Suggestions by Mennonites on How to Eat Better and Consume Less of the World's Limited Food Resources*. Scottdale, PA: Herald Press, 1976.
Lorenzkowski, Barbara. *Sounds of Ethnicity: Listening to German North America, 1850–1914*. Winnipeg: University of Manitoba Press, 2010.
Mace, James E. "Soviet Man-Made Famine in Ukraine." In *Century of Genocide: Eyewitness Accounts and Critical Views*, edited by Samuel Totten, William S. Parsons, Israel W. Charny, 78–90. New York: Garland Publishing, 1997.
Makhijani, Pooja. "A Place at the Table: Authors of Color Push Back against the Overwhelming Whiteness of Cookbook Publishing." *Publishers Weekly* (24 August 2020): 30–1.
Mama's Kochbuch. Chihuahua, Mexico: Escuela CETA, 2005.
Mangalaseril, Jasmine. "Faith and Food Intertwined." *Waterloo Region Record*. 26 November 2021.
Martens, Eleanor. "The Artist as Homemaker: A Portrait." *Sophia* 3, no. 1 (Winter 1993): 13.
Martens, Hildegard Margo. *On My Own: A Journey from a Mennonite Childhood*. Winnipeg, MB: Anderson Publishing House, 2018.
Martens, Katherine, ed. and trans. *They Came from Wiesenfeld Ukraine to Canada: Family Stories*. Winnipeg, MB: printed by the author, 2005.
Martens, Katherine, and Edgar G. Reimer. *Reimer Legacy: A Compilation of Historical Voices*. Winnipeg, MB: printed by the authors, 2015.
Martin, David. "'Mennonite' Not Eaten Here." *Canadian Mennonite* 15, no. 2 (24 January 2011): 13.

– "What Is the Spirit Saying to Our Churches Today?" *Canadian Mennonite* 21, no.17 (6 September 2017): 4–6.

Masih, Suniti. "Mennonite Indian Women and Their Culture in Society, in Education, in Workplace, and the Church." Unpublished manuscript, 2015. Used with permission.

Matahelemual, Hendy Stevan. "Spice Up Your Life." *Anabaptist World* 3, no. 5 (15 April 2022): 38.

Matsomoto, Valerie J. "Apple Pie and Makizushi: Japanese American Women Sustaining Family and Community." In *Eating Asian America: A Food Studies Reader*, edited by Robert Ji-Song Ku, Martin F. Manalansan, and Anita Mannur, 255–73. New York, NY: New York University Press, 2013.

McGuire, Marilyn B. *Lived Religion: Faith and Practice in Everyday Life*. New York, NY: Oxford University Press, 2008.

Mehta, Julie. "Toronto's Multicultured Tongues: Stories of South Asian Cuisines." In Iacovetta, Korinek, and Epp, *Edible Histories, Cultural Politics*, 156–69.

Mennonite Cookbook. Vancouver, BC: Whitecap Books, 2003.

Mennonite Girls Can Cook: Traditions of Food and Faith (blog). http://www.mennonitegirlscancook.ca. Accessed 6 April 2021.

"Mennonite Girls Can Cook Becomes a Live Comedy." *Anabaptist World*, 4 February 2016. https://anabaptistworld.org/mennonite-girls-can-cook-becomes-a-musical/.

"Mennonites & Alcohol." Theme issue of *Preservings* no. 43 (2021).

The Mennonite Treasury of Recipes. Steinbach, MB: Derksen Printers, 1962.

Mennopolitan (blog). http://www.mennopolitan.com/.

Miller, Laura. "She Dined on Black Pudding." *Slate*, 12 July 2017. https://slate.com/culture/2017/07/she-dined-on-black-pudding.html.

Miller, Melissa. "Pies at the Potluck." *Canadian Mennonite* 16, no. 21 (29 October 2012): 9.

Mintz, Corey. "The History of Food in Canada Is the History of Colonialism." *Walrus*, 12 March 2019. https://thewalrus.ca/the-history-of-food-in-canada-is-the-history-of-colonialism/

"A Mix of Mennonite, Mexican Cuisine." *Whig-Standard*. Online article (2009). http://www.thewhig.com.

Mock, Melanie Springer. "Mothering, More with Less." In *Mothering Mennonite*, edited by Rachel Epp Buller and Kerry Fast, 256–72. Bradford, ON: Demeter Press, 2013.

Molloy, Michael J., Peter Duschinsky, Kurt F. Jensen, and Robert J. Shalka. *Running on Emtpy: Canada and the Indochinese Refugees, 1975–1980*. Montreal & Kingston: McGill-Queen's University Press, 2017.

Montanari, Massimo. *Food Is Culture*. Translated by Albert Sonnenfeld. New York, NY: Columbia University Press, 2004.

More-With-Less: Thinking about Our Food ... Let's Eat! (blog). 31 August 2009. http://morewithlesscookbook.blogspot.com/2009/08/.

Moses, Lee Hull. "Recipes for a Revolution: The Enduring Wisdom of More with Less." *The Christian Century* 133, no. 25 (7 December 2016), 32–4.

Mumaw, Catherine R. "A Tribute to Mary Emma Showalter Eby." *Minding Mennonite Memory* 66, no. 3 (July 2005): 7–11, 13.

Murcott, Anne. *The Sociology of Food and Eating: Essays on the Sociological Significance of Food*. Aldershot, UK: Gower, 1984.

Murray, Stuart. *The Naked Anabaptist: The Bare Essentials of a Radical Faith*. Scottdale, PA: Herald Press, 2010.

Neudorf, Peter. "Pig Butchering." *Mennonite Historical Society of BC Newsletter* 9, no. 3 (Summer 2003): 9.

Neufeld, David G. "The Amish and Their 'New' Neighbours." Written for Amish Bicentennial in Ontario, September 2022. *Mennonite Historical Society of Ontario*. http://www.mhso.org/sites/default/files/publications/Amish%20Bicentennial%20Articles_0.pdf.

Neufeld, Dietrich, and Al Reimer. *A Russian Dance of Death: Revolution and Civil War in the Ukraine*. Winnipeg, MB: Hyperion Press, 1980.

Neufeld, Elsie K. "*Ort und Vertreibung*: My Mother of the 1920s." *Journal of Mennonite Studies* 36 (2018): 171–9.

Neufeld, Justina D. *A Family Torn Apart*. Kitchener, ON: Pandora Press, 2003.

Neufeld, Henry. "Thank you!" *Mennonite Historical Society of BC Newsletter* 9, no. 3 (Summer 2003): 7.

Neufeld, Herman A. *Mary Neufeld and the Repphun Story, from the Molotschna to Manitoba*. North Hollywood, CA: The Carole Joyce Gallery, 1987.

Neufeldt, Colin P. "Reforging Mennonite *Spetspereselentsy*: The Experience of Mennonite Exiles at Siberian Special Settlements in the Omsk, Tomsk, Novosibirsk and Narym 4 Regions (1930–33)." *Journal of Mennonite Studies* 30 (2012): 269–314.

– "Through the Fires of Hell: The Dekulakization and Collectivization of the Soviet Mennonite Community, 1928–1933." *Journal of Mennonite Studies* 16 (1998): 9–32.

Neufeldt, Reina C. "Settler Colonial Conscripts: Mennonite Reserves and the Enfolding of Implicated Subjects." *Postcolonial Studies* 24, no. 2 (June 2021): 1–19.

Neuhaus, Jessamyn. *Manly Meals and Mom's Home Cooking: Cookbooks and Gender in Modern America*. Baltimore, MD: Johns Hopkins University Press, 2003.

– "The Way to a Man's Heart: Gender Roles, Domestic Ideology, and Cookbooks in the 1950s." *Journal of Social History* 32, no. 3 (Spring 1999): 529–55.
Newman, Alex. "The Rich History and Profitability of Church Cookbooks." *Faith Today* 36, no. 6 (November/December 2018): 38–40.
Nobbs-Thiessen, Ben. "Cheese Is Culture and Soy Is Commodity: Environmental Change in a Bolivian Mennonite Colony." *Journal of Mennonite Studies* 35 (2017): 303–28.
– "Reshaping the Chaco: Migrant Foodways, Place-making, and the Chaco War." *Journal of Latin American Studies* 50, no. 3 (November 2017): 579–611.
Obituary of Anna Derksen Rosenfeld. *Der Bote* 67, no. 34 (12 September 1990): 7.
Passariello, Phyllis. "Anomalies, Analogies, and Sacred Profanities: Mary Douglas on Food and Culture, 1957–1989." *Food and Foodways* 4, no. 1 (1990): 53–71.
Pauls, Marianne Zwittag. *Memories*. St Catharines, ON: printed by the author, 2018.
Penner, Doris. "Memories of *Schaaldouak* Make Nostalgic Afternoon." *Carillon*, 15 May 2000.
Penner, Ellery. Written notes about food and Mennonites in Indonesia, 2012. Used with permission.
Penner, Ellery, and Rachael Peters, compilers. *The Cookbook Project: Celebrating 75 Years of Meals and Memories*. Niagara-on-the-Lake, ON: Niagara United Mennonite Church, 2013.
Penner, Lydia. "The Mennonite Treasury of Recipes, a Canadian Bestseller." In *Fifty Years Ebenezer Verein, 1936–1986*, 53–4. Steinbach, MB: Ebenezer Verein, 1987.
Pennsylvania-German Foodways in Waterloo County. Kitchener, ON: Joseph Schneider Haus, n.d.
Pepper, Martha L. *Called and Faithful*. Elizabethtown, PA: Martha L. Pepper, 2011.
Peters, Gerald, translator and editor. *Diary of Anna Baerg, 1916–1924*. Winnipeg, MB: CMBC Publications, 1985.
Peters, John. *The Plain People: A Glimpse of Life among the Old Order Mennonites of Ontario*. Kitchener, ON: Pandora Press, 2003.
Peters, Mariechen. "Dearly Beloved." In Dyck, *The Silence Echoes*, 57–60.
Peters, Sarah. *Walk with Me South of the Equator*. Winnipeg, MB: printed by the author, 2005.
Pető, Andrea. "Food-Talk: Markers of Identity and Imaginary Belongings." In *Women Migrants from East to West: Gender, Mobility and Belonging in*

Contemporary Europe, edited by Luisa Passerini et al., 152–64. New York, NY: Berghahn Books, 2007.

Pilcher, Jeffrey M. *Food in World History*. New York, NY: Routledge, 2006.

Plakias, Alexandra. *Thinking Through Food: A Philosophical Introduction*. Peterborough, ON: Broadview Press, 2019.

Plett, Marlene. *The Road from Edenthal: An Unhurried Journey*. Altona, MB: printed by the author, 2016.

Plett, Paul. *I Am a Mennonite*. Winnipeg, MB: Ode Productions, 2020.

Pollan, Michael. *The Omnivore's Dilemma: A Natural History of Four Meals*. New York, NY: Penguin Books, 2007.

Porter, Michelle. "More-with-Much-Less: An Anorexic's Guide to Mennonite Cooking." *More with Much Less* (blog). 3 June 2013. http://morewithmuchless.blogspot.com/.

Procida, Mary A. "No Longer Half-Baked: Food Studies and Women's History." *Journal of Women's History* 16, no. 3 (Autumn 2004): 197–205.

Rahn, Peter J., ed. and trans. *Among the Ashes: In the Stalinkova Kolkhoz (Konteniusfeld), 1930–1935*. Kitchener, ON: Pandora Press, 2011.

Randall, Margaret. "What My Tongue Knows." In Avakian, *Through the Kitchen Window*, 117–33.

Redekop, Magdalene. *Making Believe: Questions about Mennonites and Art*. Winnipeg: University of Manitoba Press, 2020.

Rempel, John. "Ritual as My Third Language: An Autobiographical Account." *Mennonite Quarterly Review* 79, no. 1 (January 2005): 7–18.

Rempel, Teodor, ed. *Letters of a Mennonite Couple: Nicolai and Katharina Rempel, Russia: War and Revolution, 1914–1917*. Fresno, CA: Center for Mennonite Brethren Studies, 2014.

Rhubarb & Roses (blog). http://rhubarbandroses-rosella.blogspot.com/.

Riekman, Becky. "Helen Kliewer Bergman." *Saskatchewan Mennonite Historian* 11, no. 3 (September 2005): 12–13.

Rindlisbacher, Simon, and Elwood E. Yoder. "500 Years after a Sausage Rebellion, Divided Groups Reunite to Remember." *Anabaptist World* 3, no. 4 (25 March 2022): 20–1.

Roes, Marion. *Mennonite Funeral and Burial Traditions: Interviews and Personal Stories*. Waterloo, ON: printed by the author, 2019.

Roth, Lorraine. *Willing Service: Stories of Ontario Mennonite Women*. Waterloo, ON: Mennonite Historical Society of Ontario, 1992.

Roth, Willard. *Mennonite Men Can Cook Too: Celebrating Hospitality with 170 Delicious Recipes*. New York, NY: Good Books, 2015.

Rudolph, Miriam. "disPOSSESSION: Exploring Mennonite and Indigenous Land Usage in Paraguay through Art." *Journal of Mennonite Studies* 38 (2020): 23–34.

Sack, Daniel. *Whitebread Protestants: Food and Religion in American Culture.* New York, NY: St Martin's Press, 2000.

Salvio, Paula M. "Dishing It Out: Food Blogs and Post-Feminist Domesticity." *Gastronomica* 12, no. 3 (Fall 2012): 31–9.

Sauder, Renee. "Food in the Midst of Sorrow." Sermon given at Stirling Avenue Mennonite Church, Kitchener, Ontario, 10 February 2019. Used with permission.

Sawatzky, Linda Epp. *Side by Side: A Memoir of Parents, Anna Enns & Heinrich M. Epp.* Winnipeg, MB: Eppisode Publishing, 2010.

Schellenberg, Angeline. "Cooking Up a Low German Blessing." *Mennonite Weekly Review* 85, no. 25 (18 June 2007): 1, 10.

Schellenberg, Lovella, Anneliese Friesen, Judy Wiebe, Betty Reimer, Bev Klassen, Charlotte Penner, Ellen Bayles, Julie Klassen, Kathy McLellan, and Marg Bartel. *Mennonite Girls Can Cook.* Waterloo, ON and Harrisonburg, VA: Herald Press, 2011.

Schlabach, Joetta Handrich. *Extending the Table: A World Community Cookbook.* Scottdale, PA and Waterloo, ON: Herald Press, 1991.

Schmidt, Agatha Loewen. *Gnadenfeld, Molotschna: 1835–1943.* Kitchener, ON: printed by the author, 1989.

Schmidt, Ed. "The Theodore Nickel Family." *Saskatchewan Mennonite Historian* 12, no. 3 (December 2006): 11–12.

Schroeder, Elfrieda. "Zwieback from Saint Johanna." *Canadian Mennonite* 24, no. 22 (26 October 2020): 27.

Schroeder, William. "Bergthal's Pilgrimage to Manitoba." *Mennonite Mirror* 3, no. 4 (January/February 1974): 9–16.

Schroth, Gwendolyn Hiebert. *Curry, Corduroy and the Call: A Mennonite Missionary's Daughter Grows up in Rural India.* Denver, CO: Outskirts Press, 2011.

Seiling, Jonathan. *Feeding the Neighbouring Enemy: Mennonite Women in Niagara during the War of 1812.* St. Catharines, ON: Gelassenheit Publications, 2012.

Shapiro, Laura. *Something from the Oven: Reinventing Dinner in 1950s America.* New York, NY: Viking, 2004.

Sharpless, Rebecca. *Cooking in Other Women's Kitchens: Domestic Workers in the South, 1865–1960.* Chapel Hill: University of North Carolina Press, 2010.

The Shoofly Project (blog). http://theshooflyproject.blogspot.ca/p/about-katie.html. Accessed 18 October 2013.

Showalter, Jewel. "Community Cookbook Author Retires from Teaching." *Mennonite Reporter* 2, no. 26 (25 December 1972): 4.

Showalter, Mary Emma. *Mennonite Community Cookbook: Favorite Family Recipes*. Scottdale, PA: The Mennonite Community Association, 1950.

Siemens, Ruth Derksen. *Remember Us: Letters from Stalin's Gulag (1930–37)*, Vol. 1, *The Regehr Family*. Kitchener, ON: Pandora Press, 2007.

Slabach, Gertrude. *A Place for Ruth: The True Story of Ruth Reimer Yoder Growing Up in Nazi Germany*. Morgantown, PA: Masthof Press, 2019.

Smith, Mark M. *Sensing the Past: Seeing, Hearing, Smelling, Tasting, and Touching in History*. Berkeley: University of California Press, 2007.

Smucker, David Rempel. "Faith versus Culture?: The Mennonite Pavilion at Folklorama in Winnipeg, Manitoba, 1980–1982." *Journal of Mennonite Studies* 33 (2015): 235–50.

Sneath, Robyn. "Imagining a Mennonite Community: The *Mennonitische Post* and a People of Diaspora." *Journal of Mennonite Studies* 22 (2004): 205–20.

Snyder, Beatrice Miller. *Pennsylvania German Customs and Cookery*. Waterloo, ON: Pennsylvania German Folklore Society of Ontario Waterloo Chapter, 1979.

Snyder, Jo. *The Vegan Mennonite Kitchen: Old Recipes for a Changing World*. Kitchener, ON: Pandora Press, 2021.

St George, Sergeant V.T. "North West Mounted Police Report." In Chornoboy, Ens, and Peters, *The Outsiders' Gaze*, 85–90.

Staebler, Edna. *Food That Really Schmecks*. Toronto, ON: McGraw-Hill Ryerson, 1968.

– *More Food That Really Schmecks*. Toronto, ON: McClelland and Stewart, 1979.

– *Sauerkraut and Enterprise*. Kitchener, ON: The University Women's Club of Kitchener and Waterloo, 1966.

Steiner, Sam. "Horst, Isaac Reist (1918–2008)." *Global Anabaptist Mennonite Encyclopedia Online*. Accessed 15 December 2022. http://gameo.org/index.php?title=Horst,_Isaac_Reist_(1918–2008)&oldid=141819.

Stier, Oren Baruch, and J. Shawn Landres, eds. *Religion, Violence, Memory, and Place*. Bloomington & Indianapolis: Indiana University Press, 2006.

Strempler, Erwin. "Uprooted, But Not without Opportunity to Go On." *Der Bote* 70, no. 38 (13 October 1993): 22–3.

Stucky, Harley J., and Alice Kaufman and Ruby Stucky, compilers. *The Centennial Treasury of Recipes: Swiss (Volhynian) Mennonites*. North Newton, KS: Swiss Mennonite Cultural and Historical Association, 1974.

Suderman, Victor P., compiler and editor. *The Sudermans from Alexanderthal, 1848–2011*. Edmonton, AB: printed by the author, 2011.

Sutton, David E. *Remembrance of Repasts: An Anthropology of Food and Memory*. Oxford & New York: Berg, 2001.

Swartz, Herb. *Stories Our Mothers Told*. Harrison, VA: printed by the author, 2006.

Szabo, Michelle. "Men Nurturing through Food: Challenging Gender Dichotomies around Domestic Cooking." *Journal of Gender Studies* 23, no. 1 (2 January 2014): 18–31.

Teichroeb, Wera. "A Child Remembers War and New Beginnings, 1941–1999." Unpublished manuscript, n.d. Used with permission.

Theophano, Janet. *Eat My Words: Reading Women's Lives through the Cookbooks They Wrote*. New York, NY: Palgrave, 2002.

Thielman, Susanne Willms. *Susanne Remembers: A Mennonite Childhood in Revolutionary Russia*. Abbotsford, BC: Judson Lake House, 2009.

Thiesen, John D. "Mennonite Nectar." *Preservings* 43 (2021): 17–20.

Thiessen, Anna. *The City Mission in Winnipeg*. Winnipeg, MB: Centre for Mennonite Brethren Studies, 1991.

Thiessen, Edna Schroeder, and Angela Showalter. *A Life Displaced: A Mennonite Woman's Flight from War-Torn Poland*. Kitchener, ON: Pandora Press, 2000.

Thiessen, Janis. *Not Talking Union: An Oral History of North American Mennonites and Labour*. Montreal & Kingston: McGill-Queen's University Press, 2016.

Thomson, Julie R. "Psychologists Explain Why Food Memories Can Feel So Powerful." *HuffPost*. 20 May 2017. https://www.huffpost.com/entry/power-of-food-emories_n_5908b1d7e4b02655f8413610.

Toews, John B. *Czars, Soviets and Mennonites*. Newton, KS: Faith and Life Press, 1982.

– ed. *Letters from Susan: A Woman's View of the Russian Mennonite Experience (1928–1941)*. North Newton, KS: Bethel College, 1988.

Toews, Mary. *Glances into Congoland*. Inman, KS: Salem Publishing House, 1953.

Toews, Paul, with Aileen Friesen. *The Mennonite Story in Ukraine*. Winnipeg, MB: Centre for Transnational Mennonite Studies, third edition, 2022.

Toews, Mrs Paul. *Spices of India*. St Marys, ON: printed by the author, 2000.

Toews, Susanna. *Trek to Freedom: The Escape of Two Sisters from South Russia during World War II*, translated by Helen Megli. Winkler, MB: Heritage Valley Publications, 1976.

Toews, Werner. *Sketches from Siberia: The Life of Jacob D. Suderman*. Victoria, BC: Friesen Press, 2018.

Trollinger, Rebekah. "Mennonite Cookbooks and the Pleasure of Habit." *Mennonite Quarterly Review* 4, no. 81 (October 2007): 531–47.

Trollinger, Susan L. *Selling the Amish: The Tourism of Nostalgia*. Baltimore, MD: Johns Hopkins University Press, 2012.

Tunc, Tanfer Emin. "Louise Spieker Rankin's Global Souths: *An American Cookbook for India* and Culinary Imperialism." *Journal of Social History* 54, no. 4 (Summer 2021): 1188–1212.

Turner, Selma Willms. *From Oma's Kitchen: From Russia to Canada with Love, Courage & Gratitude*. Abbotsford, BC: Judson Lake House, 2006.

Tye, Diane. *Baking as Biography: A Life Story in Recipes*. Montreal & Kingston: McGill-Queen's University Press, 2010.

Unger, Andrew. "'Reverse Lent' Begins Today for Devout Mennonites." *The Daily Bonnet* (blog). 1 March 2017. https://dailybonnet.com/reverse-lent-begins-today-devout-mennonites/.

Unrau, Edward. "Mennonite Pioneer Days: 1971." *Mennonite Mirror* 1, no. 2 (October 1971): 21.

Unrau, Ruth. *A Time to Bind and a Time to Loose: A History of the General Conference Mennonite Church Mission Involvement in India from 1900–1995*. Newton, KS: General Conference Mennonite Church, 1996.

UN Women, "Whose Time to Care: Unpaid Care and Domestic Work during COVID-19." 25 November 2020. https://data.unwomen.org/publications/whose-time-care-unpaid-care-and-domestic-work-during-covid-19.

Urry, James. "Mennonites, Migrations and Cookbooks: Food, Globalization and a People of Faith." Unpublished manuscript, n.d. Used with permission.

– "Time and Memory: Secular and Sacred Aspects of the World of the Russian Mennonites and Their Descendants." *Conrad Grebel Review* 25, no. 1 (Winter 2007): 4–31.

Vallely, Anne. "The Jain Plate: The Semiotics of the Diaspora Diet." In *South Asians in the Diaspora: Histories and Religious Traditions*, edited by Knut A. Jacobsen and P. Pratap Kumar, 1–22. Leiden, Neth. and Boston, MA: Brill, 2004.

Vasvári, Louise O. "En-gendering Memory through Holocaust Alimentary Life Writing." *Comparative Literature and Culture* 17, no. 3 (September 2015), DOI: http://dx.doi.org/10.7771/1481-4374.2721.

Voth, Norma Jost. *Mennonite Foods and Folkways from South Russia*, two volumes. Intercourse, PA: Good Books, 1990.

Wade-Gayles, Gloria. "'Laying On Hands' through Cooking: Black Women's Majesty and Mystery in Their Own Kitchens." In Avakian, *Through the Kitchen Window*, 95–103.

Waltner-Toews, David. *The Complete Tante Tina: Mennonite Blues and Recipes*. Kitchener, ON: Pandora Press, 2004.

Weaver, Alain Epp. *Service and the Ministry of Reconciliation: A Missiological History of Mennonite Central Committee*. North Newton, KS: Bethel College, 2020.

Weaver, William Woys. *As American as Shoofly Pie: The Foodlore and Fakelore of Pennsylvania Dutch Cuisine*. Philadelphia: University of Pennsylvania Press, 2013.

– "Food Acculturation and the First Pennsylvania-German Cookbook." *Journal of American Culture* 2, no. 3 (Fall 1979): 421–32.

Weber, Emily Kraemer. *Friendly Favourites: A Collection of Favourite Recipes from the Markham Waterloo Mennonite Girls Born in the Year of 1995*. Ontario: Markham Waterloo Mennonite Conference, 2018.

Weier, John. "Where Am I Now? (Or Why I Am Not a Mennonite)." In *Embracing the World: Two Decades of Canadian Mennonite Writing*, special issue of *Mennonite Mirror* 19, no. 10 (June–July 1990): 96.

Weiskopf-Ball, Emily. "Cooking Up Change: Family Cookbooks as Markers of Shifting Kitchen Politics." *CuiZine: The Journal of Canadian Food Culture* 4, no. 2 (2013), DOI: https://doi.org/10.7202/1019316ar.

Wiebe, Alma, ed. *Fonn Onjafäa: The Recipes of Elizabeth Wiebe*. Saskatoon, SK: by the author, 1996.

Wiebe, Esther. *Displaced: A Memoir*. No place: printed by the author, 2020.

Wiebe, Johann Abram, Henry Wiebe, and Susanna Wiebe. *Memories of Our Parents*. Kitchener, ON: Evenstone Press, 1992.

Wiebe, Joseph R. "On the Mennonite-Métis Borderland: Environment, Colonialism, and Settlement in Manitoba." *Journal of Mennonite Studies* 35 (2017): 111–26.

Wiebe, Katie Funk. *The Storekeeper's Daughter*. Scottdale, PA: Herald Press, 1997.

– *A Strong Frailty: The Life of Aganeta Janzen Block (1906–2000)*. Hillsboro, KS: Center for Mennonite Brethren Studies, 2014.

Wiebe, Menno. "From Bloodvein to Cross Lake: A 25 Year Synthesis." *Journal of Mennonite Studies* 19 (2001): 13–24.

Wiebe, Tina Dyck. "Memories Written By My Life." In Dyck, *The Silence Echoes*, 77–95.

Wiebe, Viola Bergthold. *Sepia Prints: Memoirs of a Missionary in India*. Winnipeg, MB, and Hillsboro, KS: Kindred Press, 1990.

Wiens, Elisabeth. *Schicksalsjahr 1945: Erlebnisse nach Tagebuchnotizen*. Niagara-on-the-Lake, ON: printed by the author, 1993.

Wiens, P. *"Live According to Nature": An Answer to the Pressing Need of Our Time or "How We Can Become Healthy and Remain Healthy."* Halbstadt, Ukraine: printed by the author, 1898.

Williams, Florence. "Eat Like a Mennonite." *New York Times*, 18 January 2013. https://www.nytimes.com/2013/01/19/opinion/eat-like-a-mennonite.html.

Willms, H.J., ed. *At the Gates of Moscow*. Yarrow, BC: Columbia Press, 1964.

Wilson, Catherine Anne. "Reciprocal Work Bees and the Meaning of Neighbourhood." *Canadian Historical Review* 82, no. 3 (September 2001): 431–64.

A Year of Mennonite Cooking (blog). 26 December 2009. http://ayearofmennonitecooking.blogspot.com/2009/.

Yoder, John Howard. *The Politics of Jesus*. Grand Rapids, MI: Eerdmans, 1972.

Yoder, Laura S. Meitzner, and James G. Huff, Jr. "The Best Education Happens around the Table: Four Decades of 'Mennonite Dinner' in Wheaton, Illinois." *Journal of Mennonite Studies* 38 (2020): 133–53.

Zacharias, Robert. "Learning Sauerkraut: Ethnic Food, Cultural Memory, and Traces of Mennonite Identity in Alayna Munce's *When I Was Young and in My Prime*." In *Canadian Literature and Cultural Memory*, edited by Cynthia Sugars and Eleanor Ty, 103–17. Toronto, ON: Oxford University Press, 2014.

– ed. *After Identity: Mennonite Writing in North America*. Winnipeg: University of Manitoba Press, 2015.

Index

Figures indicated by page numbers in italics

Abe Erb Brewing Company, 227n7
abundance, food, 75, 88, 175–7, 183–4, 207, 209–10, 225
activism. *See* social justice
Adorno, Eunice, 102
agriculture, 6, 25, 43–4. *See also* gardening
Albala, Ken, 116, 143
alcohol, 4–5, 36, 98, 201, 227n7
Allen, Karen, 215
Altona (MB), 32. *See also Canadian Mennonite Cookbook*
Amish: background, 9, 227n8; butter lambs, 83, *84*; cookbooks and, 115; in domestic service, 99; foodways, 7–8, 37–8; funeral meals, 212; kitchens, 103; Mississauga people and, 43; pig butchering, 220; in popular imagination, 5–6; wedding meals, 211
Anabaptists, 9–10, 113, 153, 195, 205–6, 214–15. *See also* Amish; Hutterites; Mennonites
anarsa, 185, 203, 204–5, *205*, 225
appliances, kitchen, 99–100
aprons, 82

Avakian, Arlene, 78
Aylmer (ON), 30–1

Baerg, Anna, 160
Bailey-Dick, Matthew, 144
baking. *See* bread and baking; zwieback
barbeque, 108
Bardenstein, Carol, 117
Bargen, Maria Martens, 162
Barkman, Sue, *Mennonite Heritage Village Cook Book*, 149
Barolini, Helen, 102
Bashkir peoples, 45
Baumel, Judith Tydor, 173
Belasco, Warren, 17, 78
Belize, 32–3, 52
Be Present at Our Table (cookbook), 135
Bergen, Henry, 181–2
Bergey, Lorna Shantz, 86, 103, 105, 206–7
Bergman, Andrew J., 55
Bergthold, Daniel, 66
Berry, Malinda E., 118, 238n5
Bertram, Laurie, 13–14
Bertsche, James, 66
Bhutanese Hindu refugees, 195
Block, Aganeta Janzen, 180

Index

blogs, food, 146–7
bodies, female, 73–4
bohne beroggi (mashed beans inside buns), 51
Bolivia, 51
Bolivian Mennonites, 32–3, 52, 84, 91, 102–3
Born, Elizabeth Wall, 152
Born, Hilda J., 213
borscht: absorbed into Mennonite culture, 15, 38; communion (Lord's Supper) and, 221; ethno-tourism and, 56–7; food scarcity and, 156; handwritten recipe, *119*; meat and masculinity, 110; Mennonite preferences and symbolic meanings, 35, 230n12; modernity and, 140, 141
Bower, Anne L., 138, 142–3
Brandt, Di, 17, 33; *Watermelon Syrup* (with Jacobsen and Finlay-Young), 190
Brass, Janis, 43
Braun, Connie T., 57, 84, 92, 127–8, 190, 213
Braun, Jan, 123, 208
Braun, Joe, 44
Braun, Margaret Siemens, 55, 56, 161–2, 194
Braun, Maria Klassen, 4, 86, 90, 118–19
bread and baking: adaptations by missionaries, 64; communion bread, 201; as domestic labour, 78–9, 91–2; during food scarcity, 52, 165; in Mexico and South America, 53, 55–6; ovens and, 103; *paska*, 22–3, 133, 136, 206; as political act, 165–6; raisin bread, 212; symbolic meanings, 175, 192–5, 202. See also *zwieback*
Brillat-Savarin, Jean Anthelme, 13
Brown, Hubert L., 195
Brown, Thomas, *Food for the Journey* (with Lee-Poy), 112, 123
bubbat (cake-like poultry dressing), 20
Bueckert, Aganetha, 40
butchering, animal, 86, 109, 130, 218–21, *220*
butter lambs, 83, *84*

cabbage rolls, 20, 48, 56, 133
Campbell, Maria, 43
Canadian Foodgrains Bank, 199
Canadian Mennonite (newspaper), 127
Canadian Mennonite Cookbook, 130, 142, 143, 240n66, 240n77
Cancian, Sonia, 79
cannibalism, 159, 162, 244n36
care, ethic of, 79
cassava, 53, 65, 70
Centennial Treasury of Recipes (cookbook), 82, 83
Chaco, 53–5. *See also* Paraguayan Mennonites
charity, food (mutual aid), 195–9, *197*
Chavez, Cesar, 200
chicken (noodle) soup, 4, 31–2, 41, 45, 47, 76, 87–8, 91
childbirth, 79
children: foraging during food scarcity, 162, 164, 169; missionary children, 63, 64; pig butchering and, 219
Chornoboy, Eleanor Hildebrand, 24, 104, 202, 219; *Katarina*, 190–1
Christmas, 202–5, 207
colonialism, settler, 11, 41–2, 51–2
Come and Eat (*Kommt Essen*; cookbook), 111, 137
comfort foods, 79, 122, 213
commensality (eating together), 213–22; about, 213–14, 226; animal butchering and, 86, 109, 130, 218–21, *220*; community and, 214–16, 217–18; food scarcity and, 69–70; identity and, 216; Mennonite church meal, *214*; mission work and, 20; political

meanings, 221–2; potluck meals, 85, 208, 216–17, *217*; significance of, 187; Sunday hospitality and, 218
communal (collective) food preparation, 86–8, *87*, 101
communion meal (Lord's Supper), 192, 200–1, 221
community, 21, 214–15, 217–18. *See also* commensality (eating together)
community cookbooks, 116, 123–5, 128–9
Congo. *See* Democratic Republic of Congo
Conrad Grebel University College, 121
convenience foods, 100–1, 138–9
The Cookbook Project (Penner and Peters), 28, 135–6
cookbooks, 112–48; about, 27, 112–14, 147–8, 226; community cookbooks, 116, 123–5, 128–9; crossover cookbooks, 140–1; and cultural identity and transformation, 116–18, 129–35, 137–8; food blogs, 146–7; fundraising from, 128–9; handwritten recipes and informal collections, 118–20, *119*; hybrid food traditions and, 135–7; and memory and nostalgia, 117, 132–3; modernization and, 138–41; as political statement, 141–6; publication boom, 120–1; recipe-writing, 115–16, 142; as reflection of wider society, 138; as religious ambassadors, 113; social justice (world community) cookbooks, 143–5; as textual artifact, 24, 114–18
cookbooks, specific: *Be Present at Our Table*, 135; *Canadian Mennonite Cookbook*, 130, 142, 143, 240n66, 240n77; *Centennial Treasury of Recipes*, 82, 83; *The Cookbook Project* (Penner and Peters), 28, 135–6; *Extending the Table* (Schlabach), 145; *Farmer's Kochbuch*, 136; *Food for the Journey* (Lee-Poy and Brown), 112, 123; *Food That Really Schmecks* series (Staebler), 73, 134, 234n2; *Friendly Favourites*, 123–4; *With Helen in the Kitchen* (Funk), 137; *Hope's Table* (Helmuth), 133–4; by Isaac Horst, 134, 241n98; *Kommt Essen (Come and Eat)*, 111, 137; *Mama's Kochbuch*, 136; *Melting Pot of Mennonite Cookery*, 35; *In Memory's Kitchen*, 172; *Mennonite Community Cookbook* (Showalter), 121–3, 129–30, 139, 140, 145, 147; *Mennonite Ethnic Cooking*, 131, 140; *Mennonite Foods and Folkways from South Russia* (Voth), 7, 51–2, 131, 188, 230n12; *Mennonite Girl Presents* - series, 134; *Mennonite Girls Can Cook*, 75, 129, 132, 133, 148; *Mennonite Heritage Village Cook Book* (Barkman), 149; *Mennonite Men Can Cook Too*, 110, 132; *The Mennonite Treasury of Recipes*, 72, 124–9, *126*, 130, 138–9, 140, 142, 148, 240n52; *Missionary Meals around the World*, 64; *More-with-Less Cookbook* (Longacre), 113, 143–5, 147, 148, 188, 195, 199–200, 242n131; *New Bergthal*, 140; *From Oma's Kitchen* (Turner), 131–2; *Recetario Menonita de Chihauhau*, 136; *Relief Sale Cookbook*, 198; *Simply in Season* (Lind and Hockman-Wert), 145–6; *Spices of India* (Toews), 67; *A Treasure for My Daughter*, 116–17, 144; *The Vegan Mennonite Kitchen* (Snyder), 123, 145
cooking. *See* communal (collective) food preparation; food labour

Cote, Lance, *MennoNeechie Kitchen* blog, 24, 46–7, 146
Covid-19 pandemic, 27, 50, 79–80, 89, 101, 106, 206, 217
Cree, 42, 43
cross-cultural encounters, 30–71; about, 26, 33, 70–1; culinary preservation and, 47–9; familiar and unfamiliar foods, 47–57; food exchanges and borrowings, 34–41, 50–1, 207; hybridity and, 15, 33; imagined culinary traditions and, 49–50; inclusion of non-Russian/Swiss Mennonite foods, 58–61; Indigenous peoples and, 11, 24, 41–7, 51–2; on the mission field, 20, 61–70; Russian Mennonite-Mexican foods, 30–3, 39–41, 136–7
crossover cookbooks, 140–1
Cruz, Daniel Shank, 18, 215
culinary conservatism, 48
culture: cookbooks and cultural transformation, 116–17; religious belief and practice embedded in, 16, 62, 186–7, 225. *See also* cross-cultural encounters; identity

The Daily Bonnet (now *The Unger Review*), 4, 205, 230n20
Daniel, Eva, 174
Danzig, Prussia (Gdańsk, Poland), 36
Danziger Goldwasser (liqueur), 36
David Martin/Independent Old Order Mennonites, 212
Davis, Andrew, 216
Del Rios (Winkler, MB), 32
Democratic Republic of Congo, 15, 63–4, 65, 66, 68–70, 69, 157, 221, 225
Depression, 88, 95–6, 105, 154–6, 163
Desjardins, Ellen, 17, 187
Desjardins, Michel, 17, 187
diaspora, 34

Dick, Maria Driedger, 118
dietary restrictions, 201, 214, 225
Diner, Hasia R., 13, 151, 187, 202
discipleship, 9, 144, 195, 216
Do, Dung Manh, 28, 136
domestic labour (homemaking), 68, 79, 91, 138–40. *See also* food labour
domestic service (househelp), 67–8, 97–9
doughnuts, 206–7
Doukhobors, 73–4, 210
Draper, Barb, 216
Driver, Elizabeth, 114
Dueck, Alicia J., 18
Dueck, Cameron, 18
Dueck, Dora, 98
Dueck, Helene: on bread, 193; food abundance in Canada, 176–7; food preparation and scarcity when leaving Ukraine, 168, 170–1, 171–2, 183; food scarcity in Ukraine and Soviet Union, 96–7, 163, 179–80; memory of hunger, 181; on watermelon, 189
Dueck, Irma Fast, 221
Durksen, Hedy, 127

Easter, 206–7
eating disorders, 23, 214, 225
eating encounters. *See* cross-cultural encounters
eating together. *See* commensality (eating together)
Eicher, Lovina, 188; *The Amish Cook at Home*, 74
Eidinger, Andrea, 116–17, 144
emotion. *See* fear, as food identity; food trauma; memory; mental health
Enlhet peoples, 46
Enns, Anna Duerksen, 44–5
Enns, Elaine, 42, 47, 91, 94, 215–16
Enns, L. Marie, 85

entrepreneurship, food, 104–7, *107*
Epp, Elise, 16
Epp, Mary Konrad, 191
Epp, Peter, 193–4
Ethiopia, 156–7
ethno-tourism, 15, 56–7
Evans, Jennifer, 93
Extending the Table (Schlabach), 145

familiarity and normalcy, 55–7, 179, 213
Family Kitchen (Leamington, ON), 31–2
family life, 104, 173
famine, 156–7. *See also* hunger and food scarcity
Farmer's Kochbuch (cookbook), 136
farming. *See* agriculture; gardening
faspa meal, 48, 86
Fast, Agatha, 82, 88, 155–6, 160, 175
Fast, David, 155–6, 175
Fast, Gerhard, 45
Fast, Kerry, 222; *With a Whisk, a Colander and a Rolling Pin* blog, 146
fasting, 164, 205–6, 209
fear, as food identity, 93–9; cooking to please and, 94–5; domestic service and, 97–9; food labour and mental health, 93–4; food scarcity and, 95–7. *See also* hunger and food scarcity
femininity. *See* women
Ferguson, Kennan, 124–5
Fieldhouse, Paul, 166
Finley-Young, Jane, *Watermelon Syrup* (with Jacobsen and Brandt), 190
First Mennonite Church (Kitchener, ON), 59
Fischler, Claude, 13
Fisher, Susan J., 43–4, 51, 156
food: about, 12–13; identity and, 7–8, 13–16, 19–20, 21; memory and, 21–3, 229n55; power and, 80–1. *See also* Mennonites, and food
food blogs, 146–7
food charity (mutual aid), 195–9, *197*
food deprivation and scarcity. *See* hunger and food scarcity
food entrepreneurship, 104–7, *107*
Food for the Journey (Lee-Poy and Brown), 112, 123
food identity. *See* identity
food justice, 199–200. *See also* social justice
food labelling, 4–5, *5*
food labour, 77–80, 108, 116, 201. *See also* domestic labour (homemaking); women
food-mapping, 36
food preparation. *See* communal (collective) food preparation; food labour
food preservation, 83, 88–90, 152, 189. *See also* pickles
food roots, 18, 50
food studies, 12, 223, 228n19
foodstuffs, definition, 13
food-talk, 14–15, 25, 172, 246n99
food trauma, 152, 167. *See also* hunger and food scarcity
foodways, definition, 13
foufou, 69, 70, 225
Francis, Andrew, 20
Frayne, Helen (Sawatsky), 20
freezers, 99–100
Frey, Selina, *39*
Friendly Favourites (cookbook), 123–4
Friesen, Erika, 88
Friesen, Katie, 169–70
Friesen, Ted, 76, 187
Friesen, Tena, 76–7, 81–2, 89, 156, 202, 212, 219
Froese, Matthew, 206
fundraising: cookbooks and, 128–9; relief sales, 59, 196–9

funerals, 86, 211–13
Funk, Carla, 74, 76
Funk, Helen, *With Helen in the Kitchen*, 137
Funk, Helene Dyck, 180

Gabaccia, Donna R., 48, 79, 118, 129; *We Are What We Eat*, 15
Gaede-Penner, Naomi, 191
Gandhi, Mohandas K., 109–10
gardening, 90–1. *See also* agriculture
gay people. *See* queer Mennonites
Gdańsk, Poland (Danzig, Prussia), 36
gender: about, 26–7, 77; food preparation and, 108; househelp and, 68; pig butchering and, 220; power hierarchies in household and, 104; relief sales and, 199; starvation and, 166–7. *See also* men; women
Germany, Nazi, 182–3
Giesbrecht, Edward, 91–2
Gilbert, Sandra M., 100, 211–12
Goertz, Annie, 66, 155
Goertzen-Armin, Marta, *119*
Goerzen, Anny Penner Klassen, 182, 192–3
Gold, Carol, 114–15
Goldenberg, Myrna, 172
Good, Phyllis Pellman, *Cooking & Memories* (with Pellman), 241n82
Good Books (publisher), 131, 134, 239n36, 241n96
grab bag households, 173, 246n103
Grace Lao Mennonite Church (Kitchener, ON), 60, 60–1
Groening, Margaret Heinrichs, 81
Gross, Aaron S., 192
guilt, survivors', 177–8, 181

Hacienda Roadhouse Café (Aylmer, ON), 30–1
Haenschen (exiled Mennonite boy in Siberia), 164

halvah (sesame paste dessert), 52
Harder, Ernie, 18–19
Harris-Aber, Amy, 113, 131
Hayward, Victoria, 76, 210
Helmuth, Hope, *Hope's Table*, 133–4
Hiebert, Helena Harms, 54
Hildebrandt, Maria, 162
Hind, E. Cora, 75
Hinojosa, Felipe, 17, 20
Historians Cooking the Past (blog), 27
Hmong Mennonites, 59, 60–1, 151
Hockman-Wert, Cathleen, *Simply in Season* (with Lind), 145–6
Holocaust, 172, 173, 182, 246n99
Holodomor, 151, 158, 165, 167, 245n72. *See also* hunger and food scarcity
holubschi (cabbage rolls), 20, 48, 56, 133
homemaking (domestic labour), 68, 79, 91, 138–40. *See also* food labour
Honduras, 32, 52
Horst, Isaac, 134, 241n98
Horst, Simone, 204
hospitality, 69–70, 218, 222. *See also* commensality (eating together)
Hossack, Darcie Friesen, 18; *Mennonites Don't Dance*, 82
Hostetler, John, 37, 73
househelp (domestic service), 67–8, 97–9
humour, 4
Hunchuk, S. Holyck, 152, 245n72
hunger and food scarcity, 150–84; about, 27, 152, 183–4; in Anabaptist history, 153; during Depression, 154–6, 163; ethno-tourism and, 57; from famine and political/economic instability, 156–7; feasting after, 175–7; food identity and, 95–7; food preservation and, 152; food's symbolic meaning during, 174, 189–94; food-talk and, 14–15,

172, 246n99; gender and, 166–7; impacts on family and social life, 172–3; impacts on perceptions of outsiders, 173–4, 182–3; memory of and long-term impacts, 22–3, 151–2, 177, 181–2, 183–4, 225; Mennonite Central Committee and, 160; mental health and, 167, 183; among migrants to North and South America, 153–4; morality and, 194; in remote settlements, 156; in Soviet Union, 96–7, 157–67, 177–80; survival strategies, 164–5, 177; survivors' guilt, 177–8, 181; when fleeing Southeast Asia, 150–1; when fleeing Soviet Union, 56, 151, 167–72, *170*, 173–4
hunger politics, 199–200
husbands, cooking to please, 94–5
Hussain, Arwa, 101
Hutterites, 9, 79, 120, 201, 221, 235n31
hybridity, 15, 33. See also cross-cultural encounters

Iacovetta, Franca, 25, 140
I Am a Mennonite (film), 4
identity: commensality (eating together) and, 216; cookbooks and, 116–18, 129–35, 137–8; culinary preservation and, 47–9; diasporic identity, 34; exclusion from collective identity, 23; food and, 7–8, 13–16, 19–20, 21; food identity as fear, 93–9; food identity as power, 80–92; imagined culinary traditions, 49–50
India: *anarsa* and Christmas celebrations, 185, 203, 204–5, *205*, 225; author in, 15; communion meal in, 201; food scarcity and, 154, 157; gendered power hierarchies in household, 104; male food preparation, 108, *109*; missionaries' experiences in, 62–3, 65–6, 67–8; *Mutthi Daan* (handful offering) practice, 186, 188, 195; potluck meals, 217, *217*; Thanksgiving, 207–8
Indigenous peoples, 11, 24, 41–7, 51–2
Indonesia, 62, 207, 208, 215
Inness, Sherrie A., 77, 101, 114
Iraqi diasporic women, 22, 81, 113
Isaak, Katja, 178

Jacobsen, Lynne, *Watermelon Syrup* (with Finlay-Young and Brandt), 190
Jansen, Sharon L., 115
Jansen, Walter, 159
Jantzi, Marianne, 90, 202
Janzen, Abram, 153
Janzen, Helen, 96, 154–5, 156
Janzen, Johann J., 154
Janzen, Rebecca, 203
Janzen, Rhoda, 18
Japan, 201, 221
Jell-O, 49, 138–9, 141, 176, 211
Jews, 98, 116–17, 144, 172, 177, 202, 246n99
Johnson-Weiner, Karen M., 6, 211, 212
Jones-Gailani, Nadia, 22, 81, 91, 113
justice, food, 199–200. See also social justice

Kachhap, Lily, 204
Kadi, Beatrice, 69–70
Kansas, 51, 131, 136, 191, 208
Kasdorf, Julia Spicher, 99, 196; "When Our Women Go Crazy," 24, 94; "Writing Like a Mennonite," 227n12
Kasstan, Ben, 177
Katarina (Chornoboy), 190–1
Kauffman, Tina Klassen, 48–9, 50, 96, 98

Kaufman, Alice, 83
Kelting, Lila, 132–3
King, Mabel (Yoder), 98–9
Kirkby, Mary-Ann, 120, 201, 221
Kis, Oksana, 167
kitchen, 102–4
kitchen appliances, 99–100
Kitchener (ON), 59
Kitchen Kuttings (Elmira, ON), 105–6
Klassen, Anne Penner, 174
Klassen, David, 94
Klassen, Elizabeth, 176
Klassen, Jenna, 90–1
Klassen, Otto, 55, 161
Klassen, Pamela E., 21, 81, 97
Klassen, Susanna Siemens, 161
Klassen, Victor, 20
Klippenstein, Frieda Esau, 215
Klippenstein, LaVerna, 100
Kolinsky, Eve, 171
Kommt Essen (*Come and Eat*; cookbook), 111, 137
Konrad, Anne, 48, 88–9, 92, 102, 141, 162
Korinek, Valerie J., 140
Kornelsen, Helen, 67
Kostash, Myrna, 38–9, 51
kotletten (Mennonite meatballs), 48
kringel (deep-fried bread twists), 202, 211
Kroeger, Margarethe, 119–20
Kropf, Stanley, 108
Krueger, Mary, 169

labelling, food, 4–5, *5*
Landis, Elva, 65
Laotian Mennonites, 59–61, *60*, 150–1
Le Dantec-Lowry, Hélène, 78
Lee-Poy, Mike, *Food for the Journey* (with Brown), 112, 123
Leis, Rosella, *84*
Lent, 205–6
León, Lupe de, 20
LGBTQ people. *See* queer Mennonites

lime juice, 66
Lind, Mary Beth, *Simply in Season* (with Hockman-Wert), 145–6
lived religion, 188. *See also* religious practice
Loepp, Maria Martens Klassen, 83
Loewen, Anne, 61, 64, 65, 76, 100
Loewen, Helen Reimer, 219
Loewen, Royden, 76, 130
Loewen, Susie Guenther, 144
Loewen, Walter, 194
London Free Press, 197
Longacre, Doris Janzen, *More-with-Less Cookbook*, 113, 143–5, 147, 148, 188, 195, 199–200, 242n131
Lord's Supper (communion meal), 192, 200–1, 221
Lorenzkowski, Barbara, 14
Low German-speaking Mennonites. *See* Russian Mennonites

Mace, James E., 245n72
Mama's Kochbuch (cookbook), 136
Manitoba, 43, 44, 75, 94, 124–5, 153–4
Martens, Eleanor, 83
Martens, Gerhard, 159
Martens, Hildegard, 183, 210
Martens, Maria, 30, 40–1, 104–5
Martens, Maria Reimer, 83
Martin, Bevvy, 153
Martin, Gabby, 17
Martin, Lydia Bauman, 105
Martin, Nancy, 212
masculinity. *See* men
Masih, Suniti, 203, 237n135
Maslow, Abraham, 172
Matahelemual, Hendy Stevan, 215
meals, serving, 104
meat: abstaining from, 208–9; barbeque, 108; butchering, 86, 109, 130, 218–21, *220*; masculinity and, 109–10; MCC's meat-canning initiative, 196; sausage, 5, 20, 37, 75, 205–6, 209

Melting Pot of Mennonite Cookery (cookbook), 35
memory: cookbooks and, 117, 132–3; cross-cultural encounters and, 44; food and, 21–3, 227n12, 229n55; and hunger and food scarcity, 151–2, 181–3; of women's food labour, 91–2. *See also* nostalgia
In Memory's Kitchen (cookbook), 172
men, 94–5, 104, 107–10, 199, 220
Mennomex (general store), 30, *31*, 41, 105
MennoNeechie Kitchen (blog), 24, 46–7, 146
Mennonite Central Committee (MCC), 59, 145, 160, 176, 196
Mennonite Centre (Molochansk, Ukraine), 196, 249n43
Mennonite Community Cookbook (Showalter), 121–3, 129–30, 139, 140, 145, 147
Mennonite Economic Development Associates, 199
Mennonite Ethnic Cooking (cookbook), 131, 140
Mennonite Girl Presents – (cookbook series), 134
Mennonite Girls Can Cook (blog), 24, 132, 133, 147
Mennonite Girls Can Cook (cookbook), 75, 129, 132, 133, 148
Mennonite Men Can Cook Too (cookbook), 110, 132
Mennonites: background and beliefs, 8–12; community and, 21, 214–15, 217–18; diasporic identity, 34; mission work, 11–12, 20, 61; Nazi Germany and, 182–3; settler colonialism and, 11, 41–2, 51–2. *See also* Old Colony Mennonites; Old Order Mennonites; Pennsylvania German (Pennsylvania Dutch); Russian Mennonites (Low German-speaking Mennonites); Swiss Mennonites
Mennonites, and food: about, 8, 16–17, 25–7, 224–6; assumptions and stereotypes about, 5–7; author's background, 12, 14–15, 24–5, 195–6; eating like a Mennonite, 6–7, 80, 223; ethno-tourism, 15, 56–7; food associations, 3–5; interest in, 17–19, 226; production and consumption as pleasurable, 82–3, 209–10; research sources, 23–4. *See also* cookbooks; cross-cultural encounters; gender; hunger and food scarcity; identity; memory; religious practice
The Mennonite Treasury of Recipes (cookbook), 72, 124–9, *126*, 130, 138–9, 140, 142, 148, 240n52
Mennonitische Post (newspaper), 41, 137
Mennonitische Rundschau (newspaper), 163
Mennopolitan (blog), 24
mental health, 93–4, 167, 183. *See also* fear, as food identity; food trauma
Meserete Kristos, 156–7
Métis, 44
Mexico: Christmas celebrations, 203; cookbooks, 136–7; *queso menonita* (Mennonite cheese), 30, 51, 224, 232n77; Russian Mennonite-Mexican food, 24, 30–2, 39–41
Miller, Melissa, 85
Mintz, Corey, 42
missionaries and mission work, 61–70; author's experience in Congo, 68–70, *69*; background, 11–12; commensality (eating together) and, 20; dietary adaptation, 61–2, 63, 64–6; househelp and, 67–8; impacts on North American Mennonite diets, 66–7;

importation of familiar foods, 62–4; missionary children, 63, 64
Missionary Meals around the World (cookbook), 64
Mississauga people, 43
Mock, Melanie Springer, 144–5
modernity, 99–101, 129, 138–41, 211
Mojica, Glorimar, *197*
Montanari, Massimo, 17, 50, 62, 109, 152, 164–5
morality, 194
More-with-Less Cookbook (Longacre), 113, 143–5, 147, 148, 188, 195, 199–200, 242n131
Munce, Alayna, *When I Was Young and in My Prime*, 24
Murcott, Anne, 173
Murray, Stuart, 113
mushrooms, 52, 65, 164
Mutthi Daan (handful offering), 186, 188, 195
mutual aid (food charity), 195–9, *197*

Nath, Rishita Nizel, *anarsa* recipe, 185
Nazi Germany, 182–3
Neufeld, Elsie K., 161
Neufeld, Henry, 108
Neufeld, Herman, 159–60
Neufeld, Justina, 97
Neufeld, Kornelius and Elizabeth, 191
Neufeld, Mary, 95–6
Neufeldt, Reina C., 11
Neuhaus, Jessamyn, 122
New Bergthal (cookbook), 140
New Hamburg (ON) relief sales, 197–8
New Year, 207
Nobbs-Thiessen, Ben, 46, 51, 53–4, 192
non-gender binary people, 18, 77, 107–8. *See also* queer Mennonites
normalcy and familiarity, 55–7, 179, 213
nostalgia, 56–7, 110, 117, 132–3. *See also* memory

Old Colony Mennonites, 76, 104, 198, 212, 218
Old Order Mennonites: commensality (eating together) and, 218; cookbooks and, 134; food associations with, 5, 6; food entrepreneurship, 105–6, *107*; food preservation, 89; funeral meals, 212. *See also* plain Mennonites
oliebollen, 62, 207. *See also portzelky*
organic food, 6
ovens, 103

pampushky (Ukrainian yeast bun), 56
pancakes, 51, 91, 156, 205
papusas, 59
Paraguayan Mennonites, 46, 52–6, *54*, 154, 189–90, 204
paska, 22–3, 133, 136, 206
Pauls, Agnes, 176
Pauls, Marianne Zwittag, 192
Pellman, Kenneth, *Cooking & Memories* (with Good), 241n82
Penner, Anna and John, 63, 65
Penner, Ellery, 208, 233n108, 250n82; *The Cookbook Project* (with Peters), 28, 135–6
Pennsylvania German (Pennsylvania Dutch): background, 10, 230n19; cookbooks and, 120, 134; *Cooking & Memories* (Good and Pellman) on, 241n82; cross-cultural encounters, 37–8; food performance and self-worth, 86. *See also* Swiss Mennonites
peppernut cookies, 20, 36, 51, 120, 176, 203–5, 220
perogies, 15. *See also vereniki*
Peters, Margareta Sawatsky, 87–8
Peters, Mariechen, 162
Peters, Rachael, *The Cookbook Project* (with Penner), 28, 135–6
Peters, Sarah, 64, 65, 154, 189–90, 202–3

Petö, Andrea, 14, 104
pickles, 37, 38. *See also* preservation, food
pie, 3, 4, 37, 38, *39*, 198
pigs. *See* pork
Pilcher, Jeffrey M., 62, 108, 213
Pizza Haven (Altona, MB), 32
plain Mennonites, 7–8, 103. *See also* Amish; Old Colony Mennonites; Old Order Mennonites
Plakias, Alexandra, 33
platz (coffee cake), 120, 133
please, cooking to, 94–5
Plett, Marlene, 86, 219
Plett, Paul, *I Am a Mennonite* (film), 4
plumi moos (fruit soup), 20, 36, *75*, 139, 202
Pod Łososiem/Under the Salmon (Gdańsk, Poland), 36
political statements: baking and, 165–6; commensality (eating together) and, 221–2; cookbooks and, 141–6. *See also* social justice
Pollan, Michael, 200
poppy seed rolls, 51
pork: abstaining from, 208–9; butchering, 86, 109, 130, 218–21, *220*
portzelky (deep-fried fritters), 36, 50, 51, 62, 207, 224, 233n107
potatoes, 51, 174
potluck meals, 85, 208, 216–17, *217*
power, as food identity, 80–92; about, 80–1; collective food preparation and, 86–8, *87*; food preservation and, 88–90; and food production and consumption as pleasurable, 82–3; gardening and, 90–1; memories of, 91–2; self-worth and, 83–6; women and, 81–2
preservation, food, 83, 88–90, 152, 189. *See also* pickles
prips, 149, 156, 160
processed foods, 100–1, 138–9
Puerto Rico, 50, *197*

queer Mennonites, 18, *19*, 112, 215, 222
queso menonita (Mennonite cheese), 30, 51, 224, 232n77

racism, 17, 47, 200. *See also* white privilege
Rahn, Aganetha Schartner, 166, 189
raisin bread, 212
Recetario Menonita de Chihauhau (cookbook), 136
recipes: *anarsa*, 185; *borscht*, *119*; *prips*, 149; spring rolls (*goi cuon*) with peanut sauce, 28–9; *tamales*, 111; *zwieback*, 72
recipe-writing, 115–16, 142
Red Cross, 164
Redekop, Magdalene, 7, 21, 128
Regehr, Jasch, 178–9
Regehr, Maria, 162, 178–9
Regier, Margarethe Kroeger, 119–20
Reimer, Margaret, 76
Reimer, Ruth, 171
Reimer, Wilhelmine and Jakob, 221–2
Relief Sale Cookbook, 198
relief sales, 59, 196–9
religious practice, 186–222; about, 27, 186–8, 222, 225–6; Christmas, 202–5, 207; communion meal (Lord's Supper), 192, 200–1, 221; embedded in culture, 16, 62, 186–7, 225; fasting and abstaining from food, 164, 205–6, 208–9; food as spiritual symbol, 188–95; food charity and, 195–9, *197*; food justice and, 199–200; and food production and consumption as pleasurable, 82–3, 209–10; funeral meals, 86, 211–13; Lent and Easter, 205–7; lived religion, 188; New Year, 207; specialty foods during holidays, 208; Thanksgiving, 207–8; unofficial culinary rituals, 202; wedding

meals, 86, 210–11. *See also* commensality (eating together)
Rempel, John, 192
Rempel, Nicolai and Katharina, 19
rice, 60, 154, 164, 186, 188, 208
Roes, Marion, 212
rollkuchen (deep-fried fritters), 19, 83, 120, 136, 139, 156, 198, 228n43
Rosenfeld, Anna (Derksen), 125, 127
roti, 49
Russia. *See* Russian Mennonites (Low German-speaking Mennonites); Soviet Union; Ukraine
Russian Mennonites (Low German-speaking Mennonites): about, 10–11; *borscht* and, 35, 110, *119*; cookbooks and, 129–34; cross-cultural encounters, 35–6, 38–41, 44–5, 51, 52; culinary preservation, 48–9; ethno-tourism, 15, 56–7; feasting after fleeing from Soviet Union, 175–7; funeral meals, 212; homeland, sense of, 34; hunger and food scarcity in Soviet Union, 96–7, 157–67, 177–80; hunger and food scarcity when fleeing Soviet Union, 56, 151, 167–72, *170*, 173–4; imagined culinary traditions, 49; kitchens, 102; *kringel* and, 211; Mexican food and, 24, 30–2, 39–41, 136–7; pork and, 209; *portzelky* and, 207. *See also zwieback*
rye bread, 52, 165

Sack, Daniel, 187, 214
Salish people, 46
Santiago, Lucy, *197*
Saskatchewan, 42, 43, 47, 48, 85, 96, 154–5
Sauder, Renee, 213
sauerkraut, 14, 37, 49, 202
sausage, 5, 20, 37, 75, 205–6, 209. *See also* meat

Sawatzky, Roland M., 90
Schlabach, Joetta Handrich, *Extending the Table*, 145
schmaunt fat (cream gravy), 17, 32, 228n36
Schmidt, Agatha, 171, 193
Schroeder, Elfrieda, 84
self-worth, 83–6, 100
sel-roti, 195
serving food, 104
settler colonialism, 11, 41–2, 51–2
"seven sweets and seven sours," 37
sexuality, 83. *See also* queer Mennonites
Shapiro, Laura, 141
Sharpless, Rebecca, 77
shish-kabobs, 52
shoofly pie, 37, 49
The Shoofly Project (blog), 147
Showalter, Mary Emma, 147; *Mennonite Community Cookbook*, 121–3, 129–30, 139, 140, 145, 147
Showalter, Valerie, 147
shunning, 221–2
Simply in Season (Lind and Hockman-Wert), 145–6
Sneath, Robyn, 41, 137–8
Snyder, Jo, 216; *The Vegan Mennonite Kitchen*, 123, 145
social congregation, 215
social justice: cookbooks and, 143–5; food justice, 199–200; Steinbach Pride Parade, 19, 222
sopapillas, 136
sorghum, 53, 54, 55–6, 165
soup kitchens, 196
soups. *See borscht*; chicken (noodle) soup
Soviet Union: feasting after fleeing from, 175–7; hunger and food scarcity in, 96–7, 157–67, 177–80; hunger and food scarcity when fleeing, 56, 151, 167–72, *170*, 173–4. *See also* Ukraine

spring rolls, 28–9, 59, 61, 136
Staebler, Edna, 3–4, 120, 241n95; *Food That Really Schmecks* cookbook series, 73, 134, 234n2
Steinbach (MB), Pride Parade, 19, 222
Steinbach Heritage Museum, 74, 75
Steinbach Mennonite Church, Ebenezer Verein, 125, 127
Suderman, Jacob D., 179
Suderman, Margaret, 67
Sudermann, Anna, 159
sugar, 38, 176
summer kitchen, 103
sunflower seeds, 38, 230n20
Sunnycrest Home Baking (Hawkesville, ON), 107
survivors' guilt, 177–8, 181
sustainability. *See* preservation, food
Swana, Sidonie, 69–70
Swiss Mennonites: background, 10–11; cookbooks and, 134; cross-cultural encounters, 36–8; funeral meals, 212; homeland, sense of, 34; imagined culinary traditions, 49; kitchen and, 103. *See also* Pennsylvania German (Pennsylvania Dutch)
Swiss Volhynian Mennonites (Kansas), 208
Szabo, Michelle, 108

tamales, 40–1, 111, 203
Tatar people, 44–5
tea, 38, 221
Teichroeb, Wera, 52–3, 168, 175, 183
Thanksgiving, 207–8
Theophano, Janet, 114, 117
Thielman, Susanne Willms, 161, 189
Thiessen, Edna Schroeder, 176
Thiessen, Jeanette Martig, 68
threshing season, 85–6
Toews, John B., 159
Toews, Mary, 65
Toews, Miriam, 128

Toews, Mrs Paul, *Spices of India*, 67
Toews, Susan, 165
Toews, Susanna, 173–4, 175
tourism, ethno-, 15, 56–7
A Treasure for My Daughter (cookbook), 116–17, 144
Trollinger, Susan L., 110
Turner, Selma Willms, *From Oma's Kitchen*, 131–2
tusua (insect), 66
Tye, Diane, 78–9, 95, 100, 127, 199, 218

ugali, 65
Ukraine: cross-cultural encounters, 38–9, 50–1, 52, 207; emigration from, 153–4, 191; Holodomor, 151, 158, 165, 167, 245n72; Mennonite Centre (Molochansk), 196, 249n43; Mennonite missionaries to India from, 62–3; *paska*, 22–3, 133, 136, 206. *See also* Russian Mennonites (Low German-speaking Mennonites); Soviet Union
Unger, Jakob, 56
The Unger Review (formerly *The Daily Bonnet*), 4, 205, 230n20
United Farm Workers, 200
United Kingdom, 20, 216
Unrau, Ruth, 68

The Vegan Mennonite Kitchen (Snyder), 123, 145
vereniki, 36, 38, 41, 48, 67, 74, 75, 130, 182, 224
Vietnamese refugees, 28, 136, 151, 172
vínarterta (cake), 14, 49
Vistula Delta, 218
Voth, Norma Jost, 76, 118, 174, 209, 218; *Mennonite Foods and Folkways from South Russia*, 7, 51–2, 131, 188, 230n12

Wade-Gayles, Gloria, 102
Waltner-Toews, David, "Tante Tina," 24
Warkentin, Justine Thiessen, 176
Warren, Teneile, 13
Waterloo region (ON), 38, 58, 106
Waterloo Region Record, 197–8
watermelon, 7, 8, 38, 57, 89, 188–90
Watermelon Syrup (Jacobsen, with Finlay-Young and Brandt), 190
Weaver, William Woys, 6, 37, 230n19
weddings, 86, 210–11
Weier, John, 20
Weiskopf-Ball, Emily, 124
white privilege, 16, 52, 135. *See also* racism
Wideman, Lydia and Elmeda, 105–6
Wiebe, Elizabeth, 93
Wiebe, Esther, 84, 89, 91, 102–3
Wiebe, Katie Funk, 76, 94–5, 104, 167, 180
Wiebe, Menno, 46
Wiebe, Susanna Kehler, 93
Wiebe, Tina Dyck, 164, 191
Wieler, Emilia, 42
Wiens, Agnes Harder, 67
Wiens, Peter, 209
Wilson, Catherine, 219
Winkler (MB), 32
Winnipeg (MB), 52, 58
With a Whisk, a Colander and a Rolling Pin (blog), 146
women: body, femininity, and food stereotypes, 73–6; collective food preparation and, 86–8, *87*, 101; convenience foods and, 100–1, 138–9; cooking to please, 94–5; domestic service and, 68, 97–9; food entrepreneurship, 104–7, *107*; food identity as fear, 93–9; food identity as power, 80–92; food labour and, 77–80, 116, 201; food preservation and, 83, 88–90; food-related rituals and, 210; food scarcity and, 95–7, 166–7; gardening and, 90–1; kitchen and, 102–4; memories of and tributes to, 76–7, 91–2; mental health and food production, 93–4; modernity and, 99–101; pig butchering and, 220; pressures on and self-worth from food labour, 83–6, 100; relief sale labour and, 199; serving food and, 104
world community (social justice) cookbooks, 143–5

Yarrow (BC), 80
Year of Mennonite Cooking (blog), 147
yerba maté, 55
Yoder, John Howard, *The Politics of Jesus*, 113

Zacharias, Robert, 24, 36
zwieback: about, *168*, 228n43; as comfort food, 79; in cookbooks, 130; cross-cultural encounters and, 51; fleeing from Soviet Union and, 56, 168–9; identity and, 19; as imagined culinary tradition, 49; memory and, 92; origins, 36; recipe, 72; self-worth and, 84; symbolic meaning of, 176, 188, 190–2